HONORING
THE
CUSTOMER

HONORING THE CUSTOMER
MARKETING AND SELLING TO THE JAPANESE

Robert M. March

JOHN WILEY & SONS, INC.
New York • Chichester • Brisbane • Toronto • Singapore

Copyright © 1990, 1991 by Robert M. March.

Published in Australia by Longman Professional Publishing Ltd.

Published in North America by John Wiley & Sons, Inc.

Published simultaneously in Canada.

Library of Congress Cataloging-in-Publication Data:

March, Robert M.
 Honoring the customer : marketing and selling to the Japanese /
by Robert M. March.
  p. cm.
 Includes bibliographical references and index.
 ISBN 0-471-55073-6

 1. Marketing—Japan. 2. Corporations, Foreign—Japan.
3. National characteristics, Japanese. I. Title.
HF5415.12.J3M36 1991
658.8′48—dc20   91-16374

Printed in the United States of America.
10 9 8 7 6 5 4 3 2 1

CONTENTS

ACKNOWLEDGEMENTS

I have debts to many people, in the USA, Great Britain and Australia as well as Japan for their contributions—of ideas, materials and suggestions—to the preparation of this book. I have been eager to acknowledge all of them, but a number have asked that their contribution not be made public. In addition, let me also acknowledge those Japan specialist marketing professionals from whom I have learnt so much over the last twenty years.

In the development of the book, I am especially grateful to Japan specialist Ms Judy Van Dyck of Oregon State University and to Mr Okinori Murata of Kodansha Inc., New York, for their truly comprehensive research on marketing to the Japanese in the USA. Mr T.R. Rosenberg, of Stonebridge Trading Company, Massachusetts, shared many of his more difficult experiences in Japan with insight and humour.

My debts to friends and colleagues in Japan are formidable. The single biggest and longest-standing debt is to the writer and market researcher, Mr George Fields, chairman of ASI Market Research Tokyo. His invitation to me in 1970 to be a marketing and consumer research consultant with ASI Japan first opened my eyes to the curiosities of Japanese customers. I learnt much from George. I also have longstanding debts to Dr Naotaka Torii, president of Nippon Marketing Systems and doyen of the Japanese marketing community, to Mr Itaru Suzuki, president of the Institute for Social Behavior Inc., and to Mr Shinsaku Sogo, executive director of JETRO (Japan External Trade Organization) in Tokyo. Other people whose views and contributions have influenced me include Mr Yuki Akimoto, managing director and marketing strategist for Kentucky Fried Chicken Japan, Mr Bernard Barber, executive vice-president of McCann-Erickson-Hakuhodo, Mr Roger Brookin, the eminent marketing strategist with Nippon Lever Inc., Mr Yasutaka Sai, vice-president of the Japan Management Association, Professors Kichiro Hayashi and Magoroh Maruyama of Aoyama Gakuin University, Ms Tanya Neil-Tanaka of Landor Associates, and my former research assistants in Japan, Ms Atsuko Kuroda and Ms Etsuko Hayashi, who is now completing her doctorate at my alma mater, the University of Sydney. Finally in Japan, I have a longstanding debt to the several hundred Japanese and western business people who have participated in my International Negotiation seminars over the years at the Japan Management Association. Discussions with them have helped shape my understanding of the problems of marketing in Japan.

In Australia, my biggest debts are to Mr Marshall White, who has shared his reflections and wisdom, garnered from nine years experience in serving the 'honourable customer', and to Mr Anthony Surtees, chief executive officer of Persona Australia, who has developed a truly bicultural–bilingual joint venture business serving both Australian and Japanese 'honourable customers'. Both these gentlemen demonstrate that a high order of 'Japan literacy' is achievable without mastery of the language. In library research, I was helped very much by Mr Greg McCarthy of Jetro, Messrs Hayashi and Nagumo of the Ministry of International Trade and Industry representative office, and Ms Linda Mobsby of the Australia Japan Economic Institute, all of Sydney. I am also particularly grateful to Mr Carlton Wright, national director of the Australian Design Council (and formerly with the National Panasonic Group), for providing materials and sharing his experiences, and not least to my publisher, Mr Robert Coco, for his enthusiasm—a quality not conspicuous among Australian publishers faced with a manuscript aimed at a world market.

Case studies in this book have been compiled from my own research files, unless otherwise stated.

INTRODUCTION

The Japanese are the most affluent people on the planet, and soon to be the richest. Yesterday they lived in a closed kingdom on an inhospitable archipelago in the mysterious Orient. Yesterday they were achingly poor peasants ruled by imperious warrior–bureaucrats. Today the grandsons of those peasants are masters of great economic empires, steersmen of extraordinary economic miracles. Neither are they any longer content or able to keep their island home closed, or to stay closeted in the house. They are ever increasingly abroad—buying, selling, manufacturing, investing, employing (not to mention consuming or touring or holidaying)—soon, if not already, to be your neighbour, or your customer, or your business partner, or your boss. They are set to become, in every advanced and developing country, a more pervasive, more challenging, more subtle, more disturbing or more romantic (depending on your affinities for Japanese culture) and more economically intrusive influence than any other in our historical experience.

If we look for parallels, perhaps it resembles the height of the British empire, without the military and naval might. Or we could find many parallels in the way Hollywood and United States big business came to dominate Western (though not Eastern) culture and business life through the first two-thirds of the twentieth century. But the better (and more instructive) parallel for me is the Chinese. They have, like the Japanese but over a period of many centuries, established enclaves and economic power in many countries.

Like the Chinese of the past and present, the Japanese influence is indicated not just by the presence of Japanese companies manufacturing goods designed in Japan, but also by the presence of Japanese service and support companies which have followed the great manufacturers, whom they serve at home, into the foreign markets. Like the Chinese, the power, attractiveness and individuality of Japan's culture is indicated by the growing, thriving presence of Japanese restaurants, schools, newspapers and language schools, as well as the popularity of courses on culture, business and language. It is a phenomenon of history which may be with us no more than a generation or two, and whose like we may not see again. It is a phenomenon to be understood and appreciated, and benefited from.

The contrasts with the Chinese are equally instructive. The Chinese settled permanently, but with a few minor exceptions (Brazil, Hawaii, California at the end of the nineteenth century), the Japanese have not. The Chinese have gone abroad primarily because of famine, poverty, floods or political repression at home. The Japanese have gone abroad because they were commanded to by their companies. They stay for a few years only. Most of them would prefer not to go, and are glad to go home. The Chinese overseas presence is concentrated in the Pacific Rim countries. The Japanese, although having a massive presence in the Pacific Rim, are truly worldwide: Africa, West Asia, Eastern and Western Europe, South and North America. The Chinese presence in business overseas (that is, away from mainland China) has traditionally been through family businesses. Joint ventures with indigenes is the exception rather than the rule. In contrast, and for obvious reasons, the Japanese have frequently entered into joint ventures with locals. They never intend to be permanent residents and need the connections and political influence of the indigenes.

Given the continuing worldwide spread of Japanese business many more non-Japanese today have or will have business dealings with the Japanese. The non-Japanese may have had no previous experience of the Japanese, have little knowledge of or interest in them or their culture, never have visited Japan or met a Japanese person before. This is rapidly changing. As major Japanese companies enter foreign markets, they are followed by companies which back home provided key services—banks, shipping and transportation, insurance, retailing, printing, hotels, advertising, tourism and many more. Most of these businesses look for local partners to form joint ventures, or seek acquisitions; as well, they buy services and products from local companies.

What do you need to know in order to do business with the Japanese at home or abroad, to market products to them, to sell and provide specialized services personally? If you are in a country other than

Japan, obviously you need to know at least as much as you do about your other customers. In addition, you should understand the way in which Japanese executives resident in your country have created networks of friendship and information exchange among themselves. Many decisions and many influences on purchase decisions take place via these networks.

When they first meet and talk to Japanese prospective customers or business partners, some foreign executives want to know whether marketing and selling to the Japanese is really all that different, and whether the differences are really important. What has to be emphasized more than anything else is that whatever the differences are, almost always they stem from the way the Japanese do business back home in Japan. Unlike the Chinese, that is, the Japanese have to be understood in terms of their business culture and their company culture back at head office; that is, their power centres back in Japan.

Much more than the American expatriate managers, the Japanese — predictably because they do not usually speak the local language well or share much culturally with the local people — belong to the local Japanese business community and keep in touch with what is going on back home—in the company as well as nationally. The way they behave in your country generally reflects not the way things are done in the host country but the way business is done in Japan. Back home is the source of their business values, goals and strategies, which they will most likely and quite justifiably think are superior to those in your country; their head office is the source of much of their self-esteem and of the meaningfulness of their lives.

This book is about Japanese customers, their values, attitudes and assumptions, what and who influences them, and what criteria they use to make decisions on buying. It will enable you to do a better job of marketing and selling to them at home and abroad, or save a lot of time and money, perhaps by deciding to concentrate on easier prospects than the Japanese. I have written this book not in the belief that anyone, with proper instruction (such as reading my book), can sell to the Japanese, but at least with the conviction that marketing and selling to the Japanese will be possible once you have learned some important things. A learning process might continue throughout your entire relationship with some Japanese companies.

There is also the need for sensitivity to and knowledge of the politics and power structure of the company itself and of the Japanese business community and their friendship and information networks. There is nothing fundamentally different from doing business with anyone anywhere, save that with Japanese buyers the human relationship becomes so much more important, something to be developed carefully and then permanently nourished. The best thing to hope for is that within your organization you have someone who will be able to have amicable long-term business relationships with Japanese buyers, based on good human relations skills, and some affinity for the Japanese people and their culture.

No one should go into the task of marketing and selling to Japanese buyers believing that it will not take more time than selling, marketing or negotiating has ever taken before. Japanese buyers demand a level of product quality, service and background information beyond that in any other country. If you are in Japan, you learn quickly that business survival means you must upgrade your products and service. If you are abroad, you are still dealing with sophisticated, demanding Japanese clients, but you are now dealing with them from the viewpoint of your own local, less exacting business values and expectations. Unless you are careful those values and standards will become blinkers on your ability to recognize clearly what Japanese buyers expect from you. When you are in your home country, and have had no experience of Japan, it is understandably hard to appreciate what improvements you really should make to secure the business from competition, or why you should make them—especially when your other non-Japanese clients express no complaints.

Another problem is our current perceptions and knowledge of the Japanese. Stereotypes and generalizations about foreigners can be useful. At first meetings, they can serve as provisional hypotheses about the people we are dealing with—but we should test them all the time to get to the truth of who it is we are facing. You may have heard that the Japanese are shy and awkward with non-Japanese. Until you find out about the particular Japanese facing you, act as though he were shy. If it turns out that he is not, then discard that stereotype for this particular person. Unfortunately, most non-Japanese people, unless they have a continuous intimate relationship with the country, are seriously out of date in their general knowledge of Japan. Their images may be of the 'geisha girl' or 'ninja' variety, or they regard the kimono (falsely) as everyday wear, or assume that most people live in small fragile timber homes. Images like these would be thirty years or more out of date —as would beliefs such as 'no foreigners are able to buy real estate in Japan', or ' Japanese workers are brainwashed to work long hours'.

Even if your knowledge of Japan is more up-to-date, you may be prone to let your hopes fly heavenward, or grasp one interested question as certain testimony of an undoubted intention to buy, or to regard a massive difference in *per capita* consumption between your country and Japan as a sure-fire market opportunity which you have been the very first to discover! In Japan it is better to keep your enthusiasm on a tight sceptical leash, remembering that many people have been there before you. You would not be the first to note that the Japanese consumption of beef is only one-tenth of that in the West, or to conclude that a mere 5 per cent increase would mean millions in new sales. Or to have dreamt, as have so many winemakers from France, Germany, Italy, California, Australia and South Africa, about the rosy future when the Japanese *per capita* wine consumption increases to even 20 per cent of the figure in the West. Good ideas are unfortunately prone to be commonplace in today's Japan. Japanese buyers, pragmatic, cool-headed and realistic people, have probably heard it all before. They want to know: Will it work? Does it have an application now? Does it have a track record elsewhere? Is there easily generated demand for the item? It might be less costly for you not to approach the Japanese until you have good answers to these questions.

Perhaps the most misleading perceptions of all are those that arise from the fears and threats that so many non-Japanese feel when confronted by Japanese business success and supremacy. There are many people who wistfully believe that the Japanese challenge is somehow only temporary. This tenacious myth, seemingly grounded in a desire to downgrade the significance of Japanese achievements, has been going on for a long time. Harvard University's Nathan Glazer reports that he has been watching economists watch Japan for twenty-five years, and repeatedly being taken in by analyses demonstrating that the Japanese boom was coming to an end.

Frank Gibney's 1974 book, *Japan: The Fragile Superpower*, contributed to the image of Japan as more image than substance. In 1983 Marvin Wolf's *The Japanese Conspiracy* assured us of their plot to dominate industry worldwide. The Japanese, Wolf warned, 'regularly flout the rules of ethical behaviour', their firms are forced by MITI (the Ministry of International Trade and Industry) to buy exclusively from domestic suppliers, abetted by a shield of 'Byzantine import barriers'. The 30 March 1987 cover of *Fortune* featured a special report called 'Japan's Troubled Future', written at a time when the yen was rapidly strengthening. This negatively toned report asserted that Japanese society was changing to its own detriment: 'its competitors were clamouring' for market access and so on. However, the article was written at a time when Japan was already launched into a new economic miracle of overseas investment and domestic growth.

A *Newsweek* article of 10 May 1989 caught and tried to lay to rest many of these wish-fulfilling assertions about Japan. 'Even as we fret and fume about the trade gap and Japanese purchases of US real estate', wrote senior editor Mark Whitaker, 'we keep looking for reasons why their economic surge may prove fleeting.' Whitaker pointed to three current theories about Japan's vulnerabilities which 'simply amount to wishful thinking'. One he called 'the living-standards fallacy'. When ordinary Japanese gripe about how their living standards lag behind the country's growth in collective wealth, many Americans may be tempted to think the Japanese will eventually rebel in a way that might slow down productivity'. There is simply no ground for this. The desire for constant improvement in one's living standards has been one of the great drives behind the Japanese post-war miracle, and it shows no signs of being satisfied.

Whitaker calls another theory the 'consumer revolt theory'. It is a fact that the Japanese generally have to pay at least twice the world price for consumer-products. The wishful-thinking comment is this: once the Japanese government eliminates trade barriers, the Japanese will jump at the chance to buy foreign imports, and the domestic profit margins that fund much of Japan's export drives will be lost. Feasible? Like Whitaker, I don't think this theory takes into account the costs that Japanese customers are prepared to pay for high quality and the superb service they expect.

The third theory discussed by Whitaker he calls the 'clever copycats perception'. Since the Japanese are only really good at copying what others invent or create, then, says Whitaker, 'if other countries were less free about licensing technology . . . the Japanese would be stymied'. It is true the Japanese do now license less of their own technology to the rest of the world than they take in — but in critical hi-tech areas the world is more and more dependent on Japan.

The first quarter of 1990 saw yet another apparent mini-crisis in Japan's economy, the so-called 'triple price collapse', when the value of stocks and yen declined dramatically and the cost of money increased. A *Financial Times* headline told us: 'Crash in Tokyo Clouds Japan's Economic Future' (Rodger, 1990). * A *Washington Post* headline pontificated: 'Economic Disturbance Destroys Myths', reporting,

---

* Citations to articles or books listed in the Bibliography are shown throughout in this way.

among other things, that not only were stocks and bonds losing their value, but that Japan had also suffered a trade deficit in January 1990. It is true that the Japanese trade surplus in 1989 had dropped to a 'mere' $US57 billion from $US79.6 billion in 1988 and $US87 billion in 1987. Then again, the first quarter of 1990 saw wages increase by 6 per cent, largely due to increasing labour shortages, while the US was pictured by the media as having forced Japan to open and liberalise its markets further by easing restrictions on the opening of large retail shops.

How has all this affected Japanese business and the prospects for foreign products in Japan? The truth is obvious. Japan's economy remains strong and growing. Each of the triple price collapses is linked to money, not to the real economy of production of goods. In fact, while worrying, the reality is that money is being created and changing hands without any relation to real economic forces. These include corporate investment, technological innovation, diversified consumer consumption, overseas investment in manufacturing, and the import of foreign goods and raw materials. All of these facets of Japan's real economy continue apace. Asked what effect the triple collapse had on their business prospects, Matsushita Electric, the world's largest consumer electronics firm, said it would have no effect on their target of increasing overseas production to 50 per cent of total overseas sales by 1993, from the 30 per cent of 1990. Other leading companies are on target for major growth through to the mid 1990s. To quiet fears about the triple shock, Tokyo Electric Power Company, NHK, Nissan, Toshiba and other major companies announced in March 1990 that their capital investment plans were unchanged, and represented substantial increases on investment in 1989.

Plant investment in Japan, which has grown dramatically since 1987, continued in 1990 to exhibit high growth. As far as Japan's balance of payments is concerned, the earliest that economists predict a deficit is the year 2000, but it seems more plausible that a weaker yen can only mean stronger export performance by the Japanese, a slight flattening of more expensive imports and a trade deficit even further away. Whatever happens, both Japan's domestic economy and its procurements from overseas look certain to offer boom prospects for foreign products and services well into the next century.

Why are so many people apparently enamoured of the idea that the Japanese challenge is merely temporary? For those in Western countries, where most of this wishful thinking seems to arise, the source seems to be the notion of Western cultural superiority that we have inherited, the corollary of which was the poverty and seedy antiquity of Asia. Peoples whom Westerners have been accustomed to perceiving as somehow inferior and backward are suddenly doing extraordinary things. It does not seem to make sense that they could come to overtake and surpass the 'given' of Western superiority. But the trends, indicators and figures point in only one direction: Japan and East Asia will continue to widen the gap between themselves and the rest of the world and, furthermore, their business culture and values will steadily influence and even come to dominate the way business is done around the world.

What is taking place is a transformation of the world economic order which is both unprecedented and unwelcome to many in the West. Accepting this degree of economic change is difficult indeed; everyone resists change, resists the rise of new authorities, new heroes. Those who are under threat have vested interests and cherished self-images. Our very sense of identity is wrapped up in the notion of Western cultural supremacy. Not everyone will find it easy to joint venture with the Japanese, or accept the student role, and learn the new meanings that the Japanese are creating in the world of business.

Indeed the Japanese are serious about business in a way that people in the West have forgotten. They have a twenty-four hour, life-dominating view. It is still saturated by a militaristic ethos, and the wide use of military metaphors, as individuals talk about one another as warriors or troops, and their sections and departments as platoons or battalions. There are also naval metaphors. Former Prime Minister Nakasone once spoke of his vision of Japan as an 'unsinkable battleship'. Tsunehiko Ishizuka, managing director of Sony, speaking in 1986 of the changes occurring in Japan's multinational companies, was quite explicit: 'The war fleet will still be in Japan but we will have more cruisers and destroyers abroad'.

In Japan, business executives and their families unquestioningly accept the priority of business life over the family; wives accept and adjust to the long hours and the limited involvement of the husband in family management. It is a work style also motivated by the very recent national heritage of poverty and frugality. *Bimbo hima nashi* is an expression commonly used to explain why one works without rest from morning to late at night. It means: 'The poor have no time for rest'. Underlying it is a stark fear of failure, failure in particular to survive, which is stronger by far in motivating economic behaviour than the fear of not winning that Westerners are more accustomed to.

The Japanese gratefully acquired the concept of marketing from the USA in the mid 1950s, and have set about giving it a new set of emphases. In the West, marketing in practice means the big strategies—advertising campaigns, the guiding role of research and creativity—with the rest of the marketing mix somewhat subordinate. To the Japanese these are secondary. What is important to them are: a better product, with zero defects, placed in the customer's hands in perfect condition; a flexible, responsive marketing system held together by good personal relationships; the shaping of the whole marketing effort by the corporate determination to win market share and turnover growth, even at the expense of profit; the management of the overall marketing effort by generalist managers, not marketing specialists; and a unique body of experience in marketing products, in many different countries, that has not only stimulated their new product development but also has become a dominant factor in the globalization of their businesses.

One of the major consequences of Japan's pre-eminent economic position today is to make it what Courtis (1989) has justly called 'the world's premier new product laboratory'. The surge in Japanese domestic demand that has continued since 1987 comes in part from the astounding variety of new products—both domestically created and imported—entering the marketplace. There are opportunities in Japan for good quality products from abroad, just as there are opportunities abroad, for Japanese to be attracted to invest in well-managed businesses or to provide venture capital for new products.

In approaching and dealing with a prospective Japanese buyer, there is a strong case for doing your homework thoroughly on all relevant aspects of the Japanese business and marketing environment, and the company and people you are dealing with. But if I really had to narrow it down, I would want to emphasize just two basics: one is about the suitability of your offering, product, service or investment; the other is your skills, your character and suitability as a 'people person' for dealing face-to-face, over time, with the Japanese. Both of these factors are of great importance to them, and even if other aspects of your offering are less than completely professional, they will be secondary. Developing your offering requires the thinking through of the application aspects of your product, taking it beyond the good idea phase. On the human relations side, it cannot be overstated how important the face-to-face relationship is to them.

But at the same time the Japanese almost despise salesmanship. Why is a question we will address throughout the book. But being sceptical of salesman-like pitches, and indeed sceptical in general, the truth about face-to-face dealings with them is that they can be difficult, complex, extended, repetitive, irritating, confusing, provoking, ambiguous and many more things. They can be exceedingly polite and gracious one moment, unbelievably curt and evasive the next. They can seem ready to buy at one moment, and totally non-committal the next.

The Japanese are predominantly a race of decent, shy, meticulous introverts. Their style is quiet, subdued, masked, perfectionistic—seeking a peaceful, harmonious existence, rather than happiness or fun. Generally speaking, other Asians will and do feel more at home with the Japanese than will Westerners. That, of course, is a generalization— and all generalizations are dangerous. Anyone who feels empathy, affinity, for the Japanese is a good candidate for handling business with them, for marketing and selling to them. Specifically, managers with Asian origins, or people who look Asian, will probably feel more comfortable with the Japanese, all other things being equal. Women managers often are successful with the Japanese. Women tend to be better communicators and listeners—and Japanese managers tend to feel comfortable with women in business, as long as they are not Japanese women (against whom most Japanese men are unnaturally prejudiced as incompetent in business). Most of all, perhaps, if your business involves the negotiation of large projects, not simple one-off deals, the best people to do business with the Japanese are all-round people-oriented managers, rather than purely specialist marketing or sales people. If this seeming rejection of specialist marketing or sales people raises objections and apparent contradictions among Western readers, well and good. It is one of the most important lessons to learn in marketing and selling to the Japanese customer.

Part 1

THE BUSINESS ENVIRONMENT AND JAPANESE BUYERS

1 Japanese Customers and the Third Economic Miracle

If you are to understand the values and attitudes of Japanese customers and buyers, and the nature of the opportunities and challenges they offer you, it is essential to understand the place that buying goods and commodities from abroad has had in the unfolding of the remarkable Japanese economic 'miracle'. But in fact, there is no such thing as *the* Japanese economic miracle. It is closer to the truth, rather, to say that there have been, to date, three such miracles.

THE FIRST ECONOMIC MIRACLE

The first Japanese miracle covered the post-war period up to the time of the first oil shock of 1973, and saw Japan's economy growing annually at more than 10 per cent. It was a heady era, with everyone so involved in wildly growing businesses that there was a lot of short-cutting just to get the goods out to the marketplace. Although there were many foreign companies successfully trading in Japan, their status within the business community was generally low. Japanese buyers would undoubtedly give first preference to Japanese goods, even if the quality was lower than the imported product. Imports were dominated by commodities and raw materials, to be processed in mainland Japanese factories. During this period, many Japanese business executives said that companies which only grew 10 per cent annually were simply standing still.

The oil shock brought that first era to an end, when Japanese business came crashing to earth with a 30 per cent increase in the price of imported oil and a resulting 30 per cent inflation rate in 1974.

THE SECOND ECONOMIC MIRACLE

The second economic miracle spanned the period from 1974 to 1985. The Japanese, supposedly the nation most vulnerable to oil price changes, cleared the hurdle of high oil prices through national energy economy drives, new fuel-efficient technologies and substitution of oil by cheaper fuels. Furthermore, they also had their balance of payments in the black again within five years. They lifted the level of direct overseas investment by a factor of three, enabling their blue-chip multinationals enormously to expand manufacturing and marketing by subsidiaries abroad. This second period ended with the United States re-action to Japanese car imports, and the decline in the United States' car industry, with lay-offs directly attributed to Japanese imports and well-publicized 'Japan bashing', including the spectacular public destruction of a Japanese car in Washington.

The first and second miracles saw only slow and modest progress in opening up the Japanese market to foreign companies or to imported products, or change in the attitudes of Japanese bureaucrats or buyers towards foreign goods. There had been little in the business climate to encourage Japanese buyers to buy components or finished goods from abroad in any significant way. In fact government officials and business leaders still made it clear to the nation that it was un-Japanese to buy finished goods abroad. Some senior MITI officials wrote impassioned books about the dire consequences to Japan of market opening. While Japan had recovered amazingly from the 1973 oil shock, aided by the relative cheapness of the yen, the USA and the European Economic Community began to experience increasingly large trade deficits, and to see sizeable increases in levels of unemployment, especially in segments heavily affected by Japanese imports such as cars, steel and shipbuilding. First the USA and then the EEC intensified diplomatic pressures on Japan to take steps to reduce its burgeoning trade surplus with them, although it was the USA that had by far the greatest success. This included voluntary quotas on car sales to the USA and EEC, quotas on steel, shipbuilding and bearings to the EEC, and agreements (or substantial progress towards agreements) on market openings in major fields like telecommunications, insurance, semiconductors, computers, cosmetics and tobacco. Many of the results from these market openings were material in setting the stage for the third economic miracle.

THE THIRD ECONOMIC MIRACLE

The strengthening of the yen against the United States dollar (called *endaka* in Japanese) is generally taken as the key event triggering off the third economic miracle. In February 1985, the dollar was ¥259, by February 1986 it was ¥180, a further twelve months later it was ¥153, and at the end of 1987 it was as high as ¥126. The rising trade surpluses earned by Japan, and especially the US trade deficit with Japan, were also major factors in triggering *endaka*. The countermeasures taken by Japanese industry to combat the effects of *endaka* were of major importance, since these helped to protect the export positions Japanese goods had earned overseas. Procurement of components and semi finished products overseas was one such countermeasure. Product parts and components increased from 3 per cent of total imports in 1985 to 6 per cent in 1989 ('Manufactured imports surging', 1989) — a massive increase. Profitability of Japanese companies was also greatly enhanced by procurement of raw materials overseas. For instance, the nation's largest brewer, Kirin, reported an additional three billion yen profit in 1987, stemming from *endaka*, as a result of buying its hops and barley overseas.

Moving production offshore was another factor. Heavy industry, notably steel and shipbuilding, had been more severely affected by *endaka*, and exports declined as South Korea, Taiwan and other smaller countries became able to compete successfully with higher-priced Japanese exports. The steel companies moved very rapidly to increase the pace of their overseas investment and diversification programs, with rapid moves into such new industries as semiconductors, artificial intelligence, new industrial materials and biotechnology. The shipbuilding industry so successfully rationalized itself that it had returned to the position of world's no. 1 shipbuilder—lost to South Korea in 1984—by 1987. Leaders in the move to acquire offshore production facilities included Sumitomo Rubber, with its purchase of Dunlop in Europe; Dai-Nippon Ink and Chemicals, with successive purchases of the Hartmann companies in Europe and Sun Chemical in USA, and Asahi Glass, with a joint venture in the USA; and the acquisition of European companies.

A further major factor in the third miracle was the deregulation of major industries, notably the securities industry, national railways, telecommunications and airlines, all of which exhibited significant new growth. The business diversifications programs of the steel companies and other mature industries were echoed in other industries seeking sources of new business growth, and much new venture capital started to be channelled into research and development, and new product search and development. This saw the intensification of a boom in new product introductions of all kinds, and served the cause of foreign goods well when then Prime Minister Nakasone opened up Japan's first Import Promotion Drive in 1986, with well-publicized appeals to the Japanese to buy more foreign goods.

Nakasone's appeal fell for the first time on sympathetic ears: Japanese industrial and commercial buyers started seriously to modify their buying policies so that more foreign goods and components would be bought. It was now considered to be proper and responsible for Japanese companies to buy foreign processed goods so as to help their country minimize severe criticism abroad that could ultimately affect everyone's pocket. The largest companies moved swiftly to set up large overseas procurement departments and to seek out foreign suppliers. While department store and supermarket chains moved ever more heavily into direct importing of consumer lines, JETRO (Japan External Trade Organization), an organ of MITI whose responsibility had once been Japanese export promotion, now was repositioned to be responsible for promotion of foreign imports through its worldwide offices.

The gathering boom was further caught and magnified more by growth in new construction and great demand for real estate (especially in Tokyo and Osaka), with prices increasing 40 per cent (or more) annually from 1985.

In January 1990, MITI introduced new Import Expansion Measures (MITI, 1990), which they claimed to be unprecedented in scope in Japan and in the world. These included tax credits to importers of manufactured goods, the elimination of tariffs on more than a thousand products, expanded import lending and a grass-roots effort to internationalize the Japanese economy by encouraging imports in every prefecture of the nation. 'Teams of experts', they added, 'will be despatched to all parts of the world to find suitable products for importing to Japan'. The program, begun in April 1990, is indeed truly impressive. For example, companies setting up 'comprehensive' distribution centres for imports are eligible for loans of up to 65 per cent of the cost, at an interest rate of only 2.7 per cent. Loans of up to 80 per cent of the cost of import procurement promotion 'facilities and services' are available at no interest at all.

TODAY'S JAPAN: THE OPEN MARKET

Not everyone would agree with my picture of Japan 1990 as an open market. Chalmers Johnson, Professor of Asian Studies at University of California, San Diego, is a leading critic (Johnson, 1989) of Japan's structural impediments to imported goods. For instance, Japan, he says, 'forces' its households to spend more than a third of their incomes on food, with high tariffs on beef and complete protection for domestic rice. Equally, he says, Japan's distribution system has evolved into a non-tariff barrier that artificially restricts the choices of Japanese consumers. Significantly, Johnson has nothing to say about non-tariff barriers against manufacturers from abroad—because, compared to the early 1980s, they are almost non-existent today. (For more on remaining barriers, see ACCJ, 1989.)

Despite all the problems he points to, no one can dispute that there is an extraordinary economic dynamic in Japan today, and on balance the sale of foreign imports in Japan, especially food products, is likely to be favoured rather than impeded. Indeed, this third economic miracle is close to the best news that most foreign sellers could want. The old economic nationalism that made it sinful and un-Japanese to purchase processed goods overseas no longer has currency or economic justification.

Fig. 1.1:   Origins and features of the third economic miracle

Origins	Endaka (stronger yen)*
	Industry deregulation
	Mature industries diversify
	Real estate & construction boom
	Import promotion
	Continuing globalization of Japanese multinational companies
Features	Domestic economic growth
	Imports increasing, exports declining
	Overseas investments growing
	Heavy investment in new plant, products, markets and materials

*The yen weakened in the first quarter of 1990, but was still robust compared to 1985.

At the centre of the third economic miracle are Japanese customers. This is a term I shall use in a comprehensive way to include all the variety of people listed in Fig. 1.2. There are Japanese buyers, consumers and even tourists in the domestic market, where two things stand out: quality imports are welcome and their sales are growing. There is an enormous variety of investors (often successful companies looking for diversification opportunities) and venture capital organizations with keen interest in ideas from abroad. There are Japanese customers abroad, including transients on business trips searching for new product sources or new ideas, or simply tourists with money to spend; and permanent residents who are purchasing for the use of their companies abroad, back in Japan, or crossnationally.

Fig. 1.2: Varieties of Japanese customers

A. In Japan	Examples of what they buy
Consumers	Every conceivable individual, family & household product
Domestic tourists	Hospitality, gifts, tours, etc.
Buyers/purchasing, procurement executives	All products and services for retail, commercial and industrial sectors
Investors, including general trading companies and most successful companies	Businesses at home or abroad, e.g., real estate, mines, forests, securities and new technologies.
Specialist venture capitalists	As for 'Investors' above but with emphasis on new start-up companies, usually somewhat risky
B. Abroad	
Expatriate consumers	Daily products from Japanese culture, locally made or imported
Tourists from Japan	Hospitality, gifts, tours, etc.
Buyers/purchasing, procurement executives	Products and/or services for export to Japan.
Pioneer managers for new subsidiaries, branches	Set-up of marketing/manufacturing branches or subsidiaries with all business needs
Investors, including general trading companies, successful companies	Businesses as joint ventures, or for mergers and acquisitions, usually to fit with globalization plans or export to Japan of established products, including traditional Japanese products, e.g. *sake*, Japanese beef (*wagyu*), horseradish (*wasabi*), etc. Also real estate, securities, etc., as long-term investments
Specialist venture capitalists	Start-up businesses for new technologies, services, etc (not necessarily for ultimate application in Japan)

The Japanese customer, in other words, is best thought of as 'everywhere': not just at home in Japan. Of course Japan's home market will long be the crown jewel in their 'empire' of business, but events are already unfolding to make many other countries—and especially the USA, then the United Kingdom, Australia, Holland and Hong Kong, which between them attract 70 per cent of Japan's overseas investment—the sites of growing microcosms of the domestic Japanese market. Japan's overseas investment is dominated by major manufacturing companies which exert a kind of centrifugal effect on their business environment back home. Their investment pulls competitors overseas, followed by suppliers, service and tertiary industry companies—banks, insurance companies, component makers, transport companies, advertising, public relations, consulting and so on. As this microcosm of Japanese business and commerce abroad reaches successive stages of critical mass, more of these businesses have opportunities to establish themselves profitably; that is, each of these businesses becomes a Japanese customer of services or products which local industry may see as an opportunity before the providers of those services back home become aware of it.

THE WORLD'S PREMIER NEW PRODUCT LABORATORY

Japan has a lot in common with the North American market of the 1950s and 1960s. It is a massive and dynamic domestic market in its own right, producing new products and ideas many of which may ultimately be introduced throughout the world. But, as Courtis (1989) points out, from 1988 Japan had reached the stage where it was investing more in new plant and capital equipment than the United States. Each year Japan was creating more new wealth than does the entire North American economy, and commits 'about the same amount to commercially driven research as. . .the United States'. This massive investment in new products, new processes, new markets and new materials is 'radically different from what Japan has known in the past' (Courtis, 1989). It is the economic dimension, if you like, of the boom conditions of daily business life at the beginning of the 1990s in Japan, the world's premier new product laboratory.

In this new market world, the rise of new rich social classes (discussed more fully in chapter 8) is leading to the rise of specialist, segment-specific brands and the decline of mammoth, mass-market-oriented brands. Instead of volume manufacturing and volume sales, small-lot production is becoming the norm for daily necessities, as well as fashion and prestige items. This context of new diversified customer needs and wants is a major stimulus of new product development in Japan.

It is fair to say that, while this view is generally true today, some Japanese refuse to concede changes in the marketplace. Mr Toshifumi Suzuki, chairman of the Japan Franchise Association, has this to say:

> They say that today's consumer is individualistic, diverse in thinking and tastes. I say consumers have never been more identical and sheep-like in their attitudes. The reason their buying habits look diversified is the extremely short lifecycle of most popular products. Makers put new versions on the market so quickly these days. They don't trust their own judgement. That's why they tend to buy brand-name products. From childhood, they've been dressed in uniforms and their individuality has been carefully killed off (Suzuki, 1990).

Most likely, the situation today is one of transition, with the behaviour discussed by Mr Suzuki being the still prominent vestiges of yesterday's less-differentiated, less-affluent consumer society. The Japanese 'White Paper on Livelihood' (Prime Minister's office, 1989) found clear evidence of diversifying preferences and a growing taste for higher quality, more expensive goods, the emergence of new service industries and a renewed interest in leisure. In the new climate of affluence, it reports, luxury seems almost within everyone's reach. Luxury goods are being snapped up by consumers in all but the lowest income brackets. All over Japan today, you will also find civic groups holding serious-minded symposia on such questions as creative leisure use, reduced working hours and their impact, how to use long weekends more effectively, and so on.

The enormous growth in new product development also owes much to the present near-universality of corporate diversification programs in major Japanese companies. Considerable diversification had, of course, been going on since the 1970s, but its critical role in the survival of the Japanese corporation was suddenly brought into focus by the *endaka* of 1986–7. At that time, most of Japan's leading economic research companies published predictions as to which Japanese corporations, if any, could survive *endaka* if it were to reach ¥100 to the US dollar. One major institute found that only nine major firms would survive a dollar: yen rate of ¥100. Another concluded that only one, the Matsushita Group, would remain profitable at that rate.

Corporate reaction was speedy. Nippon Steel, although no longer Japan's no. 1 company, but still its most respected and aristocratic, announced its 'Medium and Long-range Vision for Diversification' in 1987. In the next three years it announced a variety of new initiatives unrelated to steel—in electronics and information-processing technology with Sankyo Seiki, a joint venture with IBM to provide general services for small computer systems, a joint venture with C. Itoh & Co. to develop the system integration business, and Space World, a theme park built on an old factory site. These and other ventures were in addition to earlier entries into silicon wafers, food and wine importing and computer work stations. Nippon Steel wants half of its turnover to come from non-steel business by 1995. NTT (Nippon Telephone and Telegraph), as soon as it was privatized in 1987, began to develop subsidiaries at breakneck speed—in urban development, international communications and consulting—with a hundred formed in just six months. Nippon Kokan, another major steelmaker, moved into raising hogs and selling ham. Asahi Pen diversified into cosmetics. Nissan moved into down-market retailing of products like T-shirts, stationery and handbags, as well as investing heavily in new fast-food chains.

Textiles giant Toray, already diversifying since the late 1970s, is targeting all the new high-growth areas of electronics, health-care products, new materials and biotechnology. Cosmo, one of the largest oil companies in Japan, has diversified into commercial mazes, a wig rental business, self-administering medical diagnostic kits, health foods and amusement parks.

There is some evidence that some of the big companies made some unwise choices of new businesses and had their fingers burned. The 19 August 1989 issue of the *Economist* reported:

> Nippon Steel has quit the mail order business. Most of the 20 pilot plants built by chemicals and metals firms . . . are now lying idle . . . Minebea recently cancelled investment in electronics and curtailed the new division's operations . . . [Major firms] proved slow at developing the marketing skills needed to break into high-growth businesses like new materials, telecommunications, factory automation, semiconductors . . . Most played follow-my-leader, waiting for one innovator to make a move.

While the very large firms were having some trouble in meeting new corporate goals for diversification, many of the more flexible, entrepreneurial companies were performing outstandingly. Temporary Center, Japan's largest provider of temporary office staff, and the winner of the prestigious Nikkei national award for creative excellence in new venture businesses in 1987 and 1988, has funded some sixty different new businesses. They cover most of the new high-growth areas, including health foods of all kinds, executive search businesses in Japan and overseas, secretarial schools, Japanese language and culture centres, and the importation of value-added products of all kinds. Bridgestone, the world's third largest tyre maker, now gains close to a quarter of its annual revenues from, non-tyre business. Sources include bedding materials and cushions, lithium batteries, swimming schools and other sports facilities, real estate development, training programs, a Super Bolt combining plastic and metal, Calm Zone, a sound reduction panel, and Multi-Rubber Bearing (used in building foundations). Japan's second largest company, Matsushita, sees the 1990s as a high-growth era for home electronics, with high-definition TV and other new products. It is also moving heavily into industrial electronics, especially the marketing of the factory automation systems of its own creation, which have underlaid its own growth to become one of Japan's leading low-cost producers.

This sketch of diversification activities should give some more concrete focus to the description of Japan as the world's premier new product laboratory.

2 The Japanese Way of Selling, Buying, Marketing and Negotiating

In the West, they can be company heroes, their bosses are respectful and defer to them, they are lone wolves who work alone in the field on their own initiative, their incomes can be higher than that of the chief executive, and many are millionaires. Who are they? They are high-flying specialty sales representatives, earning large commissions from their individual sales efforts.

None of this is true in Japan. Individualism is frowned on as egotistical. It is the sales team effort that is important, not that of individuals. Whatever modest commissions they receive will be calculated from group performance. If you were ever to see a tough Japanese sales manager berate his salesteam—in turn bullying, scathing, sarcastic, disparaging—you would find the idea of the 'salesman as hero' laughable.

But the heart of the difference between Japanese and Western concepts of selling lies in the connection made with the customer. Sales representatives, or other members of the organization who deal with clients, identify more with the client organization than with their own. The buyer is always regarded and accepted as having superior status to the salesman. For the most part, whatever their experience or skills, they do not attempt to behave as proud professional sales executives, but as sincere, even humble, performers of whatever services or favours the client seeks—as you will see in a moment, these can sometimes have no connection with the job, at least from Western eyes. Both the salesperson and the buyer, in fact, accept that the business benefit will develop only when the core of the relationship is seen not as a rational exchange of goods or services for some consideration, but as a close personal, human relationship, grounded in the giving and receiving of favours.

BUYERS CAN BE ARROGANT

There is nothing you can do about it, and there is nothing that Japanese sales representatives would want to do about it, but . . . Japanese buyers sometimes behave like arrogant and spoilt children as they revel in the superior status assigned to them by society. In the pharmaceutical industry, ethical drug salespeople, called *puropa*, must frequently and regularly endure high-handed, autocratic behaviour from general practitioners and hospital doctors. Many of them make it clear that 'provided you don't mention anything about your products, I will let you have some orders'. Attempts to introduce information about products may be immediately cut off, in a peremptory and threatening manner. This restricts *puropa* to conversations about golf, news of the client's other colleagues and family inquiries. It is not uncommon, in fact, for *puropa* to put themselves entirely at the service of some doctors for personal favours, such as taking the children to school or kindergarten, or the wife for shopping on the Ginza.

Even if the buyer is not arrogant, social mores, which he and the salesperson accept unquestioningly, lead him to demand excellence in service and product quality, and to have the upper hand in the business interaction. 'The customer is king' is taken seriously among the Japanese, and, as is customary in all stations of life in Japan, the salesperson is exceptionally motivated to see that nothing he says could offend the buyer. In particular, questions are avoided when receiving orders from clients.

This has been a cause of great irritation to foreign managers in Japan in charge of Japanese salesmen. One foreign-owned processed food company operates on a licensing basis. Its Japanese salesmen have the task of selling marketing campaigns to licensees throughout Japan. In reality, however, the salesmen make no attempt to sell the campaigns. Not every salesman will make presentations about the campaigns, and if they do, they will be low-key, non-persuasive, using a Japanese-style modesty when they seem to disparage what they present with comments like 'This is just one possible idea'. The foreign managers complain that salesmen typically return to the office, not with campaign acceptances, but with brand-new suggestions from the licensees that are unclear, confused and incapable of being fulfilled.

The Japanese in these and many other cases believe very sincerely that their job is to identify with and support their customers, and to act as the customer liaison officer and advocate within their own company. You can see how easy it would be for some buyers (Japanese or Western) to grow accustomed to getting their own way and sometimes 'feeling spoilt'; that, after all, must also be the intention of the Japanese salesperson, that is, to spoil the customer and satisfy his whims, or whatever is needed to hold his business. A little more subtly, you may also see how it might be easy for non-Japanese to become indignant when they sense that they too are being expected to offer this very different kind of service that Japanese buyers have become accustomed to and expect.

Asking Questions

A major difficulty for Japanese salespeople is asking the client questions, especially those which might seem prying. Typically, they accept what the client requests, then go away and try to work out what he is really getting at, and why, and how to meet his demands. The same thing happens, however, within a company, when juniors receive orders from seniors.

Probably most foreigners with an interest in Japan know by now that when the Japanese say *hai* (meaning 'yes'), they are only acknowledging that they have heard what you say, not necessarily that they agree. Actually, it can be even more complicated. They can and do say *hai* to signify that they have heard, but it need not even mean that they understood. It is only when they are alone with their peers that they feel free to express uncertainty, and ask one another, 'What do you think he really means?'

In Japan, however, such situations are entirely accepted. A 'good' subordinate (or wife or child or friend) is expected to understand the other's true feelings intuitively. Asking questions that the other party would find embarrassing to answer, or which might require divulging confidential information, or which it is easy to deduce yourself from what has already been said, or from the context or background, is likely to be regarded as a sign of insensitivity or immaturity.

The Key is Service

Putting aside the very important aspects of the product, price, delivery, warranty and service package, the key to the Japanese idea of salesmanship and persuasion is devoted service over time. This aims quite explicitly to build up a weight of obligation that has to be repaid—at least by sales orders, perhaps also by recommendations to other companies or friends, and perhaps in other personal ways as well. These benefits result from the tightly networked structure of Japanese business societies (in Japan or abroad) where, as in other countries but to an even greater extent in Japan, word of mouth recommendations and 'who you know' are far more important than advertising or slick leaflets.

This customer orientation in Japan should never be thought of as a sales 'strategy'. It is an authentic part of the culture of modern capitalist enterprise in Japan. Most major companies have' made a feature of statements of company ideals or precepts that have strong ethical overtones. By far the commonest theme in these is the injunction to serve, service to the nation, to the society, to customers. This very distinctive ethic owes much to the entry into business of members of the former hereditary *samurai* class, who were disenfranchised soon after Japan was opened to the West in the late nineteenth century. *Samurai* were raised to take their place in feudal society as the responsible leading class, not concerned about money, but about honour and the nation's welfare. The first precept of Mitsubishi Corporation, for example, is 'corporate responsibility to society'. The Idemitsu Corporation includes the statement: 'We work in unity and friendliness for the common object of doing good for society'.

It is worthwhile pointing out an important regional difference in customer orientation between the Tokyo region and the Osaka–Nagoya area. Historically, as well as today, Tokyo was the centre of government, dominated by *samurai* ethical values and long-range visions, and disdainful of people in the provinces. Osaka, on the other hand, was the major commercial city, with a free-spirited approach to business, combining self-reliance and independence from the centre of government with values of frugality, practicality and a narrow merchant orientation. Even today, Osaka merchants are regarded as interested in quick profits and as possessing a gutsy mercantile courage. Tokyo business, on the other hand, is regarded as more ethical, philosophical and long-range in its approach, sophisticated and modern, and able to adapt more readily to unforeseen developments. The Tokyo region is and will remain dominant in trend-setting, setting the pace in youth-oriented, innovative enterprises (Lu, 1987).

On the personal level, the orientation of service to others starts in the home, and is taken up and reinforced in the school and society. Serving people—at home, in the office, with friends—is, to the Japanese, quintessentially human. People who massage a friend's stiff shoulders, or go out of their way to do favours to strangers, or make every effort to make customers or visitors feel at home, are acting 'from the heart'—being of service even if it 'kills them', they might say. Ms Yoshiko Nagai, for instance, has been a senior sales representative for a bed manufacturer in Tokyo for fifteen years. She has long recognized that it is impossible to be successful in direct selling to Japanese housewives if she takes a narrowly mercenary view, thinking only of making a sale and then moving quickly on to the next prospect. Every enquiry that comes in, even if it is clearly not going to bring a sale, she follows up. Personal service has top priority. From time to time, she calls on old customers who have just lost their husbands. A wife and mother herself, she responds immediately to the grief of the old customer. They take one another's hands and cry freely.

Another example is Kiyoshi Matsuda, a Japanese computer salesman in the Middle East. His Arab customers are accustomed to dealing with salespeople from many different countries, but Matsuda San always stands out from the others. For one thing, he thinks nothing of working whatever hours are necessary to solve any problems in the customer's system, even if it is a competitor's equipment. Nor does Matsuda San forget his customers whenever he has to leave the country. When he comes back, he always brings gifts not just for the manager, but for the office girls as well. The gifts are modest, but his Middle East customers are sincerely grateful for his thoughtfulness.

What are the lessons for you, the non-Japanese who would sell to the Japanese? After all, you are not Japanese, you may not speak the language nor be sophisticated in Japanese ways of getting along with people, and you may visit the prospective client only infrequently. Still, the situation is not as challenging as it might appear. For one thing, the Japanese executive expects few foreigners to understand how things are done in Japan. As long as there are basic good manners and personal maturity, they extend considerable tolerance to those ignorant of Japan and Japanese mores. Interestingly, as I pointed out in *The Japanese Negotiator* (March, 1988), Japanese executives readily answer probing questions about their companies and current situation from foreigners, which they would never do with Japanese sale representatives or other outsiders. A number of foreign executives have told me of receiving exactly the same full answers to their questions (in contrast to no answer to questions from their Japanese salespeople).

The other lesson is about having a service orientation to customers. No Japanese will expect you to be as deferential or unconditional in your approach as a Japanese. Those Westerners who feel it an affront to their self-image to behave in a deferential way to Japanese buyers may have a problem adjusting comfortably to the Japanese or to their expectations. Certainly as a minimum, the Japanese expect sincerity, not calculation. They will expect you to be thinking about their needs, and their problems, rather than about your products or your profit or

your convenience. If at least you were seen to do this, even if otherwise reluctant to follow Japanese ways—it still might work.

THE SALES REPRESENTATIVE AND THE JAPANESE

If the Western salesperson is best typified by eloquence and friendliness, it is no surprise that salespeople should be so distrusted in Japan.
This is a country where the man who is quiet and speaks little is
regarded as manly, while he who speaks well is distrusted. This
attitude owes a lot to the old *samurai* traditions. Samurai embraced
sayings such as 'Talk is the root of misfortune', 'In your speech honey,
in your heart, a sword' and 'Keep your mouth closed and your eyes
open'. The earliest homilies on merchant behaviour in Japan, dating
from the fifteenth century, were no less damning: 'Idle talk is prof-
itless', said the sage merchant Izumiya, 'if you want to become rich.'
Zen Buddhism has always required its students to stop intellectualiz-
ing, that is stop verbalizing, if they wish to have 'direct knowledge of
reality'. The equally influential Confucian tradition taught that one
could only realize one's destiny by submitting to the dictates of
heaven, and rhetoric or pushy persuasion had no part in that.

Much of this is still true for Japan today. Young Japanese are still
taught by parents and teachers to be reserved, not to speak up. Parents
admonish their children to avoid 'sticking out', in line with the well-
worn adage: 'The nail that sticks out gets hit'. They still show diffi-
dence and hesitation with strangers, still lack assertion in standing up
for their individual rights, are unreserved only with their closest intimates. Unlike so many of us with a Western upbringing, the Japanese
have no familiarity with (and usually little affection for) intellectual debate, or the idea that 'truth' can be arrived at or expressed verbally.
There is nothing in their cultural tradition like the Western concept of
the diplomat–negotiator, of the 'drawing-room chevalier' who is able
to move from country to country, mixing with the citizens in an affable
cultivated manner. It is a cultural background woven from these and
other elements that inhibits the development of a concept of the persuasively skilled salesperson. One Japanese business consultant puts
it this way:

> . . . the Japanese intrinsically have a deep-rooted suspicion of what is
> clearly defined or stated. We believe truth is in the grey zone. For in-
> stance, if you say 'My marriage is simply wonderful', we suspect you are
> not telling the truth. However, if you say 'My marriage is an entire

mistake' we also doubt its validity. But when you say 'My marriage is a wonderful mistake', we now feel you are talking and telling the truth. (Kobayashi, 1985)

Kobayashi's message is as relevant to business and the selling situation as it is to any other in Japan. In a few words, the message is: cool the sales talk and the big claims. Be modest and balanced in talking about yourself, your company and its products.

Buying for Integrated Manufacturing Systems

The wisdom of dispensing with sales talk and claims is strikingly brought home when you try to sell components or parts in Japan. This runs you directly into a powerful and now highly evolved system which integrates the supplier with producer and customer. (see Baillie; 1986; Chiesl & Knight, 1985; Manoochehri, 1984; Reich, 1987). Stemming from the philosophy of quality manufacture propounded by Edward Deming, today it includes the notions of the quality-control cycle, involving designers, suppliers, producers and customers, zero defects, the quest for the elimination of defective parts, *baka yoke*, or procedures for the avoidance of 'foolish' mistakes, and the just-in-time (JIT) system designed to smooth production flows by producing the required item at the time needed, and in the quantities required.

Because of the strategic importance of the supplier in making this type of integrated system work effectively, would-be suppliers are put through a long and tough evaluation process by Japanese buyers. This typically means revealing corporate information that may have never before been given to outsiders, repeated testing to ensure that the product will meet requirements, and that the relationship, unlike in the West, will be mutually close and co-operative. This is usually a major learning experience for Western suppliers, whose previous experience with component buyers has been cost-oriented rather than quality— or co-operation-oriented. In the Japanese system, producers feel they must share highly confidential information about usage, quality, tolerances, potential production processes, production scheduling, etc., with the suppliers. Before they do that, they need to satisfy themselves that the information will be treated confidentially and not divulged to competitors. (The reverse also applies.)

Selling components into this kind of integrated manufacturing system, it will be clear, is closer to the negotiation of a joint venture or merger than it is to most of the kinds of selling and marketing considered in this book. It therefore requires commitment at the highest level of the foreign corporation. (See Case study 2-1 for a further example of a supplier-buyer relationship in Japan.)

The complexity of the more advanced procurement systems can be illustrated by studying those of Sony and Nissan. Sony Corporation calls their approach one of 'global localization'. This means that, simultaneously, they promote the self-management of procurement in their thirty-five overseas factories, while the headquarters procurement group in Japan provides support to them to improve their procurement function. This support includes the transfer of skilled personnel overseas, training in Japan of local plant staff, establishment of a tight global information system, and the use of a unified coding system for components, etc. In practice, plants overseas procure some parts locally and some from the international procurement office in Japan. Local procurement is increasing.

Sony's basic philosophy of procurement is clearly spelt out in English-language documents which they will supply. As Mr Yoji Maeda, of the HQ Procurement Group puts it, Sony acquires new suppliers and their parts through their Qualification and Approval (QA) System. First, new parts are tested and qualified by the QA Division of the HQ Procurement Group to determine whether they satisfy the designers' specifications and quality levels. Second, prototype products incorporating the parts that pass the first stage are assembled and tested for performance. Parts satisfying the designers' specifications should then normally be approved. In Japan, 90 per cent of incoming parts are provided by suppliers who have been vetted through the QA system. This system is being introduced into the eleven plants in South-east Asia, and will be introduced globally in the future.

Nissan Motor Co. Ltd provides a comprehensive booklet entitled 'Selling to Nissan' which every would-be supplier to Nissan should acquire. Even more than Sony, Nissan's overseas manufacturing facilities have the authority and responsibility for purchasing their own parts and materials, and actively encourage enquiries.

THE MARKETING CONCEPT IN JAPAN

The marketing concept, with its emphasis on the centrality of customer needs, and on conceptual and analytical tools for the application of the marketing concept in practice, was taken over and quickly mastered by the Japanese in the 1950s. However, there are many differences between the Japanese and the Americans in the application of the marketing concept that need to be understood. These differences include:

- Americans advocate specialization in marketing; Japanese business executives look down on specialists.
- Americans advocate objective, research-based decision-making; the Japanese are more 'subjective', distrust research, make more gut-level decisions about marketing.
- Americans see marketing people as in fast-track careers, with potential to make it to the top; Japanese see them as narrow, academic, unpromotable.
- Americans have specialist marketing managers managing the entire marketing function; the Japanese have general business managers in charge of all 'marketing' activities.
- The Americans have co-ordinated and centralized specific activities under unified marketing departments; the Japanese still tend to have decentralized separate, independent specialist departments: for advertising, research, new product development, planning, etc.
- Americans subordinate sales departments to overall marketing direction; the Japanese subordinate marketing and marketing service departments to the sales department.
- Americans give marketing departments the primary responsibility and authority for marketing decisions, the Japanese give it to general business managers or to heads of sales departments.
- Americans give central emphasis to 'big' marketing strategies and comprehensive, integrated marketing planning; the Japanese are more piecemeal in approach, have few 'big' strategies, are more tactical and responsive to the whims and requests of big wholesalers and retailers.

One way to explain these differences is to note that the Japanese concept of a general manager, the most desirable ambition for a young executive, is as an all-rounder who has been rotated throughout the organization over the early years of his career, until he is seen to be ready for general management. This concept of the generalist, along with the downgrading of specialists, is universal in Japan, and is reinforced by the practice of on-the-job training for marketing (and other functional areas) with emphasis on learning practical ways to promote sales and get along well with customers, rather than academic study. The Japanese generalist orientation (which also means that no job specification exists) means in practice that, in the case of customer complaints handling, for instance, one individual will do all the follow-through, whatever the problem. A Japanese car sales representative might be expected to undertake minor adjustments to a vehicle still under warranty. Under no circumstances would he rest content with showing the customer the location of the repair shop.

An important principle in understanding the Japanese approach to marketing stems from a time-honoured expression, *genba wa tsuyoi*, or, freely translated, 'the strength is with the field'. This is accepted as the epitome of common sense in organizational life. *Genba*, the field, has the meaning of 'where the action is', and the injunction to take notice of the *genba* is a warning to anyone who would plan for others first to understand exactly what the *genba* situation is. In corporate life, an important *genba* is the sales force and the channels of distribution it services. Japanese managers know perfectly well from experience how strong this particular field is. The manager who would try to force the sales department to introduce a product which the sales people feel will not be successful is doomed to failure in Japan. The sales team will simply not push it. Their hearts will not be in it. Once that happens, no one in the company has any capacity or power to induce the sales department to push it in spite of its misgivings. This is a very different situation from that usual in the West.

Another key difference affecting the way marketing is organized and carried out is that the most important corporate goal of the company is to sustain or achieve high sales turnover and market leadership, with profit goals subordinated. This is very different from American obsession with profitability. The market share emphasis in Japan makes for major differences in practical business management, especially by allowing the manager to direct new businesses towards building sales and market share, with only a caveat 'not to lose money'. As well, the Japanese emphasis puts the general managers in charge of achieving results which, in the West, would be more the responsibility of the marketing managers. Marketing practice in Japan is thus embedded deeply in a context of general management. Or, put another way, marketing in Japan is merely a set of tools and orientations in the hands of smart but not professionally trained staff, under the control of general managers. It is not the responsibility of some specialist divisional manager (who would in any case be suspected of being incompetent for the tasks of general management).

CHALLENGES FOR THE WESTERN SELLER

Dealing with a people as dedicated to personalized customer service as the Japanese provides challenges that should not be underestimated. Personally, one challenge comes in terms of contrasting personal styles. Extrovert, 'stereotyped' salespeople may find it a little more challenging than usual to manage introverted, sceptical, 'unfriendly' Japanese buyers. The Japanese disdain of 'salesmanship', if you do launch out into product rhetoric, may be offensive. If your style tends in this area, you will probably need to modify it. In particular, you may need to speak less, use or tolerate silence more, give your Japanese buyer more personal space (don't physically crowd him), expect that he knows his job (even if on first sight he does not inspire you with confidence) and is only doing what he must do; and don't expect to become friends, or even friendly, too quickly.

From discussions with many foreign executives dealing with the Japanese on complex issues (such as component supply, joint venture formation, technology or licensing distributor agreements), I have formed the impression that a fairly predictable model or process of adjustment to the Japanese side is involved. In some ways it is like the process that the dying are believed to go through, from disbelief to resignation. In other ways, it is similar to the diffusion of innovation process. The stages in the Western executive's adjustment to Japan seem to be like this:

1 You begin in honeymoon mood with great business optimism, curiosity, interest and some fascination (in fact, if you don't have these in the beginning, you will probably never make it with the Japanese).

2 Initially, you feel respectful and trusting of the Japanese side, even if some things happen that you can't quite make sense of.

3 You become puzzled and bewildered, as these odd or funny things continue to happen, such as promises that seem to be made failing to materialize.

4 You become irritated, shocked, angry and contemplate giving up (this will stay with you for a long time).

5 Your fighting spirit rescues you as you pull yourself together to enjoy a brief period of power and autonomy.

6 That doesn't last, and now you become depressed, bitter and melancholy. Now you really do look the unthinkable—the complete severing of the relationship—squarely in the face, even though you know that you probably cannot find anyone else to take your pros-

pective customer's place in Japan. In this mood, you may feel most acutely that you have been tricked by the Japanese, secretly accuse them of double-dealing, of leading you on, of unethical behaviour.

7 Eventually the gloom begins to lift, and you begin to see the Japanese side and their demands in a sober and realistic fashion, their strengths and weaknesses as well as your own self-delusion. You slash the big number forecasts you had once made of Japan's short-term potential, and say ironically to yourself: 'Welcome to Japan!'

CASE STUDY 2-1: RELATIONSHIPS WITH JAPANESE CUSTOMERS AND SUPPLIERS

by Shojiro Makino
President
Grace Japan KK

Most of us are familiar with multilayer distribution channels, particularly for mass-consumed products. Between manufacturers and retailers there are often three or even four layers of wholesalers and sub-wholesalers, with each retailer and wholesaler covering limited product markets. These multilayer distribution channels have evolved as the most economical and efficient means of serving a market environment that has long been characterized by relatively small *per capita* income, crowded living quarters and heavy reliance by consumers on public transportation and travel by foot.

The same systems apply even to industrial goods. Because of the existence of many small buyers, the industrial manufacturer finds it extremely difficult to sell directly to such buyers economically. Excepting products which require a high degree of technical service and follow-up, the majority of industrial goods manufacturers still rely on the existing layers of distribution. In addition, these channels, especially the wholesalers, perform functions such as delivery, sales calls, point of purchase advertisement, collection of accounts receivable, working capital financing and market information feedback.

Contractual Relationship

Another important characteristic is the 'assumed' continuity of contractual relationships. Normally in Japan contracts between two individuals or firms, often not written, are assumed to be continuous unless some drastic changes take place to shake the foundation of the relationship. This assumed continuity often carries real cash value. It is considered to provide effective insurance against the uncertain outcome of written contractual relationships. Any specific conflict is resolved to maintain the essential continuity of relationship. As you may know, the Japanese prefer to resolve problems through compromise, reconciliation and third-party arbitration, instead of going to court. Accordingly, firms are reluctant to switch their suppliers and customers because the continuity of a business relationship carries higher value than discounts and other benefits offered by new suppliers.

Organic Relationship

In industrial product marketing, Japanese customers demand that manufacturers become a vital part of some organic customer–supplier relationship. Here, reluctance and/or unwillingness to meet the demand often result in failure to obtain business. In American industrial marketing, managers try to make deals with purchasing managers of their industrial customers by juggling three product variables, namely, price, delivery and quality. All these variables are treated as economic trade-offs. Since delivery and quality are often set at the level of the 'adequate industry standard', price becomes the only negotiating point between supplier and purchasing agent.

Not so in Japan. During the last thirty years and particularly perhaps the last fifteen years, Japanese manufacturers have developed manufacturing systems that challenge the conventional wisdom of industrial engineering, manufacturing operation and operations research. Suppliers must strive for zero-defect quality and a delivery schedule set by customer plants. Before suppliers are accepted, purchasing managers and quality control managers of the customer carefully check suppliers' production and quality assurance systems to evaluate whether the suppliers are capable of meeting their rigid standards. Believe it or not, supply prices are very often set by customer plants or negotiated between supplier and customer to ensure that the prices are 'reasonable'. Also, suppliers are expected to provide additional services, such as absorbing surplus manpower and early retirees from their customer plants. Obviously, it is not simply price that determines the relationship.

These interactions which form a special customer–supplier relationship can and do often impede the foreign manufacturer to enter a particular market. This is not only limited to the case of government monopolies but also applies to the private sector. The famous Japanese 'just in time' system (*kamban* system), developed by Toyota, was only possible through customer–supplier interactions where the supplier becomes a vital part of the organic relationship.

Quality

There are some significant differences in quality control and quality improvement areas between Japanese and United States manufacturers. In general, the American manufacturing system tries to inspect quality into products, while the responsibility for quality control of customers is often shifted to suppliers. Quality and productivity are not treated as trade-off variables. Instead, quality is assumed to determine productivity.

A strong need to improve product quality is also built into the Japanese manufacturing system, as customers demand and get, almost without exception, both quality improvements and scheduled price reductions from suppliers. The latter are pressured to improve product quality and cut production cost as they ride down the fabled experience curve. Price increases are rarely permitted, unless suppliers vastly improve products or develop new products that help customers cut their production cost and improve product quality. Japanese customers are seldom satisfied with 'an acceptable quality level' or 'adequate-industry standard'.

Case One

To illustrate the difference between quality considerations in the typical United States and Japanese production systems, I will present our own case. Grace Japan K K, a wholly-owned subsidiary of W.R. Grace & Co., was established in 1961. We specialize in sealants for food and beverage cans, among others, and are totally integrated in manufacturing in Japan. Initially, the technological superiority of our products enabled us to take almost 100 per cent of the market. The fact that our major customers had technical ties with companies like Continental and American Can also helped us establish this strong position. Then, Japanese competitors began to enter the market and gradually eroded our market share, at first by price-cutting and next by providing better services. However, the superiority of our products enabled us to maintain the leading position until the early 1970s.

When a leading can manufacturer developed a special seam process for their cans, they needed sealants with improved or different properties, and therefore came to us to develop such a product. For about five years we kept telling them our standard in the United States. During the period, we were not smart enough to know that our customer was improving the can-end lining speed up to 800 per minute and its quality standard from one defect per 50,000 to one out of a million or better. Our product began to have difficulty in meeting the rigorous requirements. In the meantime, a competitor at the request of this customer undertook to develop a new compound in a collaborative R&D. Earlier Grace had flatly refused to enter into such agreements as such a project would have necessitated the disclosure of all know-how, formulations, manufacturing processes, etc. When we began realizing, somewhat belatedly, what was happening, we started to send urgent requests to central R&D laboratory in Lexington, Massachusetts, for the improved product along with greater details about specific technology. These requests were often met with complete disbelief. Grace collectively failed to appreciate the importance, and did not like the idea of becoming an integral part of the supplier support system of this major customer. Around 1976, literally overnight, we lost the major part of the business to competition.

Case Two

We are currently one of three major suppliers of a certain chemical product to a top car manufacturer. It took three years to become a candidate supplier, in spite of the fact that we introduced a new product which no one was supplying. It took another year before finally being admitted to the select circle of chemical products suppliers. Although our product was a uniquely new material not available from any existing suppliers, the car manufacturer decided, to our dismay, to give them the opportunity to meet our specification, properties and characteristics in order not to disrupt a longstanding relationship.

Before final approval was given, a total of two dozen people, mainly technical, visited our plant at Atsugi on several occasions to inspect our quality assurance system and procedures and existing manufacturing facilities, and to review the proposed system and procedures for scaling up. We were requested to submit two documents, one called 'Company Profile' and the other called 'Cost Estimate'. In addition, we were asked to present our policy on quality assurance, our organization chart, quality assurance systems and procedures, manufacturing facilities, history of product development, manufacturing processes, inspection specifications, QC and quality improvement, quality assurance systems and procedures for scale-up production, etc. I went ahead and filled out all the forms and provided all the information without getting prior approval from our New York headquarters. I knew there was not time to explain and I knew, if I explained, they would ask me to commit *harakiri* before furnishing all this information. We were absolutely and totally stripped down. There was not a secret left. Nevertheless, later I convinced my bosses that the long-term benefits of the relationship thus formed with Nissan were worth sacrificing for perhaps a better price, at least for the short term.

In conclusion, the intimate knowledge of the traditional buyer-dominant relationship behaviour is the key to successful marketing by foreign firms in Japan! As emphasized, continuity of the contractual relationship, written or unwritten, different industrial marketing and manufacturing systems, product management, quality control and quality improvement are a few important components of the buyer-seller relationship which is distinctly long-term-oriented.

Part 2

FACTORS FOR SUCCESS OR FAILURE IN SELLING TO THE JAPANESE

3 Success and Failure in Japan

What makes for success or failure in selling to Japanese customers? Here are some different answers to that question, drawn from the experiences or conclusions of foreign companies already successful in Japan:

> . . . tailor your products to the demands, tastes and particular requirements of Japanese customers . . .cautiously select Japanese counterparts to complement your original strength . . . make heavy up-front investments and re-tailor product lines and specifications to local needs . . . delegate authority to local management . . . (McKinsey & Co., 1983; also cited in Nakajima, 1987)

> Make a serious study of the Japanese market with particular emphasis on Japan's changing economic and social patterns . . . Tailor [your] wares to Japanese tastes and requirements . . . Move as swiftly to exploit opportunities in the Japanese market as Japanese firms do to exploit opportunities in ours . . . keep a much closer eye on Japan's increasingly innovative technology, and, where feasible, borrow from it assiduously (Christopher, 1986).

Hachiro Koyama, president of one of the most successful foreign companies in Japan, Johnson's Wax, says that though there are 'dozens of factors which make foreign companies winners or losers . . . the most important factors [are] long-term commitment' by which he means 'a hard long-term commitment of capital investment and resources. . .thorough homework and preparation before entry and years of perseverance before operations become profitable'; and the other is adaptability or flexibility. This means 'adapting to local customs, business practices and the local culture in general'. Don't believe, he warns, that you can transplant 'your way' in Japan. There, it is 'adapt or die' (Koyama, 1985).

David Schmidt, president of Levi Strauss Japan, says that, based on his company's trial and error experience, 'five factors must work together: (1) long-term commitment, regardless of adversity; (2) commitment to a quality organization; (3) building and maintaining a strong brand image; (4) developing the right distribution mix; and (5) a detailed and thorough concentration on product, ours and our competitors' (Schmidt *et al.*, 1986).

It is obvious that there is a good deal of consensus among foreign business leaders and Japan business specialists as to what makes for success in Japan. How successful have foreign companies been in Japan? The evidence is very clear. Since the late 1960s, foreign companies in Japan have outperformed their Japanese competitors on key indices. For instance, the most recent results show that the net after-tax profit of foreign companies averaged 1.9 per cent, rising to 2.2 per cent for manufacturers, as against comparable figures of 0.8 per cent and 1.3 per cent for domestic Japanese companies. The sales-to-ordinary-profit ratio for foreign companies was 3.5 per cent, far exceeding the 1.8 per cent for all Japanese companies. In manufacturing, the average goes up to 4.3 per cent, and if petroleum is excluded, the figure jumps to an astonishing 6.8 per cent. These differences have held up consistently in the 1970s and 1980s, indicating at least that, once a foreign company has established itself in Japan, it performs exceptionally well. Indeed, in research of my own in 1977–78, comparing the performances of foreign firms in Japan, Australia, Malaysia, Indonesia and Philippines, more firms in Japan reported that they 'always' achieved corporate profit and sales objectives than was the case in other countries. Many Japan subsidiaries of foreign companies, moreover, are regularly reported to be the group's most profitable overseas subsidiary. These include Coca-Cola, Nestlé, Johnson's Wax, Ciba-Geigy, Max Factor, Kentucky Fried Chicken and many others. So there is enough evidence to indicate that if you can succeed in Japan, it is indeed going to be worthwhile.

Actually, the situation is probably even better than painted above, because you need to make a distinction between companies still in the pioneering stage, when they are invariably in the red and being funded by headquarters, and those which have reached the stage of operating regularly in the black and generating their own funds for development. It is not clear how many foreign companies are still pioneering in this sense, but one can get some inkling from the fact that in the late 1980s 200 or more foreign companies each year withdrew from Japan, out of a total of perhaps 4500 to 5000 companies (two-thirds of this number would be joint ventures where the majority stock is held by Japanese companies).

This generates a new question. What enables a company to move from the unsuccessful red-ink, pioneering stage to the successful black-ink, autonomous stage? Let me draw on the findings of my own research (March, 1977, 1978, 1980) over the last twelve or more years. This, plus consulting work to a number of foreign companies in Japan during the 1970s and 1980s, reinforces my conviction that, in most respects, these findings are still valid today. The key factors include: how long the subsidiary had been operating in Japan, attitudes of the head office towards Japan, the quality of the pioneer chief executive officer in Japan, the marketing strategies employed, product superiority and the corporate connections to the Japanese business environment.

For instance, I found that the successful companies, established on average in 1954, as against 1965 for the unsuccessful group, had more than three times as many employees, a well-established Japanese-style organization and decision-making style with high-quality Japanese personnel and far fewer expatriates (notwithstanding greater size). They were leaders in a secure market niche, more technologically innovative than Japanese competitors, with secure distribution channels and a well-established sales force. They had strong internal controls on cash, accounts and procedures. All of these, however, were fairly evidently consequences or concomitants of success. The origins of success proper, I reasoned, lay in four factors: the quality of the pioneer manager, parent company attitudes to the Japanese operation, the use of niche-oriented marketing strategies and the use of effective means for understanding and adapting to Japan.

THE QUALITY OF THE PIONEER MANAGER

This factor probably struck me more than anything else. These outstanding pioneer managers displayed the greatest perceptiveness about Japan, were of very superior intellect, personally warm, charming and acutely sensitive to others. These were the factors that enabled the sophisticated adjustment to Japan, as illustrated by the following interview quotations (March, 1978). The first is from an interview with a European manager.

MANAGER: Japanese are normally introverted, European managers are extroverted, so if you bring them together then normally the Japanese will be on the losing side. But they know their market better, they are just not able to argue in the same way as the Europeans are doing, so one of the jobs of the chief executive here is to make clear that the Japanese are not as stupid as they sometimes seem to be. My job is as a defender of the organization, and a motivator . . . I would even say that the company must be organized here in such a way that it is also functioning when the boss is in . . . he should motivate them to do something, to give new ideas, but he should not become too deeply involved . . .

INTERVIEWER: That seems to be the traditional role of a Japanese president, just to give a general framework.

MANAGER: One certainly must, and being trained in a different society one will always direct and control, but in a totally different way. They should not see this too clearly; you must lead them into what you want. If I were to call my middle managers and say, 'This morning I had a beautiful dream and we are going to do this and that, in this direction, and that is an order'—everybody would say 'yes', but nothing would be done! (ha, ha, ha). In the early days, I would tell them: 'I am just back from a trip to our customers, and I saw such and such— I think this is a good idea to do this.' They would all say 'yes', and we would decide what to do. Yet, after two weeks, I would ask how it was going, and they wouldn't be started. I would get angry and say: 'But everyone agreed to this, so do it!' Then eventually I would find out that it is just not possible. So one must lead them like this, give them much information, what you think, discuss the matter and say: 'Let us find the best possible way together'.

This interview is with an American manager.

INTERVIEWER: Could you try to crystallize the key points in your success in Japan—the company's success?

MANAGER: First of all, I would say that we did not make any difference between Japan and any other country. I was convinced that it was as difficult or as easy here as it is everywhere. Everybody talks about how suspicious the Japanese are, trying to keep the foreign makers out and all this 'hidden trade barriers' stuff. I found out that it is 90 per cent crap. They don't like the Japanese, they don't talk the language, they don't like to eat *misoshiru* (a traditional soup), they don't like the philosophy, they say the Western way is the only one, and there are ethical problems—Jesus Christ and Confucius have not much in common really. It can't be helped. But I'm in Asia and I'm not here as a missionary, but as a businessman, so I live with Confucius, of course. I think this was one reason. The Japanese, they are not great on psychology in respect of analyzing, but once they feel you are nice and mild and you don't dislike them . . . if you dislike them, they feel it at once, you can't hide it. Quite often they say to me, 'God damn you, *shachoo* (president), you have blue eyes!' They forget it, you see. Even when I talked broken Japanese at the beginning, that did not matter. Fluency is not important.

INTERVIEWER: They feel comfortable with you?

MANAGER: Exactly. And then it is really pleasant for them to have a foreign president—also very convenient for them, since then they always have a scapegoat. If they have to do something disagreeable, they just tell people, 'the *"hen na gaijin"* (odd foreigner) told us to do it'. You play this role so that you don't feel you are in a strange environment. My basic attitude was always that Japan is our home ground. That helped more than anything.

An Outstanding Japanese Pioneer Manager

These interviews indicate the sensitivity, adaptability and tolerance needed by successful foreign managers in their dealings with the Japanese, inside or outside their own organization. But before leaving this subject of the pioneer manager, it is only fair to say something about a Japanese manager who stands out as a superlative pioneer manager for a foreign enterprise, McDonald's Japan. The humour and humanity of former lawyer Den Fujita, chairman of McDonald's Japan, say so much about the personal qualities needed to set up an innovative business in Japan (Fujii, 1986).

> Den Fujita, 60, is a graduate of Tokyo University in law, who initially wanted to become a diplomat. But he was told that anyone with an Osaka accent would never be successful in the foreign service. So he established a trading company.
>
> Mr Fujita travelled often to the US on business. On one of his trips, friends tried to interest him in the fast-food business . . . (and) Ray Kroc, McDonald's founder, finally persuaded him.
>
> Mr Fujita told [a foreign audience] that he brought McDonald's to Japan to make the Japanese eat more beef . . . '[they] looked', he said, 'so seedy, pale-faced, short . . . shabby and not dignified'. By feeding beef to the Japanese, he hoped to make them 'more competitive in the international world'. Of course, he added, 'fat girls are inevitable' as a result of fast foods.

Human relations, according to Mr Fujita, are essential to success in Japan. 'Foreign businessmen need to study the complicated psychology of the Japanese . . . . For instance, the English language should be understood as a tool to take advantage of Japanese inferiority.' At McDonald's, employees speak some English to make the Japanese feel that the product is foreign.

If a product is made in Japan but it looks like it was made in the United States, then they will accept it. Sugar coating is necessary and then they can swallow it.

Mr Fujita's greatest fear is pizza . . .they could be serious competition. Every morning he looks at the newspapers to see if there is any news of pizza. He is relieved when he finds none.

There are about 1.6 million babies born in Japan each year and some 800,000 deaths. That would be a net gain but not according to Mr Fujita. He figures he gains 1.6 million new customers. 'These babies are my customers. The people who die are not my customers.'

Den Fujita is a highly educated, self-made businessman with immense charisma and a wonderful sense of humour. Pioneer managers, he reminds us, may need to be people a little out of the run of the conventional manager.

PARENT COMPANY ATTITUDES TO THE JAPAN OPERATION

The attitude to Japan of key head office executives (that is, the chief executive office or international vice-president) is one of the most important factors in success here. In some companies, this key home executive has particularly positive and affectionate attitudes; many have served in Japan, or have visited frequently; a few were born or educated here. These positive attitudes directly affect the degree of optimism felt about Japan prospects and about the level of investment to be made, as well as making the job of the Japan manager so much easier, because 'they both speak the same language'.

In contrast are companies where the key home executive has negative and sometimes hostile attitudes to Japan and the Japanese. This creates many problems for the local manager. Gaining approval for new projects is difficult, because they are seen as more risky, or because they involve trusting Japanese partners more. There was one anti-Japanese international vice-president who spent three days a year in Japan, but three weeks in Australia, even though the Japan business had ten times the Australian turnover (and could have had twenty times with more investment).

In another case, the United States parent's chairman was enthusiastic about Japan and kept pushing the local manager to present plans for new projects. But at the same time he was warned by the head of the international division, 'Don't show the chairman any plans, otherwise he'll be on my back wanting to get this thing going.'

Again the message is clear. If you want to be fully successful in Japan, you need total head office support.

NICHE-ORIENTED MARKETING STRATEGIES

Most foreign companies operate in highly competitive industries, some with rapid rates of change due to technological innovation. Most of the market leaders are Japanese, and they vie for leadership with one another, sacrificing immediate profits to increase or maintain market share. Moreover, they have often been one-product companies committed to a mass market, growth-at-all-costs philosophy, and investing little in additional products. This concentration has inevitably meant that the foreigner has had to choose a niche-focused marketing strategy, creating specialized products with distinctive characteristics. This has been the main track to success of foreign companies in Japan.

MEANS OF UNDERSTANDING AND ADAPTING TO JAPAN

Given the massive size of the Japanese business environment, the task of learning about it, understanding it and feeling at home in it can be daunting. What steps do foreign companies and executives take to understand and adapt to Japan?

There are at least three different strategies employed:

Invite Key Japanese to be your Advisors

Japanese who are strategically located in the business world—bureaucrats, politicians, bankers, scientists, consultants, wholesalers, etc.—will be better able than you to see the prevailing trends, opportunities and threats of importance to you. Retaining such people, by extending them stock or directorships, is common practice. But simply developing friendships with a wide spectrum of Japanese, outside Tokyo as well as within, can also be an important and continuing source of information.

Systematic Buyer Research

Some of the smarter foreign companies in Japan have deliberately invested in a variety of informal and formal research about Japanese buyer preferences and attitudes, in order to develop what one has called 'touch and sensitivity'. This can cover not only tastes and preferences, but also communication-related issues, in order to develop an understanding of the correct nuances for communicating with Japanese buyers. The point underlying this is that learning about Japan—its culture, tastes and preferences, about communication nuances—in everyday life is almost out of the question for non-Japanese, unless they have exceptional affinity for Japan, and make a determined effort to develop such a broad-based understanding.

Involve your Japanese Staff in Decision-Making

Involving Japanese staff in decision-making might seem plain common sense. Unfortunately, it does not always happen. Poor communication with them, difficulties in explaining key concepts and political issues within the company are part of the problem. Another is that many Western managers like to 'kick ideas around', 'bounce ideas off others'—but Japanese are not accustomed to this and usually mistake the Westerner's intention, with language problems compounding the situation.

However, both in Japan and abroad, there are increasing numbers of Western-educated Japanese and Japanese-educated Westerners who can make a useful contribution to decision-making about marketing and selling to the Japanese. The challenge, then, is for the manager to listen to and make sense out of suggestions which in many cases will be alien to his usual mode of thought.

Appendix 3.1 at the end of this chapter contains responses by eighty Western managers of foreign companies in Japan to the question: 'What advice would you give to a new foreign company setting up a Japan operation similar to your own?' These responses provide a useful set of ideas for those contemplating marketing and selling to the Japanese in Japan.

THE LESSONS FROM FAILURE

Unfortunately, for all the allure of big profits, the study of success rarely results in anything other than inspiration. The real lessons on how to succeed in difficult markets like Japan come from trial and error, from blundering and making mistakes, then recognizing them as such and correcting them, before it is too late. Complete failure comes when we fail to recognize and learn from mistakes and blunders, which then accumulate and eventually force withdrawal from the market.

The seeds of failure can be sown right at the very beginning of the foreign corporation's interest in Japan. As pointed out earlier, the attitudes to Japan of head office executives have a lot to do with success or failure in Japan. If head office from the start is lukewarm or ill-informed about Japan, entry decisions will often be made by teams from head office who, unfamiliar with Japan, entirely overlook critical issues. One is the task of recruiting quality personnel, the success of which depends in part on the philosophy of business and the quality of top management in the new venture. Another is the kind of impression to be made on prospective Japanese buyers. The most important factors are the quality of the top people in the new enterprise, and the image and 'respectability' of the corporation itself.

Product Adaptation Mistakes

Failures to adapt the product to Japanese tastes, or workplace requirements, are common. Most of these come back to just a few key differences, including:

1 *Difference in physique.* The Japanese have shorter limbs and relatively longer bodies; head shape is different; hands and feet are narrower and shorter. Such differences affect everyday clothing and industrial equipment such as tools and safety clothing.

2 *Colour and fragrance taste differences.* The Japanese prefer colours and fragrances lighter than Europeans, more delicate than other Asians. They especially avoid heavy fragrances. Many failures in shampoos, perfumes and toiletries have been attributed to failure to adapt to local consumer tastes.

3 *Animal fats.* Foreign foods with high fat content, such as chocolate, ice cream, yoghurt or cheese, tend to be avoided by the Japanese. The failure of Cadbury Dairy Milk Chocolate in Japan is said to have been because of its high milk fat content, in contrast to the very low fat level of the leading Japanese milk chocolate, which is crisp and brittle. However, United States ice cream brands such as Lady Borden, Baskin & Robbins, and Haagen Daz have all been successful because they took

the Japanese low tolerance for animal fats into account. The same is true for the French cream dessert maker, Danone, another successful foreign brand.

Marketing Strategy

If a product fails to be accepted by the consumer, no amount of excellence in advertising, etc. can help. But there are also cases of excellent products failing in the marketplace because of inappropriate marketing. The demise of Colgate in Japan in 1975, after having successfully gained up to 12 per cent market share of the Tokyo area toothpaste market, is one of the 'best' examples. Most trade opinion on the reasons for failure was that Colgate's attempts to increase its market share by price-cutting, which actually cut into wholesalers' margins, rapidly led to wholesalers refusing to carry the line.

In the early 1960s, there were many unsuccessful attempts to introduce American products into Japan. H.J. Heinz attempted to introduce tomato ketchup but was unable to overcome traditional attachment to soya sauce. General Mills established a joint venture with Morinaga Confectionery in Japan to market cornflakes, but were unable to supplement the traditional Japanese breakfast. In both these cases, we can say either that they were ahead of their time, or that they did not persevere, since eventually tomato ketchup and then cornflakes did take off in Japan.

While not exactly a failure due to marketing strategy, there was the case of Singer Sewing Machines in Japan in the 1960s, when it had the lion's share of the Japanese sewing machine market. According to reports, when a slight downturn occurred in the market, Singer attempted to sack some of their Japanese staff. This lead to public outcries against the 'heartless' Americans, savage media attacks on Singer and the suicide of at least one employee.

SUCCESS AND FAILURE IN EXPORTING TO THE JAPANESE

Much has been written about the success or failure of foreign subsidiaries in Japan, but there is very little about the success or failure of exporters to Japan. One reason is that the real marketing effort is undertaken by the Japanese distributor; since the foreign side is rarely involved directly, and has little or no say in making marketing policy, there seems little point in informing foreign audiences about what Japanese distributors do. In the USA, moreover, if one judges by what is being written, it is direct investment, not exporting, that business executives seem to want to read about. The little that is written about exporting often takes the form of self-critical articles with titles like 'They're cheap, they're late . . . they're American products' (Lorence, 1987). This particular article ends with a conventional list of five steps not to good exporting, but to setting up your own subsidiary in Japan!

Many commentators in the USA lament the lack of export orientation:

> US entrepreneurs [writes one pair of specialists] tend to be focused on product and technology given a known domestic market niche, and have little interest or knowledge of broader opportunities. Even if [they] are perceived, often ability to reach for them seems to have complexity and risks beyond the young organization's means (Cavugeil and Nason, n.d.)

Even in Australia, where domestic market size is miniscule compared to the USA, 'complexity and risk' also inhibit export performance. The leading Australian researchers on exporting, (1985) Barrett and Wilkinson (1985), say that non-exporters 'lack useful information about overseas markets and [have] difficulties in locating satisfactory overseas agents . . . [are affected by] exchange rate fluctuations, have working capital constraints and inability to offer competitive credit terms to overseas buyers'. Significantly, they provide much insight into export capability when they report that, based on their findings: '"Export oriented" firms are more likely to be larger firms, firms with some foreign ownership and firms which prepare written plans. They are also likely to have more top executives who are better educated and overseas-born' (Barrett & Wilkinson, 1985).

Obviously, export capability involves mastery or understanding of complex new markets and unknown people, and managerial and risk-taking abilities, as well as experience of strange cultures. In the case of Japan, we can expect these factors to be even more important, particularly when we hear warnings such as those of long-time Japan-side businessman Richard Bush (1981). Factors he cites that scare off would-be exporters from Japan include pre-warning of the difficulties others have faced, the reputation of Japan's 'unfair treatment of foreign goods', the 'mysterious distribution system that only Japanese can understand', etc. The late Mark Zimmerman, one of the best experts on doing business with the Japanese, who managed an American pharmaceutical manufacturer in Japan for many years, was not very attracted to exporting either:

Exporting to Japan is a thankless business, often resulting in disappointingly limited market shares and sales . . . I'm almost inclined to advise that (except in the case of high commodity agricultural products, raw materials, and unique products that are impossible for the Japanese to imitate) exporting to Japan is only a realistic option when undertaken as a market-testing device prior to local manufacturing in a joint venture or other direct investment in manufacturing . . . (Zimmerman, 1985).

Without actual experience, it seems difficult for many businesspeople to appreciate exactly what Zimmerman is getting at. I can offer here at least one comprehensive case study of exporting to Japan, the 'Chateau Case', which reveals better than any analysis the challenges that foreign exporters might expect. That case, plus my focus in this book, is not just about dealing with agents or distributors in Japan. There are many businesspeople outside Japan today who are doing or want to do business with Japanese individuals and companies resident or passing through their home country. These businesspeople quickly discover that dealing with the Japanese, in Japan or abroad, is different, and want advice on how to handle them. Even more so than the export managers who visit Japan occasionally, these businesspeople abroad may have absolutely no knowledge, experience of the Japanese and Japan, and frequently no interest either.

The Chateau case, plus the warning from Bush and Zimmerman, seem good grounds for considerable caution in planning long-term export distribution in Japan. There are many lessons to be learnt, but there is no case for a general avoidance of the Japanese market by exporters. Those who can expect to do best in Japan, however, will probably be large, already successful exporters elsewhere, with high-quality, culturally sensitive managers, able to inform and train themselves to deal with subtle and demanding distributors and end-users.

Support Systems for Potential Exporters

In spite of the difficulties, there is a variety of help at hand for the potential foreign exporter in Japan. JETRO, as mentioned elsewhere, provides its very useful TOPS system to help identify candidates as agents or distributors. The foreign Chambers of Commerce in Japan— United States, British, French, German, Canadian, Australian, etc.— provide access to a great deal of information and expertise from people who have already been successful there. Then there are the Japanese companies and trading houses themselves, your potential agents and distributors who will have much assistance to offer if they are convinced that your product stands a fair chance of succeeding in Japan.

On your side, you may want to bear in mind some of the lessons of the Chateau case.

Remaining Barriers in Japan

Since Richard Bush wrote in 1981 of the complaints then current of the difficulties and unfair treatment accorded foreign exporters, there has been a revolution in the status of the foreign export product. Six market-opening packages of new policies, legislative and tariff changes from the Japanese Government have greatly improved the market opportunities for foreign goods. These have included tariff reductions, greater self-certification for compliance with Japanese product standards and codes, the participation of foreign representatives on Japanese policy advisory councils, simplified import procedures, new government agencies open to foreign bidding and an ombudsman system.

Although more remains to be done in a number of areas, including cars, biotechnology, chemicals, cosmetics, computers, forest products, medical equipment and some others, the areas of 'difficulty' have been greatly reduced since 1981, while the new import measures introduced in 1990, and described in the introduction to this book, demonstrate the seriousness of the Japanese approach to import promotion.

Other Limitations on Exporting to Japan

Returning to the issue of the lack of popularity of exporting in the USA and elsewhere, another factor is the loss of control over marketing that occurs when a foreign agent takes over. In export markets other than Japan, exporters with marketing skills stand a good chance of retaining influence on the marketing policy and campaigns. This is rarely the case in Japan, where agents expect to take charge, consider that your experience elsewhere is irrelevant to the tough Japanese market, and leave you in a position equivalent to that of a dependent supplier. In this case, it is the agent alone who decides what customer benefits or themes are to be stressed, even what promotional materials are to be used.

Does this mean that you are then totally in the hands of the Japanese agent? The answer is almost certainly yes, although there are a few things you can do, should you wish to. The main one is to maintain excellent long-term personal relationships with senior Japanese managers throughout the agent company, so that you may be kept informed of what is happening. Still, you cannot count on this. The reason is that the Japanese side, if it has the kind of market or channel power that you need to get your products or services sold in Japan, will also be highly active in handling a variety of other agencies and concerns besides yours, not to mention new projects under way, and the major 'firefighting' that is part and parcel of every business. It will, needless to say, know exactly what the state of the market is and what are the demands on its own resources.

Whenever you might recommend some new venture or action, given this context, considerations that will inevitably arise include: how important to their overall business your component or contribution is; how feasible is your proposal in light of the current situation; and what time and resources are currently available to devote to your proposal. Decisions not to devote time to your requests or demands will probably be made fairly easily, whereas decisions *to* devote time will be made rather more slowly.

The issue for the Japanese side will then be how to convey this to you, if at all. Most commonly, little or nothing will be said when the decision is negative or suspended, in part because Japanese male pride dictates that one does not make needless explanations (since this might seem like the mere making of excuses), in part because the capacity to explain the complex issues is frequently beyond the English language ability of the Japanese concerned, and in part sometimes because the Japanese side takes the view that, as they are the side with superior status, there is no necessity for them to make explanations (this is likely to be relevant to the extent that you have failed to establish good personal relationships with the Japanese).

KEYS TO SUCCESS

I believe that three factors are the keys to dealing successfully with the Japanese. These are: adjusting to and even using aspects of the Japanese communication style, developing and maintaining good personal relationships with an array of Japanese, and having a good understanding of how Japanese companies work, of their politics and how they make decisions. These factors are equally important in Japan or abroad. I believe that most of the failures in dealing with the Japanese are to be attributed to failures in these three areas. And the truth is that few non-Japanese dealing with the Japanese can claim to have any innate or developed capacities in these respects. They must be worked on.

Sir Hugh Cortazzi, a former British Ambassador to Japan, wrote of the late Mark Zimmerman that: 'he recognized from the beginning that if he was to make a success of his time in Japan he had to learn to like and understand Japan and the Japanese . . . He had to understand Japan as it really is' (Zimmerman,1985). I agree unreservedly with this. If you don't work hard at being interested in, understanding and learning about the Japanese, the chances of failure will be measurably strengthened.

THE CHALLENGES OF PERSONAL RELATIONSHIPS IN JAPAN

The fact is that dealing on a regular basis with the Japanese is often described as a thankless, confusing or mystifying job, sometimes even as humiliating. One finds this even at top levels of management.

A friend, the Western president of an overseas subsidiary of one of Japan's largest computer companies since 1980, once said to me, 'I find a Japanese company so much more human and much more intelligent in its business planning than American companies. But the human relations I still don't comprehend. A man that I have seemingly friendly relations with one day, the next is suddenly cold and distant. I don't fathom them at all.' The week after he told me he had resigned! The difficulties of the human dealings had finally got to him, he said. He never knew where he stood with the Japanese senior managers he was dealing with, even though, intellectually, he knew that they were fair and decent men.

Another case, which I reported in *The Japanese Negotiator* (March, 1988), was an English commodities dealer in Tokyo, for whom relationships with Japanese clients were 'like mental fencing'. He never felt he could get close to them, was always alert and waiting for something unexpected to happen. For all the differences in their positions, they were both victims of a Japanese failure to fully reveal themselves.

Come down the corporate ladder, into the everyday marketplace, and the situation can be even worse. I remember a number of Japanese remarking that 'selling in Japan is a humiliating experience'. There is a lot of oral evidence to support this view, and it is particularly true for the Japanese sales representative (as we have seen). In comparison, Westerners are treated relatively benignly, according to their status, and according to whether the relationship between your company and the Japanese is still in the courting stage. This should not be counted on, however.

The ordinary non-Japanese executive in Japan as an export manager, or as an entrepreneur seeking to establish a new business among Japanese clients (in any country at all), has to face Japanese who are not excited by his offers, who are secure in their superior status as buyers, who have been trained to regard all proposals with a cold and sceptical eye, and, not least, never to trust 'sales talk'.

Do you know that many Japanese would expect you to be humble and self-deprecating about yourself and your product? This will certainly sound offensive to many. Still, if you recognize in advance that the Japanese will accept your self-deprecation as merely Japanese-style good manners, and not believe for one moment that your product is a lemon, there is no real problem. Everything you claim will be carefully evaluated in any case, so (appear to) be humble and win some points for good manners . . . Is it any surprise that dealing with the Japanese should be a painful subject for many and psychologically wounding for the more sensitive person?

THE LIMITATIONS OF GOOD ADVICE

Much of what I have written is good advice as far as it goes, with the qualification that it is based on the experience of major Western multinational companies in Japan, and directed towards companies of similar size and international spread. It is formula advice: 'This is what they did. Follow their example.' Quite simple, with no tedious qualifications about exceptions, or years in the wilderness of red ink, about time horizons, or lucky breaks of timing, about the contribution of the high-quality Japanese partners or exceptional pioneer managers who made it possible.

From the Japanese viewpoint, if you are a major United States or European company, a multinational and/or market leader, you will probably already be known by name, and easily evaluated or investigated. Your company will probably command ready respect. For companies that are neither household names, market leaders nor multinational, or are small or medium-sized, who come from countries neither in Europe or North America, or are entirely unknown to the Japanese, the situation can be quite different and more difficult. It is for such companies in particular that this book has been written.

For this group of companies or entrepreneurs, whether they are marketing and selling to the Japanese in Japan or abroad, much current advice about doing business with the Japanese is limited not merely because it assumes one is large and well-known, not merely because it focuses only on doing business with the Japanese in Japan, but also because it is invariably based on or justified by success stories of major companies who established themselves in Japan in another and easier time. Moreover, very little has been written about companies which have either failed completely or have made mistakes along the way to becoming stable and profitable in Japan. When you realize that up to 200 foreign capital companies close down each year in Japan, the question as to why they fail has to be asked and answered. It is not enough to talk *sotto voce* about relationships, corporate and personal, that came unstuck.

True, analyses of failure are occasionally presented. Mr Sadao Oba has written that the biggest causes of failure by foreign firms in Japan are: failure to adapt to the Japanese marketing system, underestimating the strength of local competitors, failing to understand the Japanese or to accept good advice and appointing an unsuitable representative. George Fields, the crosscultural market researcher, no doubt with memories of the many foreign product failures he has seen, emphasizes how important it is to 'start from the product'.

The proper study of failure ought to lead us to understand that businesses fail anywhere for a diversity of business reasons, not just those related to marketing or the product or distribution. One sizeable factor in Japan has been the uncritical dependence on a Japanese distributor or joint venture partner, who, it had wistfully been thought, would make all the right decisions that the naive foreigners could never have made in the cultural maze of Japan. The jury may be still out on whether it is best to entrust your business in Japan to a local partner. However, foreign business has been demonstrating its disappointment with Japanese joint ventures since the mid 1970s by steadily increasing its stockholding in existing joint ventures, by buying enough from the Japanese partner to given them a majority shareholding and thus full control over marketing. There are ample examples—with Unilever buying Hohnen out and Abbott Laboratories buying enough from DaiNippon Pharmaceuticals to gain a 60 per cent controlling interest and thus the full control of marketing they had long sought.

Anyone who claims that going it alone or teaming up with a Japanese joint venture partner is the best or only way is simply not being realistic. Sometimes it can be the very best thing to do, as Kentucky Fried Chicken, Southland ('7–11' chain) and Caterpillar Company have found out in their long-term and very successful joint ventures with

Mitsubishi Corporation. Sometimes it turns out unsatisfactorily, as I cite throughout this book.

The good sides of having a Japanese partner may include the added prestige your brand acquires from the association (as when General Foods teamed up with Ajinomoto); the distribution power your product gains from being piggybacked with their existing products (Californian and Australian wines have benefited from having major brewers like Kirin, Asahi and Suntory as their distributors); and the minimizing of the drain on your managerial staff resources in industries where executives may be your major resource (the direct mail industry is a good example) or where entry cost is low.

On the negative side, however, you might have to include: the assignment of second-class personnel to handle your agency after the people with whom you originally dealt turn out to have no operational involvement with your product; the partner's overload of foreign agencies leading to poor attention to the marketing needs of weaker individual agencies; faulty, conventional or uncreative judgements by the Japanese; and a variety of interpersonal communication problems arising with the Japanese side as you try to push them to pay more attention to your product.

Much of this can be compounded if your company, instead of being a Fortune 500 member, is merely a medium-sized or small company from a country that some Japanese regard as less advanced, intelligent or prestigious than themselves; on a day-to-day basis, you might sometimes feel you are being treated as a second-class citizen, kept waiting, treated in a rude or condescending manner, or given subtle messages that you are an inferior and ought therefore to know your place.

These problems are not ones mentioned in analyses or reports of the experiences of Fortune 500 companies in Japan. One important reason for this is that so much has changed about Japan's place in the world since most of those cases occurred, and since most of those books about them were published. In particular, many Japanese business executives have become more assertive and sometimes even arrogant, as they revel in their market and bargaining power and enjoy their new status in the world of international business. Many of them are making things harder for the increasing number of foreign executives coming to Japan for the first time, often from companies very modest, even minuscule, in comparison to the Japanese they meet. The Japanese, who have always operated on the basis that the buyer has superior social status to the seller and is entitled to behave loftily, haughtily and demandingly, are reinforced in this when they confront foreigners from small companies in small countries—Australia and New Zealand are good examples.

The Japanese are not necessarily the best people to make predictions about what will succeed or fail in Japan. When McDonald's started up in Japan, many Japanese predicted that it would surely fail, because 'Japanese will never eat standing up'. This was a conventional conceit of many Japanese at the time, but it was not in fact true, since some noodle shops had traditionally been *tachigui* (standing eating). And in really no time at all, *tachigui* became the smart thing to do in Tokyo for young Japanese with the ultra-fashionable hamburger. Akio Morita, whose brainchild was the Walkman portable stereo radio, encountered enormous resistance within his R&D department to the idea. No one believed in it, and he had to exercise a rare direct command in order for the development work to be undertaken. It is commonplace in Japan (as well as in other countries) for companies to rely more on the opinions of their retailers and wholesalers than on consumer market research and trust their own intuition about what products are likely to succeed in the marketplace.

Of course this is confusing advice for foreign would-be marketers. If you can't trust the Japanese, who can you trust? The problem is really no different in any other country. Not every Japanese or Englishman or Swede is an expert on their own country or on the opinions of their fellow countrymen. When you want information about Japan, don't just trust the first opinion you get. Ask many people. Moreover, ask the best-educated Japanese. Your hotel porter, or taxi driver, or even your interpreter, don't necessarily have good judgement or current knowledge, although they will mostly share the desire to be polite and helpful to you by giving you some kind of confident answer. If you have ever been lost in Tokyo, trying to find your way somewhere with an inadequate map, you will have surely had the experience of having many people confidently give you instructions, only to find that most of them were completely incorrect! One of the big problems for unsuspecting foreign executives in Japan, as some of the case studies in this book demonstrate clearly, is that some Japanese partners in a new joint venture will provide estimates of future sales which subsequent experience will reveal to have been hugely inflated. Being pleasantly sceptical about everything you are told in Japan is one of the most important strategies you can adopt, especially if you are prone to be optimistic and impetuous. It will help to keep you psychologically healthy, as well.

Outside Japan, a new breed of foreign business executives exists which deals with the Japanese and their companies overseas. They want to market to and sell to Japanese companies abroad, as suppliers of services, parts and supplies. Unlike the foreigners who go regularly to Japan or live there, these people may have no interest in or knowledge of it. Moreover, Japanese companies, although important, are only one of many market segments that they are responsible for. The problem for them will be the early discovery that selling and marketing to the Japanese overseas will present challenges and questions that they are not able to provide answers for, either out of their past experience or from talking to others. As well, there is a conviction amounting to a demand that, when the Japanese are living and working abroad, they should behave in a culturally modified way. When they do not—and generally speaking they do not—local businesspeople are nonplussed, and nationalist sentiments that translate readily into anti-Japanese sentiments do arise.

CASE STUDY 3-1: BREAKTHROUGH IN JAPAN: DCE'S EXPERIENCE[1]

Key Points

- Total ownership of the Japanese venture turned out to be more effective than joint venturing.
- Deciding to manufacture in Japan provided important customer benefits.
- Notwithstanding local manufacture, the emphasis on foreignness proved an advantage in Japan.
- With an effective corporate structure in place, DCE's top managers believe that they have barely scratched the surface of the Japanese market.

Last year the dust control equipment maker, DCE, increased its sales to Japan by 70 per cent. This year it expects a further 50 per cent increase. Roger Harrop, the company's managing director, has encountered no non-tariff barriers in Japan. Are they a myth?

DCE—one of the goodies BTR acquired when it bought Thomas Tilling in 1983—has been selling dust control equipment in the world's major industrial markets for many years. As the second largest after the USA, Japan was an obvious market for it to tackle; and its first move in that direction took place in the early 1970s, when it appointed a Japanese agent.

The agent was a specialist installer of powder handling plant; and the hope was that he would both incorporate DCE equipment into the projects that he tendered for and sell it by the unit to existing factories. Any industry where dust is either a hazard (because of its explosiveness) or worth recovering (e.g. powder paint or gold) or a nuisance is a potential user of DCE equipment, although food and pharmaceuticals account for about 40 per cent of sales. Prices range from around £1000 for a small standardized unit up to £50,000 for specials.

The agent was clearly geared more to project work than to ordinary, bread-and-butter standard unit sales—with the result that sales were highly erratic. 'It was', says Tony Llewellyn, DCE's marketing director, 'feast or famine.' Whereas what the company's works in Leicester above all required was a steady drip-feed of orders, preferably for standard products.

The agent, moreover, was more interested in immediate profit than in developing DCE's business in Japan long term. Prices were set at an unrealistically high level.

Clearly the principal–agency relationship was unsatisfactory; and it was felt that a different kind of partnership—a joint venture—might work better. That is to say, it might encourage the agent-turned-joint-venturer to adopt a longer-term view. So a new company was set up. Each partner owned 50 per cent, but the company was effectively still run by the agent. That was in 1976.

The new arrangement, however, did not work noticeably better than the old, and in 1979 DCE bought out their partner, making the Japanese company a wholly-owned subsidiary. This brought it into line with DCE's practice in other parts of the world; it has long had wholly-owned sales companies in Germany, France, Denmark and Holland, a manufacturing company in the USA and companies in Australia and South Africa which assemble from knocked-down kits. Only in Japan had it been thought necessary to go for joint venture instead of total ownership; a reflection, perhaps, of the awe which the Japanese market inspires in distant Westerners. In fact, as DCE was eventually to demonstrate, the awe was misplaced.

Initially, even when wholly owned, DCE's Japanese subsidiary did not develop smoothly, and it is only since it parted company with its original managing director and recruited another, in 1982, that business has taken off. DCE recruited the new MD, K. Ando,[2] through the consultancy PA who, says Roger Harrop, managing director of the parent DCE since 1983,[3] 'have a reasonably good reputation in Japan'.

The change of boss in Japan was followed shortly by some radical policy changes. First, as to pricing, DCE pursues a premium pricing policy world-wide—reflecting, it argues, superior quality and backup.[4] But in Japan under the previous dispensation, prices had gone over the top, and DCE was losing business as a result. So it now cut its prices and announced that it would not increase them for two years. (Its principal Japanese customer had not increased its prices for very long while.) Even after the cuts, though, DCE's prices were still, deliberately, above the competition's.

The wisdom of this pricing policy was confirmed by DCE's assessment of that competition. There were two licensees of its American competitors— with whom it is very successfully competing in the States; their products were, Mr Harrop reckons, of the same quality as DCE's but technically not as advanced. As to the other, more purely local competition, it was thought to be of inferior quality.

Mr Llewellyn, casting a careful eye over the competition at the 1984 Japanese Powdertech exhibition, was 'heartened—and surprised' at the competition's relative weakness as to product design.

The second major policy decision was to manufacture in Japan; that is to say, to buy in some components from local Japanese suppliers, instead of simply assembling complete knocked-down kits imported from Britain as it had previously—and as DCE's Australian and South African companies still do. The intention is slowly to build up the local content as and when the local suppliers prove themselves on quality and delivery.

The advantage of local manufacture is primarily on the score of delivery to the customer. It takes five weeks to make a dust collector—but another eleven to deliver one from the UK to a customer in Japan.

In addition, Japanese suppliers bring with them Japanese standards of service and quality. 'It's their honour that's at stake,' says Mr Harrop. 'The supplier will supply quality that's better than you ask for, and he will deliver early if he thinks it will be of benefit to you.'

The first two prospective suppliers whom DCE approached both insisted on coming, at their own expense, to the company's headquarters in England to find out exactly how they could best serve DCE. How many British sub-contractors, Mr Harrop wonders, would similarly bestir themselves, even to make their much shorter journey?

Part-sourcing of components in the countries in which the goods are sold is not necessarily to the home factory's disadvantage. If the market is both very large and several thousand miles distant, on-the-spot manufacture there usually means that one sells more product (because one is more competitive) than if every nut and bolt were exported from home. The smaller percentage of home content may be offset by higher volumes. DCE's American company sources 60 per cent of its product content locally; but DCE Leicester is kept very busy supplying the other 40 per cent. Sales in America, says Mr Harrop, 'are going like a train'.

The one thing that has held up the development of local manufacture in Japan has been finding the right man to head up the production side. For this post direct advertising in the press was thought to be more appropriate (and also more economical) than using a consultancy. But the task did take nine months. Japanese do not change jobs very readily and are not too happy at moving to foreign firms; on the other hand there is quite a pool of available talent among the recently retired, happy to embark on a second career.

Since Japan is a key market for DCE it has investment status as far as advertising is concerned. That is to say, it gets a budget, funded largely by the UK, in line with its potential, not with its current sales. Later, when sales have grown, the Japanese company will wholly fund its own advertising.

DCE's principal ad agency is, unexpectedly, German: Ernst & Partner of Dusseldorf. Since factories do not buy dust control equipment unless they have, or until they recognize that they have, a dust problem the main objective of DCE's advertising is awareness; and Ernst had developed powerful awareness ads of which the dominant component was a slogan or motif drawn in dust—which they deployed, to prize—as well as awareness—winning effect in Der Spiegel.

'Other dust control companies have written slogans in dust', says Mr Llewellyn, 'but they have tended to be rather banal. What distinguished Ernst's work was its words, its graphics and its high standard of photography.'

DCE was so taken with the quality of Ernst's work that it began to use the agency internationally (including in the UK); and its second agency, Levy Flaxman of New York, also uses the message-in-the-dust technique, but with, of course, an American treatment.

But if Germany and the United States called for a local input so, even more obviously, did Japan. Shiggi Konno, the managing director of BTR's Japanese company Sanshi Enterprises and a non-executive director of DCE Japan, introduced them to the Nippon agency. Nippon was appointed more on the strength of its attitude— 'they asked the right questions'—than because of its initial creative work. Indeed some of its earliest messages-in-the-dust were thought by DCE to be too whimsical for the Japanese market.

The final, accepted message was one that would never have occurred to a Westerner—on the grounds that it was too Western! Nippon proposed, simply, the symbols for alpha-plus. Mr Harrop: 'One of the Japanese perceptions of the West that is not appreciated over here is that foreign goods are seen as being superior by definition. (Never mind if in practice they sometimes aren't.) The alpha in our ads means that we are the best. The plus is that extra something that being foreign gives us. Emphasizing our foreign-ness is the last thing we would do in Germany or France, where we try to be as local as possible, and it is exactly the opposite of what we would have thought of doing ourselves in Japan.'

The alpha-plus ads have now been running for a year in the two major industrial dailies in Japan, *Nikkei Sangyo* and *Nikkan Kogyo*, and the campaign is planned to be stepped up in 1986.

Loyalty and industry are evidently the distinguishing characteristics of the Japanese company, irrespective of who owns it. Mr Harrop: 'They get very little annual holiday. No one goes home before eight or nine at night. Even the female clerks will work all hours. And Saturday is a whole work day.

'When I go out there they usually have a little party—a buffet supper—which the whole firm attends. (Their English improves as the party progresses!) It might finish around 11 p.m. Then they go back to the office to make up the time they have lost during the party!

'They like to feel part of the family, and to be told what's going on in the company. They expect me to give them a presentation—and they take copious notes of everything that's being said. This degree of dedication is 'just part of the culture'.'

And it is obviously worth cultivating. Both Mr Harrop and Mr. Llewellyn visit Japan three or four times a year; and in the coming year it will receive a similar number of visits from DCE's production liaison man, Tony Wells, to help set up the production facility.

A marked difference between Japan and the West concerns the role of the sales force. DCE Japan does have area salesmen, but Japanese customers like to buy through trading houses (even though this will be more expensive for them than buying direct from the manufacturer), so the salesmen spend much time promoting the trading houses.

Liaison with the Japanese ad agency is undertaken locally, although Mr Llewellyn did have a hand in the choice of agency. Indeed Mr Ando was initially keen to do the advertising himself; it would save money. 'But he now appreciates what we can achieve through using an agency's resources.'

A further distinguishing characteristic of Japan, which Mr Harrop is apt to emphasize to his own shopfloor, is its almost obsessive attention to product quality. 'We're very proud of our product quality here,' he says. 'But it is in Japan that it's really tested. If a piece of equipment is delivered to a Japanese customer with so much as a scratch on the back he'll return it.'

Both Mr Harrop and Mr Llewellyn clearly believe that they have barely scratched the surface of the Japanese market. They have looked at the competition and found it unfrightening. They have to pay a 12 per cent import duty, but do not reckon it a problem. As to non-tariff barriers, they have come across no evidence of any as far as their kind of goods is concerned.

Mr Harrop, indeed, is rather sceptical about their existence even in the sectors where European exporters are at their most querulous. He cites the rise of the BMW. He has noticed over the past year that BMW cars have become much more common on the streets of Tokyo. 'Suddenly it has become the prestige motorcar—and it's the ambition of every Japanese businessman to have one.' He attributes this sudden cachet mainly to BMW's marketing skill. And if BMW can do it, why not Jaguar?

If British exporters do not succeed in Japan, it is more likely to be due to lack of commitment than to any fiendish oriental plot to keep them out. 'One thing that always strikes me', Mr Harrop says, 'as I'm sitting in the Okura Hotel having my breakfast, is that the only foreign voices I hear are American, French or German. When you do hear a British voice it's somebody from the embassy or an insurance man—never from manufacturing.

'The majority of British manufacturers, it seems, are not prepared to do what's necessary. They believe they have only to find themselves an agent and wait and see what happens. It just isn't like that.'

On the other hand, success involves 'nothing clever'. You just have to have 'the best products', the right set-up—and perseverance.

Thanks to their possession of the third of these attributes, DCE did eventually achieve the second, enabling them successfully to market what they confidently believe to be the first.

1. Extracted from *Business Marketing Digest*, formerly *Industrial Marketing Digest* (UK), First Quarter, 1986.
2. 'Mr Ando's first name is so long "that everyone calls him K".'
3. Which he joined from Tecalemit, where he ran a division.
4. Technical backup includes a 'library' of 10,000 different kinds of dust accumulated in the course of the company's sixty years of making dust collection equipment.

CASE STUDY 3-2: THE CHATEAU CASE

Key Points

- Capitalizing on entry into the Japanese market has proved to be a long-term project for Chateau.
- In retrospect, the foreign sellers believe they were duped into expectations of the Japanese market in the medium term that they now see they will not achieve for perhaps fifteen to twenty years.
- The challenges of regular account management over the long haul can be very different from the honeymoon-like goodwill of the early days of a company–company relationship.
- There are serious questions about the economic merit of this company selling into Japan over the medium term. In other words, they now feel they could have devoted their resources to other export markets with a far better return and fewer problems.

Chateau Wines USA started to export to the Japanese market in 1983, after two years of negotiation with one of Japan's larger whisky distillers. At that time, Japanese *per capita* consumption of wine was 0.5 litres, while today (1990) it is 0.7 litres. This compares to the Californian average consumption of around 20 litres. In 1981, USA (and California in particular) did not rank in the top five countries exporting wine to Japan. France dominated the Japanese market, as it still does, but today Californian wine exports to Japan make it no. 3 behind France and Germany—quite an achievement. Again, in 1981 Chateau's total worldwide export volume was only 20,000 cases, so they were hungry to develop their export sales beyond Canada and South America. They wanted to get into Japan.

In 1981, a lot of Japanese business groups, representing major companies in the liquor business, were travelling through California wanting to make agreements to import wine to Japan. Chateau had a team of Japanese on their doorstep every two months or so, looking interested and asking every question imaginable—prices, costs, products, technical information. Then, for the most part, they would disappear, never to be seen again. Chateau quickly grew tired of this. Even when their Japan consultant, who knew the liquor business in Japan well, told them that he had one of Japan's largest distillers interested in importing Chateau wines, their first reaction was apathetic disinterest. It was only when Tyrrell, the consultant, persuaded them that Yamato Whisky were serious that Chateau decided to meet and talk. The negotiation ran from early 1982 through April 1983. Looking back over that 'courtship' phase, Chateau's export director, Clark Siebold, says they learnt four things:

1 About Contracts

The Japanese did not want a legal contract in the American sense. They wanted a long-term relationship built on mutual trust and respect. 'We learnt the hard way,' said Siebold. 'We spent month after month bashing our heads against a brick wall of about forty-two pages of legal jargon—and ended up with a two page letter of intent! Since then it has never been worth anything when we run into problems. It just made our legal department feel good! In any case, we have since come to believe that a Western-type contract is worthless and unenforceable in Japan.'

2   About Information

'The two year negotiation period was like being permanently in the dentist's chair,' says Siebold. 'The Japanese have the most amazing ability to extract information from you. It's all one way.'

At the same time, they were checking on other facets of Chateau's organization: corporate philosophy, to what extent the quality control department was reactionary or precautionary, people employed, turnover, etc.

'At the end of this courtship period,' said Siebold, 'the Japanese knew more about us than I once had.'

In looking back on that trying period, Siebold cautions others to decide in advance what you will or will not tell the Japanese. If you feel that you want to retain some confidentiality, Siebold says to simply say that you are not at liberty to tell them—your hands are tied.

Siebold illustrates: 'I am not at liberty to tell you how we get 400 grams of strawberries into a 200-gram jar. But we may be able to tell you when we get to know you better. 'But he added, *sotto voce*, ' Chances are you won't want to tell them when you get to know them better!'

3   Be Clear on your Objectives

Chateau learnt how important it was for their subsequent relationship to have a clear plan for the market, which, though it must be flexible, should at least state minimum or fallback positions. It should include statements about:

- why you want to be in the Japanese market;
- what your volume and market share expectations are;
- what your profit objectives are over time; and
- what minimum level of price, volumes and profit you want in order to make a 'go' decision.

In the case of Chateau, at the time of negotiation, they were in a position of strength that they never subsequently enjoyed. Yamato Distillers were at that time losing market share, so their need to diversify into the developing wine market was strong. Their idea was to get a Californian winemaker to supply them first with a Yamato house brand, to Yamato specifications and entirely marketed by Yamato.

On the other hand, Chateau wanted to position and develop their own Chateau brand in the Japanese market. They had no interest in supplying the wine for a Yamato brand if it did not also mean that the Chateau brand was being vigorously promoted and sold into Japan. The final agreement covered both of these activities.

4   Promises, Promises

Dealing with a large Japanese organization like Yamato usually means dealing with the development department. They are not marketing or sales people; their sole role is to acquire new products and technology for the company.

Says Siebold: 'We slowly found out over time that we were simply talking to the wrong people! That created many difficult problems of unjustified expectations on our part. We discovered eventually, for example, that the development department might make grandiose promises to us, but they were meaningless if they did not have the backing of the sales department.

'You can imagine how keen we were to get into the relationship when they made preliminary sales forecasts like 300,000 cases by year 3. Boy, did we drool! We had finally hit the big time, we all felt. But what happened? Their marketing and sales people got together, and said there was no way they could deliver the volume forecast by someone else—that is, the development department. To cut a long story short, by year 3 we had only achieved 10 per cent of the forecast given to us initially by Development. We had been suckered in.'

Siebold relates that, in anticipation of the considerable sales envisaged at the time of signing the letter of intent, Chateau had agreed to fix all prices for three years, at a level which would have been generous to both sides, if the promised volume had been delivered. As things turned out, Chateau were on the losing end. 'I am convinced they sell you high to get the prices down, which they did,' says Siebold. 'We failed to get the commitment of the sales department up front. We were naive.'

The initial promises created many other problems. The first year's shipments were so enormous, often jumbojet loads, that Yamato ended up with stock that they were not to sell for almost three years. As the months and early years wore on, it was obvious that something was wrong, but 'we had enormous problems trying to work out what was going on', said Siebold. 'The difficulty with the Japanese is that they don't like to admit failure. Eventually, we were independently able to work out what the contributing causes of the poor sales were.'

These included: the Yamato Wine label, which Yamato themselves had designed in spite of Chateau protests, failed to represent the wine as a quality product to the consumer; their large sales force was given no product knowledge, and was not motivated to spend time on products other than whisky; retailers had no confidence in the product; and the contamination of European wines with antifreeze in 1985 affected the whole market. In any case, whatever department of Yamato was involved, their sales forecasts kept changing and changing.

Original negotiation, 1982	300,000 cases
Letter of intent, April 1983	75,000 cases
Revision, May 1984	70,000 cases
Revision, August 1985	35,000 cases
Actual sales in 1985	25,000 cases

Going Overboard on Service

In keeping with their original information orientation, Yamato people kept up a stream of enquiries and requests to Chateau concerning production and product development. According to Siebold, Chateau's small R&D department has spent up to 40 per cent of its time in recent years simply attending to Yamato requests, and for a long time Chateau were prepared to make this extraordinary effort in expectation of rapid market development. These have included requests for research and quotations on aluminum cans for wine, cans for vending machines, quarter-size bottles, 3-, 4- and 5-litre packs and changes in bottle shape. The biggest problem with this continuing flow of requests was, says Siebold, 'that they would drop one project and start a new one before the previous one was fully answered . . . then, as time went by, they would start reviving old questions, like: "How much will it cost to do so and so today?" Then we would have to update the costings, give them the new figures, and again the project would go into limbo.'

On one occasion when Chateau requested a price increase, due to rising freight rates, Yamato refused to discuss it. They said that it was important that both sides share in ('what they called', said Siebold) 'profits'. Siebold added caustically, 'What they mean in practice, by the way, is "share losses". They don't share any profits except ours!'

On this particular issue, they eventually agreed not to share the increase but, after two days of discussions insisted on by Chateau, to an equal share of the 'profit' from an improvement in the exchange rate.

Handling Arrogance and Rudeness, Warm-heartedness and Friendliness

Siebold established a sound, friendly relationship with one of the Yamato directors in the early days, and that has continued to the present. Unfortunately, the import agency managers he has had to deal with over the years have not been anything more than superficially friendly, and the most recent one is arrogant and condescending, often speaking to him as though he were a schoolboy. To Siebold, the Japanese act as though his, Siebold's, sole purpose in life is to serve them, and they attempt to wring the maximum effort and service out of Chateau.

All the noble sentiments expressed in the honeymoon days of the relationship mean nothing to the day-to-day relationship, but Siebold does not fully understand why he is treated the way he is. Perhaps part of the blame lies with him. He has by his own admission made a number of mistakes (such as failing to send samples that were requested, lying about laboratory results which were in fact non-existent and being found out by the Yamato people); the service he has received within his own organization has frequently been sloppy, and he has appeared at all meetings over the years together with his Japanese-speaking American consultant to advise him on the real meaning of what the Japanese are saying, to resolve any crosscultural misunderstanding. This consultant's presence, he now suspects, has somehow offended the current Japanese manager.

At a deeper level, Siebold suspects that this particular Japanese, in his heart, looks down on Americans (and other whites) as inferior people, as second-class citizens. 'Look at how much better dressed they are. $100 silk ties, cuff links that make my wife's jewellery look like trash,' says Siebold.

Another factor, says Siebold, is that Chateau also placed more demands on the Japanese than do, say, their no. 1 wine suppliers, the Germans. 'We are hungry, we put up a lot of recommendations, we visit two or three times a year. In contrast, the Germans only visit once every two years and make no effort to promote their product further in Japan. So it would be understandable if they felt bombarded by us, and were just retaliating.'

On the other hand, Siebold's director friend within the company seems to be keeping a watchful eye, from afar, on the relationship, and has suddenly appeared, on occasion, 'like a guardian angel', when Siebold felt they were being treated too badly and pushed too far by the agency manager.

What Chateau have Learnt from their Experiences

'We have asked ourselves a lot of questions about Yamato, especially how genuine they are about all the requests,' says Siebold. But at this stage, he is not able to give a clearcut answer to his own question, although he is very cool-eyed now, having passed through all the courtship, culture shock and pain barriers, to be resigned and sceptical, with only modest hopes well into the medium term.

Siebold lists the following points he has learnt over the past nine years of dealing with the Japanese:

1   *It is a long-haul relationship that has to be worked at continuously.*

2   *The relationship is never easy in the personal sense; frustrations seem never-ending.*

3   *Communication sensitivity is a top priority.* Simple, seemingly throwaway questions from the Japanese should always be thought-through carefully. His failure to think carefully about a question he was asked casually as he got into a taxi—'Say, do you sell bulk wines?'—lead him to answer 'no', without asking or having time to ask why the question was being asked in the first place. That failure cost him a very large order in bulk wines which the Japanese placed that year with one of their competitors.

In general, questions should be analyzed meticulously: What are they really getting at? Why are they asking the question?

In the early days, Siebold gave simple answers to simple questions, and this lead to complex chains of questions demanding eventually more work than if they had understood all the implications in the first place. Perhaps it is also his own learning experience, but today, Siebold says, he can quickly generate a checklist of 100 questions or more to be answered so that Japanese requests or queries can be dealt with. 'And you can be sure', he adds, 'that if I didn't do that, when I came back with my simplistic answer, they would! Because they have never, ever asked a simple question.'

4   *Japanese business politics is omnipresent.* 'Although we are never told much about it', says Siebold, 'even our small business, hardly 1 per cent of their turnover, is constantly if subtly influenced by their internal politics, as the fortunes of differing factions within the company keep changing. There are wine factions and anti-wine factions. The composition of teams we face keeps changing. The pet projects of one faction leader get shelved suddenly when a new faction takes over. I'm sure a lot of the aborted projects we have spent good money and time on have been victims of factional infighting.'

5   *Managing frustration.* Handling the Yamato account is more demand-

ing and frustrating than any other, anywhere, for Chateau's Siebold. How is he able to keep himself sane and balanced, then? I asked. His answer emphasized: first, always to be on top of the heavy administration involved in managing the account, 'an enormous volume relative to our sales'; second, to be himself always, for that minimizes the pressure on him; third, when he encounters rudeness, he doesn't take it any more, but speaks up for himself and calls on his director friend whenever troubles develop; fourth, until recently he used a professional, bicultural consultant who acted as a buffer between him and the Japanese, to give insights into their behaviour that he is not capable of achieving, who could communicate more tactfully with the Japanese than Siebold himself (but he recently terminated the relationship after nine years, finally feeling confident that he can handle the account entirely on his own); and, finally, a little childishly but understandably, he plays games to embarrass the Japanese—by creating situations where he is going to do something better than them, such as in a sporting or social or performance situation, or where he embarrasses them, for instance, by having his business cards ready to exchange with newcomers when they do not have theirs with them.

Final Words of Wisdom

'I've tried to look within myself and seek causes for our adventures and misadventures. "What are we doing wrong?" For instance, we tried for a long time to make a big virtue out of not taking price increases when we might have and ought to have, pointing out to them how decent we were. I now see this as folly, and crude egotism. Maybe the managers I have to deal with are failures, and the import agency department is a kind of corporate Devil's Island. Who can say? The Japanese employ double standards all the time in their dealings with us, like the sharing of losses but not profits. There have been many cases where they have refused to yield with us on the very point they had insisted we yield to them. It's Big Brother with a vengeance!

'Current words of advice to would-be exporters to Japan are far too positive and optimistic,' continues Siebold. 'We need to open people's eyes to the difficult, long-haul job it is here, that it's highly unlikely that they will do well in the first five to ten years. All that Japan offers is the allure of a huge market—but cracking it is, as an exporter, one of the biggest corporate challenges any company can face anywhere!

'Then there is the problem of educating the people in my company to deal with the Japanese. Of course, it is important for our people to be more meticulous. That has to be learnt. But they also have to learn to be more sceptical. Let me finish with this story. We had a group of Yamato salesmen out to visit us, and they ended up at our production facility. There was a final party, and the Japanese team leader made a great inspiring speech. "Let me tell you what we will do for Chateau wine in Japan," he said in a stentorian voice. "We will sell it all over Japan! We will build a great distribution system! We will tell every retailer how good Chateau wines are!" Everyone was excited. They all shouted "*Banzai*" three times.

'The next day our production head rang me, and told me how excited he and everyone was, about what the Japanese were going to do. "Isn't this fantastic?" he asked me. I mumbled something, and hung up.

'Then I suddenly realized—it was all bullshit!—it was a real flash of insight.

We Americans are so naive, so easily deceived by this sort of thing, what the Japanese call "*tatemae*". Now I knew that it really meant nothing. Oh, they were sincere, no doubt about it—but the Japanese would have already forgotten everything they had said, it was just their way of being nice. But I was virtually alone in my company, and maybe in the whole state, in understanding that our most terrible problem is with ourselves—that our big egos and incurable optimism make easy marks of us all. Sobering, when you think about the future.'

CASE STUDY 3-3: CANDY GONE STALE

Key Points

- A Japanese buyer tries to intimidate a foreign direct seller/exporter, but calm persistence creates space for agreement.
- There is need for prior agreement on arbitrating differences, including means for testing product quality and ingredients.

An English candy manufacturer supplied two large shipments of different candies to a Japanese department store without problem. A third shipment was ordered, but there was a four-month delay while the English waited for detailed instructions on packaging designs, eventually received by airmail and telex.

Two months after receiving the third shipment, the Japanese complained to the English that the candy on this occasion was not acceptable to them, much of it was substandard, and all contained a colouring agent prohibited in Japan. They demanded that full compensation be paid.

Recognizing that the issue was only resolvable face to face, the English general manager flew to Japan on his own to discuss the claims. The Japanese met him on arrival, looked after him solicitously, but were business-like at all times.

In the first meeting, involving more junior people on the Japanese side, a detailed inspection was jointly made of the rejected stock. The Englishman then discovered three things. One, the Japanese had not sold any of the third shipment, making him wonder if failure to sell the product had motivated their claims. Two, the Japanese were expecting him to take their word that the candy contained a prohibited colouring. Three, they were also insisting that most of the product was substandard, whereas he could see clearly the amount that was substandard (by which they meant that the shape was sometimes distorted). There was a lengthy and awkward discussion with these junior Japanese about the need for an objective and fair method for assessing (a) how much stock was substandard, and (b) whether there was any prohibited agent in the product.

At the second meeting, the Japanese presented findings from their laboratory tests confirming, they said, that the prohibited colouring was present. The Englishman was convinced that this was impossible, and asked for part of the samples that the Japanese had reportedly tested to be shown him. These were, he was told, no longer available. After much discussion, agreement was reached that samples were to be split into three parts—one to be tested again by the Japanese, one to be tested by the English and one by an independent laboratory. Just before departing for London the next day, the Japanese again met the Englishman and presented further 'evidence' that the prohibited colouring matter was present. He remained adamant that all tests must be undertaken before reaching a decision.

Once back in London, laboratory tests there showed that the colouring was not present, so the Englishman insisted on the settlement formula originally discussed in the first meeting—namely, that they would make payment only for the amount of substandard stock jointly identified when he was there.

The aftermath of this experience was a severe shaking of the Englishman's confidence in his ability to deal with the Japanese.

He had, he said, developed a healthy respect for their group bargaining ability, but he considered that their ethics were not the same as his. Asked if he would ever do business with them again, he said that he would not supply anything unless he could be satisfied that Japanese standards of presentation and quality could be met, and that clear specifications were agreed on. Moreover, he would want to establish in advance ground rules for arbitration of disputes, especially a method for scientific testing of product ingredients, and for decisions on 'substandard' product.

Although he had been a one-man team against eight Japanese, he was not displeased with the way he had handled the situation and the pressure they had imposed. He had been gentlemanly, patient, stubborn, not overly intimidated. Nonetheless, he had not felt relaxed with them, feeling that he did not understand what they were thinking, and not being able to read their personalities. They were difficult and tough negotiators with whom it is difficult to be frank or open.

'British business experience', he concluded with characteristic British understatement, 'has left me inadequately prepared to deal with the Japanese.'

APPENDIX 3.1

'What advice would you give to a foreign company setting up a Japan operation similar to your own?' The following are verbatim responses to this question from the chief executives of foreign companies in Japan.

'1   Good luck!
2   Be prepared to make a very significant investment to get a small toehold in the market.

3   Consider some forms of tie-up with a local company with distribution muscle'.

'Be patient for it takes time to understand Japan.'

'No half measures. If you decide to set up operations in Japan, you must go all out, invest without hesitation. Set up national sales network, give good after-sales service.'

'It is probably too late to go it alone, so find a first-class Japanese company anxious to develop into new areas but lacking technology, and form a partnership—your product and marketing knowledge and his market (Japan) knowledge, government contacts and pool of first-class staff not normally available to a foreign company.'

'Do not get the impression that the Japanese market is unlimited; it is very much segmented. Do not underestimate the competition and be aware that competition can arise very quickly if it does not yet exist. Try to balance what you can contribute to the local market and what the Japanese market (in our case the second largest in the world) can contribute to your group's operation.'

'Do a lot of homework first—then ensure that you hire the right personnel. Another cause of major problems is that foreign firms hire personnel on their English-language ability only. "If a man speaks good English, he gets the job." Such people are normally a long way from being the best.'

'Be sure you have something unique to offer. Time is running out for me-too-ism.'

'Don't.'
'1   Adequate funding.
2   Top-flight manager with backing of parent company.
3   Plan on a three- to five-year start-up period.
4   Allow the company to adapt to Japan—*vice versa* is impossible but often tried.'

'Concentrate on the wholesale side of banking rather than retail. Remember that in Japan there is a life-long-employment system under which it is extremely difficult to get rid of staff who later prove unsuitable or who become redundant.'

'Create an independent profit/responsibility-minded outfit. Send or hire on the spot top-calibre foreign executives (young) with the desire to spend *many years* in Japan.'

'Hire good retired Japanese executives as advisors and young, good-calibre Japanese to be trained to become executives.'

'It is essential to get the best possible Japanese staff. There is a tendency to regard them as a high-cost expense whereas they should be regarded as an investment.'

'1 Commit to a long-range financial plan, invest in the consumer franchise, advertise consistently.
2 Explore use of local distributors—joint venture or part ownership.
3 Plan to assign foreign managers for a relatively long period in Japan—eight to nine years.'

'It takes time and perseverance.'

'Leave management and control to Japanese entirely since a foreign company can't understand Japanese customs fully (very hard due to different customs, i.e. Rome is Rome).'

'Rely strongly on local Japanese advisors in accounting, legal and sociological fields. Local idiosyncracies are still as important as ever.'

'Don't believe all you are told about the difficulties. There are problems but that should not prevent you making progress if you have patience and determination coated with politeness. A commitment to Japan and awareness of their problems rather than emphasizing your own is important. Above all, your product must be genuinely competitive, the Japanese like quality and market leaders.'

'The top man shoud be a foreigner who has had considerable experience in Japan and speaks the language.'

'Thoroughly investigate all aspects of the operation as it applies to Japan and get competent personnel to manage.'

Look for a partner who has good connections but is not group-affiliated with competitors. Also, make sure that the partner is about the same size as the foreign company.'

- Difficult to transfer experience [from one country or culture to another].
- A good blend of national and expatriate staff of high quality.
- Continuous efforts to upgrade quality and effectiveness of organization/personnel.'

'1 Make sure your products/processes/unique selling points have acceptance in the Japanese market before you start.
2 Make sure your business can afford the high costs of expatriate employees, top-quality Japanese management personnel, etc.
3 Make sure your business has sufficiently long-term prospects to attract and hold high-quality Japanese personnel.'

'Firstly, set up a small office purely for studying the particular market in depth. Learn the language if possible, then certainly the general culture. Have at least one Japanese on staff. Secondly, make as many good contacts as possible. Learn the strengths and weaknesses of the competition, and what the market really wants. Thirdly, *plan* carefully and, if there is real justification, launch on the market with maximum resources. Fourthly, aim to invest and become deeply involved with Japanese companies.'

'High-quality and high-performance products and employ capable Japanese engineers.'

'Think.'

'1 Direct investment is better than joint venture.
2 Try to acquire 100 per cent of a Japanese competitor and use this company as your base of operations.'

'Not to do it any longer as competition is overly keen and it takes a relatively long introductory period until the operation becomes known and thus profitable.'

'Study the market carefully before deciding how/when/why to start. Listen to the advice and learn from the experiences of others who went before and, above all, show respect for the "Japanese way".'

'Have reasonable fluency in the language—understand how the various corporations are interrelated—how your Japanese sales force thinks—come equipped with a large amount of patience and a willingness to learn from everyone.'

'Long-term perspective is required.'

'To behave, as much as possible, as a Japanese company.'

'I am not likely to be helping competition, but if foreign executives don't speak Japanese they must have some Japanese executives who are fluent in English. This really applies to any company regardless of products marketed.'

'Be able to set up with complete capabilities from the very beginning in order to compete head to head with Japanese competitors offering the same services, products, etc., including price.'

'Cost it accurately first, so that you don't pull the plug on a viable venture because some cost accountant didn't do his job properly at the outset—set your goals and let local management do the planning.'

'Find a good partner.'

'Don't ever go halfway. Take time to learn. The Japanese system does work. Don't overload with foreigners. Don't get "interpreters", get nationals who have abilities beyond speaking English. Bring your best resources—the payoff will be worth the effort.'

'Strong local management, patience, long-term planning, heavy media advertising.'

'Don't believe "It's different in Japan" and it can't be done your way. It can, with minor modifications and determination not to be beaten. Be very patient, it takes longer to get things started. Don't read books on how to do business in Japan, find out for yourself.'

'Do not be misled by impressive market potential statistics on Japan. You may be successful in every international market you have been in but do not be overconfident or complacent—Japan *is* different.'

'Set up an organization with a national as top executive, supported by the best local staff available. Research the market carefully and spend time and money in training top executive in local procedures, cultural differences and some language capability.'

'Have patience (and money)—learn to accept and respect the Japanese system (labour—finance—government restrictions, etc.)'

'Think big.'

'Don't.'

'Consider 100 per cent ownership; employ top Japanese, also for executive position pay them well and treat them in Japanese way wherever possible; foreign executives should speak some Japanese to get around but Japanese employees should master English to some extent.'

'Very carefully select Japanese company partner who will provide top-calibre people and one that has success in working with foreign companies. Insist on the new venture becoming independent from parents as quickly as possible. Separate union, personnel admin., etc.'

'Control only a few fundamental items, do not try to control in detail.' 'Learn as much about the market as possible. Have lots of patience. Try to use the Japanese system—don't fight it. Quality and reliability are essential. Remember that many foreign business criteria do not apply in Japan.'

'To go ahead.'

'1 Take a well-established and respected national partner (minority).

2 Insist on partner supplying personnel manager. Ninety-five per cent of problems are people and particularly *union* problems.

3 Spend time talking with long-term expatriates, ask them to relate their mistakes—of which we have all made many.

4 Aim to match profit of similar corporations; don't look too high—quick profits do not obtain in a competitive market.

5 Staff sensitive areas with expatriate staff initially—appoint Japanese understudy as soon as possible with a view to taking over eventually.

6 If not large enough to support expatriate accountant in early stages, have accounts done by international auditors such as Price Waterhouse.

7 Establish "company regulations" from day 1 (the Japanese love them) and base them on those of a well-established company. This will avoid future negotiations for working conditions as the company grows.

8 Prepare for the fact that an instruction given may not be carried out at once. The Imperial Navy had a slogan: "Tell an officer three times, a sailor six times".

9 Attend every possible seminar relating to running foreign corporations. Sophia University conducts many such—in English.

10 Have a good translator on staff, but insist on reports being written in English. All educated Japanese are capable of reading English but are reluctant to speak it or write it.

11 Do learn some Japanese.

12 Avoid the "this is how we do it in the West" syndrome. We are no longer in the West.

13 Try and trust employees at all levels; the "need to know" method just will not work here.

14   Never talk about shareholders' profits. You will be told that your first duty is to honour your social obligations to employees, the shareholder being welcome (almost) to part of what is left in the kitty.'

'Establish wholly-owned operations—apply Western marketing concepts.'

'Assume that the targets set in original plan will take about one year longer to accomplish than envisaged. Send a sophisticated, solution-oriented, flexible country manager who has the credibility and confidence of Head Office and has proven adaptability to new situations.'

'Must have exclusive rights to distribution of highly desired and competitive items.'

'Concentrate on few items and develop slowly in pace with your local staff.'

'Management personnel should have working knowledge of Japan's geography and manufacturing processes.'

'Be realistic in assessing market potential and marketing approach—have patience.'

'Don't look for short-term results. Accept that initial investment will be nearly double that of any other market.'

Part 3

UNDERSTANDING JAPANESE CUSTOMERS IN JAPAN

4 Strategies for Japan Market Entry

Looking at Japan from the outside, it might not seem that their business executives or their markets are any more dynamic than one's own. But that would be an illusion, like looking at them through the small end of a telescope. Seen from up close, Japan and the Japanese are truly formidable. They are both precise and quick at what they do; everything—people and machines—seems well organized and superbly maintained. Other countries are not like this, so it is no surprise to find two distinct attitudes in foreigners who approach the Japanese market: one self-confident and purposeful, that relishes the opportunities Japan offers; the other unsure and hesitant in the face of Japanese commercial power. Each of these attitudes lends a special meaning to the expression 'entering the Japanese market'.

THE CONFIDENT ENTRANT

Large corporations tend to be confident about Japanese market entry, particularly if the goal is to set up a branch, subsidiary or joint venture with a view to manufacturing. In either case, even to contemplate entering Japan, multinational companies can be expected to have ample self-confidence, based on their international and Japan-side reputation, and substantial previous overseas experience.

There would have to be a clear market opportunity in Japan for their product or service offering, plus enough skilled managers to assign to the Japan operation without damaging activities elsewhere. Best of all, in today's economic climate in Japan, there would not be many major foreign companies left in high-growth areas who have not been approached by different Japanese companies interested in setting up a Japan-side joint venture. (See Robertson, 1987, for a useful review of issues in setting up joint ventures in Japan.)

THE HESITANT ENTRANT

On the other hand, smaller corporations and entrepreneurs, or large corporations whose market opportunities in Japan are, though clearly potentially profitable, not substantial compared with results achieved elsewhere, are often less sure about the market possibilities in Japan. They may be unknown in Japan, less confident about their ability to operate there or about their ability to attract or choose an appropriate local partner/distributor. We know from experience and research that businesses like these have the least self-confidence and the greatest reluctance to pursue opportunities in Japan.

Many of these 'unconfident' businesses are those that use long channels of distribution in their home country, are thus distant from their end customer at home, and so, by a special logic, find it hard to see the potential of their products independent of their trade-oriented or demand-creating strategies. Products of this kind are also often adapted very precisely to the needs of particular segments at home, and so may not appear to be easily modifiable to different Japanese needs. Again, some companies regard their Japan market potential as overly sensitive to and inhibited by high ex-factory price and freight costs.

Foreign executives can be hesitant for other reasons. Some feel they lack any kind of support system in Japan—they know no one and feel vulnerable and easily exploited. On the surface, this is a problem of inadequate preparation and homework, although on closer examination it usually stems from lack of other overseas and crosscultural experience. The obvious remedy is to employ people in international business who have experience and sensitivity for dealing confidently and comfortably in alien environments, and specifically Japan. Such people would know that banks, commercial attachés, JETRO, executives from your country who are old Japan hands, same-country businesses in Japan not competitive with you who might be partners for cooperation, etc., are all willing to help and support the newcomer. They constitute an almost 'instant' support system within Japan.

Whether or not internationally experienced people are involved, many successful exporters and joint venturers to Japan have also used bilingual, bicultural people as consultants to help them over the many difficult communication and negotiation problems that frequently (if not invariably) arise with the Japanese. These problems can include face-to-face communication problems with Japanese executive, problems in identifying suitable candidates for distributing or joint venture agreements, or problems in finalizing agreements without them seeming to take 'forever'. When such specialist consultant support is not used, and the executive is not internationally experienced, it is true that many can lose interest in the Japanese market as a result of such initial difficulties.

JAPAN IS WORTH THE EFFORT

In spite of the 'Japan is too hard' image, foreign businesses (small and large), entrepreneurs and exporters were increasingly successful in Japan throughout the 1980s, and will certainly be even more so in the 1990s (See ACCJ *Journal*, 1981). There is a basic format to making good market entry decisions, which is outlined below. If some logic and thorough evaluation of this kind is done, Japan offers one remarkable plus: it is by far the most profitable market in the world for multinational corporations. According to a survey conducted jointly by the *Wall Street Journal*, the *Japan Economic Newspaper* and Booz, Allen & Hamilton, '56 per cent of business leaders in US and Canadian firms, and 64 per cent of executives in European firms, said their profitability was higher than in other countries' (*Japan Times*, 1989).

The report went on: 'Despite Japan's image as a closed market, businessmen in this poll found it significantly more open in terms of government regulation than Europe and about as open as the United States . . .' This did not happen overnight. In earlier research (e.g., March, 1978) among foreign (i.e, non-Japanese) multinational corporations, Japan was by far the most profitable market in the Pacific region. I have heard many anecdotes since the 1970s that Japan has long been *the* most profitable market for United States and European companies.

High profitability does not, of course, come from stagnant or mature markets. It comes from the extraordinary dynamism of Japan, from shortening product lifecycles, constantly emerging new consumer/buyer needs and market niches, and the intense competition for delivering the new products that satisfies those needs. As Courtis (1989) said, it is the world's premier new product laboratory. And premium-pricing policies targeted to a quality-seeking marketplace don't hinder profitability either.

As a foreign business executive or entrepreneur, uncertain about what opportunities exist in Japan for you, you should feel some surge of confidence knowing, as pointed out in chapter 1, how important the search for new products is to most Japanese companies. New product development is the pre-eminent mission of most businesses in Japan today. Virtually every significant company has permanent new business/product development teams detached from everyday routine. Their task is to find and develop the new businesses/products that will bridge the future gaps in corporate income as existing products mature. At the same time as this gives them extraordinary sensitivity to emerging market segments within Japan, it also alerts them to their competitors 'breathing down their necks', and to the race between them to break the parity barrier—that is, to find the product difference that would make their brand stand out from the others, and no longer appear at par.

Unlike most markets in most advanced economies, the competitive race in Japan is not concerned with lower pricing as a point of market leverage for branded products. Nor is it concerned with, or even given any credence to, the view that competitiveness, differentiated image or parity breaking come out of the barrel of advertising/promotional 'guns'. The product is unquestionably 'hero' because successful 'heroic' products—functional, well designed, serviceable, reliable, defectless— are what Japanese customers want.

Opportunities are Here

In this turbulent environment of dynamic markets, remorseless competition and exacting customers, does a Japanese company really have the time and interest to consider working with you to launch your product in Japan? If you talk to Japanese executives, or merely read the vernacular business press, you soon learn that they are truly victims of the turbulence of their competitive marketplace because they are never sure that they know what is going on. Are they really up to date with new developments? Are they losing out to their competitors?

Again, we should be careful not to overestimate the abilities of all Japanese companies to sustain the flow of 'hit' products. Many of them, in fact, have little idea how to develop new products, especially what they often call the 'software' side—that is, not the product's basic functions, but the added differentiating features. Failure to find parity-breaking features in existing profitable products also intensifies the search for entirely new products. So the answer to my first question is likely to be very positive, depending on the apparent potential of your product/business for the Japanese market. Instead of feeling that Japan ought to be in the too-hard basket, you might be closer to the truth by speculating that 'they probably need us'.

MARKET ENTRY DECISIONS

Market entry decisions are among the most complex one can make. In the case of Japan this is especially true because, as the record shows, it takes more time, more product adaptation effort, more consultation, more chewing over options, and more market and channel evaluation work, before final decisions are made. The pre-entry feasibility and opportunity analyses demand commitment, persistence, a comprehensive approach that is not simply focused on narrow marketing issues, and a generous investment of time. After all, the Japan you are going to study—a specific market for a specific product at a specific time, encapsulated in a complex, subtle, often ambiguously structured culture and society—will in many respects be like an unmapped and unlit universe, and those of its denizens who become useful informants for your purposes will be few in number.

The nine steps outlined below are more a checklist of points you ought to have covered by the time you have finished, rather than a statement of the order in which things have to be covered. As I point out elsewhere, the data for some of these steps can be obtained in your own country before even visiting Japan, while other data have to be obtained on the spot. But the issues are so complex, and the difficulties of formulating the right questions so challenging, that the early stages will be, and ought to be treated as, brainstorming exercise without boundaries or proper starting points: perhaps as a monster jigsaw puzzle. Here are the nine steps:

1   *Assess corporate needs and goals.* Does being in Japan contribute to corporate strategy in, say, corporate growth, human resource development, technological innovation or regional planning? Is there a long-range strategy, a vision of what Japan can contribute?

2   *Evaluate resources and constraints.* Do you have the people, products, technology and commitment needed for ultimate success in Japan?

3   *Understand the Japanese business and marketing environment.* What kind of a business and marketing world is it? What trends are emerging that could affect your business? How do you do business in Japan?

4 *Evaluate Japan's market potential.* How big is the market? How much of it could you realistically capture? Who are the market leaders? What are their strengths and weaknesses? What is the current level of technology/product quality? What new opportunities are emerging?

5 *Corporate entry strategy.* Will it be a 100 per cent subsidiary, a joint venture (50/50? 51/49?), a branch office to represent you or handle your imports, a distributor agreement with a Japanese company or a licensing agreement?

6 *Market entry strategy.* The portmanteau question is: which products should be introduced where (nationally, Tokyo, other regions?) at what price through what distribution channels promoted in what way? Will your own people do this or will a Japanese distributor or partner take responsibility?

7 *Support-system development strategies.* What long-term corporate friendships ought you to cultivate among banks, leading industrial groups, distributors, major customers, other foreign companies or consultants?

8 *Negotiation strategies for entry.* What degree of flexibility in overall corporate goals, break-even targets and financial requirements should you be prepared to exercise? What degree of marketing or other control should you aim for over your Japan operations? What preparations should you make, and what should you know about the Japanese company you negotiate with?

9 *People and human resource strategies for entry.* Will the company send the right people to Japan, people who fit in with the culture and know the company business thoroughly? How will human relations be handled in the Japan operation? What type and quality of people should you employ in Japan? Generally, what changes in *your* attitude, philosophy and behaviour should you make in order to deal with the Japanese people?

THE SEARCH FOR A PARTNER

Part of Japan's recent growth as an import-rich economy has been the growth in agencies and organizations helping businesses (usually without charge) to locate possible partners. In addition to the services provided by banks, your country's commercial attachés or even chambers of commerce, JETRO offers a computerized database service designed to help overseas exporters find the right partners in Japan. Known as JETRO TOPS, or Trade Opportunity Service, it seeks to match the foreign company's needs with Japanese companies which have already indicated that they want to be introduced. This service can be provided before you leave your own country.

In earlier days, would-be exporters to Japan thought mainly in terms of trading companies as appropriate distributors for their products. Today, however, there are many other and better alternatives. Major retail chains import directly, usually through their buying offices abroad. Daiei, Japan's largest retailer, has fourteen overseas buying offices—eight in Asia, three in the USA, and one each in London, Paris and Sydney. The Sony group has four companies involved in direct importing, in addition to its electronics manufacturing. These are: Sony Plaza, importing clothing cosmetics, confectionery and sundries; Sony Trading Corporation, importing aerospace products, system kitchens, furniture and fittings, commercial machinery and beverages; Sony Enterprise Company, importing athletic machines and tapes; and CBS/Sony Family Club Ltd, which has a very large business in Japan selling imported clothing, housewares, stationery, outdoor and sporting goods.

A different type of potential partner is also emerging in Japan. Although not always easily identifiable by name, they are mostly venture capital companies, or new business entrepreneurs associated with venture capital groups. One, for instance, is the Venture Enterprise Center (VEC), a non-profit organization established to help develop new businesses based on innovative technology. Companies or individuals who apply for assistance are subjected to intense scrutiny by senior executives and scientists. VEC has not yet assisted foreign companies, but there is no impediment to applying for assistance, especially joint Japanese–foreign ventures. Another venture capital company is Temporary Center Inc., whose remarkable story is related in case study 4-1.

Your Product is the Key

There are currently around 30,000 new products introduced to the Japanese market annually. There is no adequate way to convey how extraordinarily diverse, innovative, creative, cute, kooky, practical, thoughtful, etc., these products can be (new product development in Japan is discussed in the next chapter). Leonard Koren's book, *283 Useful Ideas from Japan* (1988) presents 'an abundance of clever useful ideas . . . textured sidewalks for the blind, vibrating taxi seats, vending machines that speak' and many more. And the flow hasn't stopped. It increases its surge. Some recent products include: pantyhose impregnated with perfumes, or lace versions decorated with synthetic pearls, or, if you have a spare ¥200,000, the real thing; pre-paid telephone cards that you can set to a number, then the card, when inserted, automatically dials the number; Apatite chewing gum (¥500 for eight sticks) that reduces plaque as it replenishes calcium; or recent new products in the shape and size of a pen including radios, paper punches, electric shavers, clothes, vibrators and placebo pipes (to help give up smoking).

Whatever industry it serves, the key to success in Japan is your product. Even if your presentation or your support package offer are mediocre by Japanese standards, even if you discover that you have failed to do your homework or understand what you are getting into, it will usually not deter the Japanese. What they will be looking for is the diamond of market potential hidden in your 'uncut' offering. They will expect that a lot has to be done on any foreign product before it is suitable for Japanese customers. They know that they must, and will, take full responsibility for the launch and promotion of the product. But while they may take time to get the product right for the Japanese market, at the same time they will probably take what appears to you to be shortcuts to test-marketing. In American marketing practice, new product candidates usually are moved through a rigorous step of tests and evaluations before finally being placed in test market. The Japanese, on the other hand, get to market far more quickly; then, if the product proves to have potential, and especially if wholesale/retail channels accept it, move quickly into full campaign backing.

ENTRY STRATEGIES: CORPORATE AND MARKETING ISSUES

Is Head Office Really Behind your Planned Japan Entry?

There is a clear step-wise character to organizing yourself to evaluate the opportunities and threats of entering the Japanese market. Logically, the first step is to understand why you want to be in Japan, but for the best chance at success you need your top management really behind it. The question is: are they? Are they confident that they can be successful there? Do some, at least, understand Japan or have some kind of positive vision of what they would like to achieve there? Or is it, after all, a middle-management initiative, with top management lukewarm or merely fence-sitting?

Assuming that the potential market in Japan is very large, experience suggests that companies which fail to clarify their hopes and aspirations in Japan, and/or fail to spend time learning about Japan, are much more likely to drop out of Japan if short-term results are unsatisfactory, or if decisions radically different from those made in other foreign countries seem necessary for survival. The decisions I have in mind here include the longer break-even periods required in Japan, the higher initial investments, the substantial product modification usually required, the frequent exceptional demands by the Japanese for consistent quality in products, the demand for a stable corporate game-plan that treats personnel as a permanent (not disposable) resource, and sometimes the greater autonomy requested by local management.

Knowledge and Attitudes Audit on Japan

If your company is starting from a position of limited knowledge about Japan and doing business there, you may find the use of a 'Japanese market audit form' useful. I use an extended version of this, and it has the salutary effect of demonstrating how much you have to learn and study. There are two parts: your knowledge of Japan, and your personal opinions about Japan and attitudes towards it.

JAPANESE MARKET AUDIT FORM

1 KNOWLEDGE OF JAPAN
   What do you know about the following aspects of business life in Japan? Rate your knowledge of each characteristic as Good, Fair or Poor, and add any comments to each as you go.

   The contemporary business environment
   Social customs in business
   Personal friendships and relationships
   How to manage Japanese staff
   The quality of Japanese staff
   Politics and its relation to business
   Political stability
   Economic stability
   Strength of nationalistic feelings in business
   Japanese attitudes to foreign business generally
   Japanese attitudes to foreign goods
   Japanese attitudes to foreign people

Japanese attitudes to your country and products
Knowledge and image of your country in Japan
Contract law and attitudes to contracts
2 PERSONAL OPINIONS AND ATTITUDES
Answer Yes or No to each of the next statements, and write the
reasons for your answer in each case.

I feel confident about doing business in Japan.
I have some prejudice against the Japanese.
I would like to be our full-time representative in Japan.
I usually feel uneasy dealing with the Japanese.
The local culture will be easy to adjust to.
Doing business in Japan will be too difficult for us.
I feel confident negotiating with the Japanese.
We can't spare the money or the people to develop this market.
There are easier markets to concentrate on than Japan.

You can use your answers to these questions to help you clarify how much or how little you know about doing business in Japan. For the exercise, give yourself a rating for each part. If your knowledge is very shaky or non-existent, it will be time to start serious study. If your opinion rating indicates low self-confidence or a reluctance to get involved in Japan, should someone else in the organization take responsibility? At least, you can set goals to educate yourself or seek advice or assistance. The questions in the form are also useful as conversation starters when you talk—as you should—in Japan with expatriate old hands about the challenges of doing business there.

Making Preliminary Business Contacts

As already mentioned, there are many sources of information and help for would-be market entrants to Japan, whether manufacturers, joint venturers, exporters or technology licensors. Most foreign governments have foreign commercial services and attachés with specialized knowledge of Japan, and valuable publications. The USA, Canada, the EEC and Australia in particular provide extensive services to their nationals, but virtually all of their publications are available to non-nationals. Ports and states of these countries also have offices in Tokyo and are involved in trade and investment activities in both directions.

On the Japanese Government side, JETRO, which is under the administration of MITI, is the principal agent helping foreign enterprises wanting to do business in Japan. It provides a valuable set of publications and educational videos. Another MITI organ, the Manufactured

Imports Promotion Organization (MIPRO), operates the World Import Mart in Tokyo, and has some offices overseas, including Washington DC.

Among business organizations specializing in Japan, one of the most valuable is the American Chamber of Commerce in Japan (ACCJ), which has played a major role in the opening of the Japanese market, and has a variety of useful publications, especially the monthly ACCJ *Journal*. For younger entrepreneurs and executives, membership of the Australian Business Association, which was founded by young Australians who had set up their own businesses in Tokyo, is also open to non-Australians. It concentrates its educational activities on young entrepreneurs actually resident in Japan.

Japanese trading companies, which have offices in most countries, handling the sales of a number of foreign goods in Japan, also undertake market surveys and arrange contacts with both potential customers and prospective joint venture partners. However, the trading companies are huge organizations that cannot provide the detailed marketing and technical attention that foreign manufacturers or exporters usually require. Even so, they can assist with introductions, while the smaller Japanese trading companies (many of them very specialized) may be helpful.

Both foreign bank branches in Japan and Japanese banks have experience and skill in helping prospective market entrants, in both financial and non-financial areas. Banks in Japan perform similar functions to banks elsewhere, except that the main bank performs a somewhat focused role, especially by co-ordinating borrowings from a variety of institutions as required, managing fund-raising in the bond market, and generally acting in a somewhat more protective way if times turn bad—this can even include introducing new clients to the company or loaning key staff. There are thus some good reasons to develop a main bank early in your entry strategy formulation stage. On the other hand, entrants who seek venture capital rather than conventional bank loan products may find that not every bank is prepared to assist.

In general, prospective entrants will find that there are a very large number of people and organizations available to help, guide and advise them and, equally important, to become friends with for the long haul.

ENTRY NEGOTIATIONS AND HUMAN RELATIONSHIPS

How will you handle the business meetings and negotiations with the Japanese? There are a number of background differences between you and the Japanese that can immediately influence the frame of reference you bring to your discussions. One is the interest the Japanese will show in your corporation, its history and achievements. This is rather more interesting to them than information about you personally, and will remain so throughout your dealings with them, although they will appreciate learning about your career experience and, as friendship begins, something about your personal and family life.

Again, as I pointed out in chapter 2, because the status of sales and marketing people in Japanese companies is not high, they are unlikely to figure prominently as decision-makers (if at all) in your meetings. Rather you will deal with general or business managers who will concentrate on the product. Concentrate, did I say? They will almost certainly end up knowing more about your product—how it is made, how it can be used, its performance—than you do, via repeated questionings, sometimes just to check that you are telling them the truth. Again, you will probably find that the composition of the (large) Japanese team facing you changes frequently.

All of this makes for a testing time. How you will handle the undoubted stress of repeated, repetitive questioning, a different style of human relations and perhaps your own shortcomings in preparation for strenuous and demanding meetings, is an important element in achieving a successful outcome and laying a solid foundation for the future.

Not everyone has the skills, approach or motivation (or stamina) to make a success of dealing with the Japanese. On the other hand, you do not need to superhuman. There are three basic sets of skills to look for in finding a manager to handle negotiations with the Japanese effectively. These are:

1 the skills necessary to complete the business tasks effectively,
2 a genuine interest in Japan and the Japanese, and
3 the ability to handle yourself well under stress.

Skills Appropriate for the Task

You need to be an experienced manager and to have proved that you can manage, get along smoothly with people and handle complex projects; you should also know your company and its products and technology thoroughly. If you have these requirements (and the concomitant good communication skills, especially listening), they will quickly become apparent to the Japanese without you having to say much at all—and will set them at ease. Speaking Japanese, being a marketing specialist, having a shining manner or persuasive skills—none of these are very important.

Genuine Interest in Japan and the Japanese

You need to have some positive, even 'romantic' interest in Japan, its history, culture and people. Curiosity, a sense of wonder, a desire to learn, are more important than bookish knowledge or dogmatic opinions. Again, genuine interest is something that soon communicates itself, and reassures the Japanese that they are dealing with someone who will take a learning approach to doing business in Japan.

Good Self-manager

Being in a foreign country, having daily long meetings with people you don't understand too well, constantly facing things that you don't understand but that at first sight are vaguely menacing or threatening, at times being on the verge of expressing annoyance or irritation and holding yourself back with effort—all of this is stressful. Furthermore, the food will be strange, there may be no one to speak to in your own language at the end of the day, your sleep may be disturbed. Usually, people who are good stress managers when abroad, do sleep soundly at night and can eat anything, are people who tend to move into the international business area. Certainly, the more experience you have had doing business in other foreign environments, the more capable you will be of managing yourself well in Japan.

The competent foreign executive in Japan, if functioning as lead negotiator, cannot get along on just one or two of these strengths. You need all three. A good self-manager with interest in and fondness for the Japanese cannot succeed if he is not a knowledgeable manager. If you are a competent manager and manage yourself well you will soon let on if you have no basic interest in Japan and the Japanese. And so on. On the other hand, someone less than perfect in these terms may be entirely admirable as a support for the company spokesman.

JAPANESE IDEAS OF GOOD HUMAN RELATIONS

Ideals of good human relationships are definitely undergoing a major shift in Japan. The younger generation of managers (say under 40) are less reserved, more direct in speech, more rational and less emotional than the older generation. But the ideas of the older generation about human relations are still pervasive, especially when it comes to what is regarded as appropriate behaviour for dealing with entertaining customers or other high-status people. Nishikata Masumi, a senior Japanese businessman, puts it this way:

> In Japan, a particularly common mode of entertainment, notably with customers, is to throw off ceremony entirely and behave in a 'foolish' manner. 'Let's leave discussion of the boring details (*'katai hanashi'*) till later', they say . . . When the atmosphere has been thoroughly thawed out, they might then say, 'As you can see, I am just a frank and open person, transparent, no front or back, so let's have a drink or two together' . . . With the conversation brought together in this way, both sides demonstrate their common interests to one another. (Nishikata, 1980).

While many Japanese intellectuals and some young radicals see this kind of behaviour as bordering on hypocrisy and even servility (and you may do the same), it is very representative of the Japanese desire to forge a strong emotional connection with the people they do business with. This emotional connection is not just friendship, for it is founded on the (for the moment unguarded) revelation to one another of the artless (and so authentic) reality of one's personality—a revelation so rare in the intensely formal business society of Japan that it is treasured as a special favour from one person to another. One message to the non-Japanese in Japan, I suppose, is to recognize that the Japanese do not feel comfortable with being sophisticated after hours— they like to innocently 'let their hair down' (they say: 'slip out of formal dress'—*kamishimo o nugu*) and show themselves as they are, for there is otherwise no space in Japanese life to find out what someone is really like behind the mask or formal exterior. Getting drunk together, showing boyishness during after hours (with innocent pranks), are also available to foreigners who seek genuine human connections with the Japanese. And should you not indulge in alcohol, or are dealing with some Japanese who do not drink, the search for and discovery of common interests (who knows—stamp collecting, bushwalking, tennis, golf?) may provide the linkage you need to break down the strong, everyday reserve that most Japanese manifest.

CASE STUDY 4-1: A NEW TYPE OF JAPANESE PARTNER FOR FOREIGN COMPANIES

Until recently, foreign companies entering Japan probably looked for a partner among trading companies, manufacturers, wholesalers or retailers. But a new type of partner has emerged—entrepreneurial venture capitalists like the remarkable Temporary Center Inc., or TC.

TC, although founded only in 1976, is Japan's largest personnel agency and one of the largest in the world. Originally providing temporary office help, it is today a diverse, impressive international corporation. Headquartered in Tokyo, it has eighty offices in Japan and sixty offices throughout Asia, Oceania, the United States and Europe (as at March 1990).

In addition, through extension of its original business into other personnel and education areas, plus diversification into new business areas, and entrepreneurial involvement in new projects, it is also involved in some sixty rapid-growth joint ventures in Japan and other countries. Most of these latter have been developed in support of independent entrepreneurs or small businesses whose ideas have been attractive to TC.

Original Business Extension

From the original temporary help base, TC has expanded into executive search, recruiting and outplacement consulting services on both a national and international basis. As an outgrowth of their primary focus, TC has developed language and vocational training courses, originally to provide high-quality education for temporary staff. These have grown into complete training programs, including bilingual secretarial training, Japanese language courses and culture centres, serving Japanese and other international companies in Japan and abroad.

New Business Diversification

TC has repeatedly won the prestigious Nikkei Award for Venture Business Skills since 1987. With its stated goal and commitment being 'to implement the best ideas of today's entrepreneurs', TC operates as a venture backer and business co-ordinator. If an idea has potential to them, TC entrepreneur partners are typically expected to invest in the joint venture also and to manage the business. The range of new business ventures is very wide: import–export, consulting, real estate, education, restaurants and catering, arts and entertainment, publishing. Here a few of the businesses that came on stream in 1989:

- Den is a new concept store in Japan combining a restaurant—serving Japanese food with Western wine—with a boutique selling top-quality United States and European brands of fashion and accessories new to Japan. Den (under a different format) has also opened in Los Angeles where the goods it sells are traditional Japanese crafts.
- Ten Hearts is a new restaurant chain in Japan, specializing in yum cha (dim sum), using prepared materials flown in daily from Hong Kong.
- Aura Japan specializes in the sale and rental of second-hand classic cars, especially Rolls Royces and Bentleys.

- Interiito is an overseas English learning system. Young Japanese spend a year abroad living with the locals and enjoying the local lifestyle—sports-oriented—while learning English. This is already available in Hawaii, Singapore and Geneva, with Los Angeles and Sydney soon to be added.
- Tomoko Culture School provides education for Japanese (and other) women in ballet, jazz dance, tai-chi, piano, calligraphy, aerobics, etc. To date, it has branches in Singapore and Hong Kong.
- Orchid Japan imports orchids into Japan, with other high-class flowers to follow.
- Suebest Japan imports herbal tea blocks from China which are not drunk but placed in the bath! It is reputed to reduce fatty tissue and make the skin smoother.
- Atempo hires out chamber music quartets in Tokyo for dinner parties and other special occasions, and is involved in musical promotion and education.
- Temporary Art-Now leases pieces of quality sculpture to offices and for building foyers; manages public events such as city celebrations; and organizes and manages travelling art exhibitions, especially through TC offices and subsidiaries overseas.
- Japan–England Culture Centre is a finishing school in London for young Japanese ladies. They spend one year studying current affairs, history, culture, etiquette and manners and Western flower arrangement, making regular visits to the ballet, operas and exhibitions, and playing and learning refined sports—horseriding, tennis, swimming.
- Wins is a bilingual secretarial college in Tokyo and San Francisco. Young Japanese spend twelve weeks in the overseas centre earning their qualifications. It also conducts Japan orientations for foreign companies in Tokyo.
- Business Language Institute Inc. in Los Angeles (in conjunction with another TC joint venture, Christopher Columbus Travel College) provides one-year courses for young Japanese women.
- Nippon Interhover is a joint venture with Marubeni and Nissho Iwai which imports golf and ski practice centres into Japan. These centres are sold into the Nissho Iwai national chain of the Swing Shop (golf practice shops), as well as to other golf and sports schools.
- Kei Silk imports high-quality silk products from Thailand for sale in Japan.
- Karugamo Rice Balls is a Tokyo home-delivery service, using minicars, for value-added rice balls (popular for lunch in Japan).
- Yuri Na Kikaku is a business concentrating on eduational innovations, its first product being a reversible children's book which has been well accepted.
- Shaffle is a health services organization, based on the ideas of oriental medicine. It has created a new soft oriental aerobics suitable for middle-aged people, and offers courses in stress management, fitness, meditation and relaxation, and the use of herbal medicines. Teachers for all these courses are sent to companies.
- Commuterbus Business English School is a morning-only bus from re-

moter areas commuting to the city centre. During the hour or so trip passengers take a regular English-language course.

Other Recent Business Developments

BBC is a powerful, eight-company joint venture in which TC, with 35 per cent of the capital, takes the leading co-ordinating role. Its other partners include Nippon Steel, Yasuda Fire and Marine, Chichibu Cement, Yamaichi Securities and Toyo Engineering. BBC consults on business restructuring, new business development, venture capitalism, overseas mergers and acquisitions and real estate investment, and diversification for mature industries. The biggest project of BBC to date is the development of a floating city on Tokyo Bay. Called the 'Noah Project', this will actually be a 46,000-tonne ship fitted up as a complete business mini-city, including offices, hotels, sports facilities, shopping and restaurant malls and theatres.

JIC, short for Japan Incubation Capital, is a seven-company joint venture specializing in the development of computer software. Again, TC has taken the position of leading financier and project co-ordinator.

Other Features of TC's Activities

Given Japan's supposedly chauvinistic business society, perhaps one of the most extraordinary features of the TC approach to business is their emphasis on and trust of youth and the ideas and skills of women. Within TC itself the average age of staff is only 27, while at least half of the individual entrepreneurs involved in joint ventures are women, mostly in their twenties. On the board of directors, two or three members are in their sixties, but the remainder range in age from 37 to 45.

CASE STUDY 4-2: THE WHEELCHAIR JOINT VENTURE

Key Points

- The inclusion of a Japanese trading company in the negotiations for a manufacturing joint venture was of great value.
- Protecting intellectual property is an important consideration in deciding on the Asian location for a manufacturing joint venture.

The Fine Wheelchair Company had been a family-run business until 1980 when it became public and listed on the German stock exchange. Originally established in 1933, it has become no. 1 in the limited market of rehabilitation equipment. Since 1953, however, it has established subsidiaries in the USA, Canada, Mexico, England, France and Switzerland, and now a foothold has been established in Japan giving them access to the rest of Asia. The company had become the market leader in Western countries, but they felt they needed to establish a presence in the Far East because their Asian competitors (the Taiwanese in particular) were encroaching on their world market. The company primarily markets wheelchairs, and recently the Taiwanese have begun to manufacture chairs that can be sold at a lower price. The company is proud of its high-quality equipment and had not explored the market for low-cost wheelchairs, so the Taiwanese began to obtain a large market share in some underdeveloped countries where Fine's products are too expensive. The Taiwanese chairs are of a much poorer quality, though they are direct copies. They have cheap labour but not technology. In underdeveloped countries, there are not the same government health care and benefit programs, which are primary customers in the richer Western countries. Therefore, they don't purchase from Fine.

In many countries such as Sweden, West Germany and the United States, handicapped people own four or five wheelchairs for different purposes, and this is the target market for Fine in Asia. More recently, the Taiwanese have entered these same markets with their low-quality, inexpensive products. This was the time Fine decided to take action against this competition. They also became aware of the large market for a low-priced wheelchair. Fine decided that a procurement or manufacturing source in an Asian country was necessary to compete with the Taiwanese. The labour cost of a wheelchair is quite high so low-cost labour had to be a key element of the selected country. Fine had looked at Singapore, Korea and Hong Kong but chose to establish some kind of partnership with a Taiwanese wheelchair manufacturer, which turned out to be an unsatisfactory option. The Taiwanese had no research and development experience, no quality engineering experience and none of the required technology. They were very experienced in one area only: how to copy another company's product. There are many special ingredients in a high-quality wheelchair, such as techniques for welding, brazing and chemical specifications, and this was just what the Taiwanese companies would want. After negotiating with them, Fine concluded that they could not be trusted with this valuable technology, and had very little to offer in return. For these reasons, they chose instead a Taiwanese bicycle-maker, which only lacked adequate distribution techniques. The bicycle market in Taiwan was depressed at the time and this company was looking for a way to diversify.

Just when Fine had intended to join this bicycle-maker, the value of the US dollar dropped drastically, making it more practical to manufacture a low-cost chair in the USA. They still wanted a presence in Asia, however, so they selected Japan, which is the biggest market for these low-priced chairs, although the market is probably ten years behind that of its Western counterpart.

After learning more about Japan, Fine executives felt that Japan was as good for marketing as for manufacturing, and such things as quality control, research and engineering skills were better quality than those in Taiwan. They also reasoned that if a joint venture could be formed in Japan it would provide access to many other Asian markets. Finally, they found a prospective partner in Nagoya, who happened to be Japan's largest wheelchair manufacturer, called ZMI.

One of the unique aspects of the joint venture finally established is that it includes a third party, a Japanese *sogo shosha*, or general trading company. It was the marriage-broker for the wheelchair companies.

There were several reasons for choosing to use this trading company. It acted as go-between for the actual negotiation, and there was no disagreement to speak of. The joint venture was floated as a *kabushikikaisha* under Japanese law and is called Fine Company Asia. Fine International was allocated 60 per cent of the shares, ZMI 30 per cent and the trading company 10 per cent.

Though the joint venture was incorporated under Japanese law, the basis for the agreements was created around Western law. This was necessary because Californian law surrounded the technological transfer agreement from the German company. This area was quite sensitive, but the trading company helped resolve any disagreements.

Evaluation

The negotiation lasted about two years and, according to Fine executives, it would have been much more difficult without the help of the trading company. This virtually eliminated any cultural communication problems that may have arisen.

To keep harmony in the relationship, a steering committee was formed in which the members of each partner of the joint venture would take part. Regardless of stockholder power, the members had equal say in decisions.

Once established, Fine Asia was turned over to its Japanese managers assigned from ZMI.

Source: interviews conducted by marketing students, Aoyama Gakuin University, Tokyo, June 1985.

5 Developing Products for the Japanese Market

Without the right product, properly adapted to Japanese tastes, there is probably no way to enter the Japanese market successfully. Even if this statement is also true of other countries, there are some special problems in Japan: the established tradition of preferring quality and readiness to pay premium prices for it; the extreme difference in cultural, religious and historical background that makes Japan far more difficult to understand and adapt to than most other countries; the sophistication and fussy tastes of Japanese consumers; and the intense competition that will often see copycat, but improved, competitive products on the market soon after yours has demonstrated that consumers want the product.

In *From Bonsai To Levi's*, George Fields (1983) told what is a now classic story of General Mills failure to persuade Japanese housewives to use their rice cookers to bake undoubtedly delicious cakes. The barriers were 'two formidable interrelated cultural factors': one, the rice cooker was in almost constant use, since rice is also eaten during the day, while left-over rice is kept warm. The other reason was the fear of contaminating the rice with cake flavours, such as vanilla or chocolate. Rice is so central to the Japanese diet that they are highly sensitive to its 'purity' (that unique blandness that permits it to be teamed with strong flavours, such as prepared fishes or pickles).

Since Fields related this story, the penetration of infrared and other cooking ovens suitable for cake baking has increased considerably in Japan, but not so prepared cake mixes. In upper-middle-class neighbourhoods, however, specialty shops devoted to supplying ingredients, equipment and education for home baking have appeared and prospered, serving housewives who, using the free time they gain from having, among other things, automatic rice cookers, now prepare their own ingredients for cakes and breads at home. But why, then, has there been no general rise in home-baking? One factor certainly is that, apart from upper-middle-class housewives, who are prepared to be experimental and innovative, Japanese housewives serve highly conservative tastes in their spouses and children, and do not have much confidence in their own cooking abilities, which concentrate on very simply prepared traditional items or, increasingly, on buying in precooked or fresh products at supermarkets or fast-food outlets. So many Japanese eat out, in fact, and have such an enormous variety of restaurants and foods to choose from, that these practices are likely to continue.

Rice itself since then has taken on a new lease of life as a core concept for new value-added products, spurred on by increasing community health concerns. Using unpolished rice (*gemmai* in Japanese), Kellogg's has been successful with a breakfast cereal called 'Gemmai Flakes', while national brand pastry-goods makers have created many different *gemmai* breads, cakes and cookies.

Not every market opportunity in Japan requires tangling with the material culture. Ore-Ida Foods Japan entered the market in 1984 with five different types of frozen potatoes. Adapting to Japanese tastes, they lowered salt content, reduced package sizes by one third, and offered all products in a pre-cooked format. This meant that any of their frozen products could be quickly prepared in the one kitchen appliance available in virtually every Japanese household: the oven toaster. Seeing an opportunity for their hash brown potatoes, 'Golden Pattys', to be eaten at breakfast, where rice consumption had fallen dramatically in the face of easier-to-prepare and digest bread, they achieved a heavy sales increase and high-name awareness within months of the start of a television campaign.

THE SEARCH FOR NEW PRODUCTS

The new product explosion since the mid 1980s has its roots in the temporary slowing of economic growth in the early 1980s, which stemmed in turn from the oil shock of 1979. Japanese companies at that time were looking for products that could be sources of new revenue, but they focused then on revamping existing products, adding features or gadgetry, or to building brand image, rather than on a search for genuine new products (*honmono no seihin*). The search for new ideas was widespread, but narrow in focus, much of it a sifting over of products and ideas from the Japanese past. There was also a brief corporate dalliance with energy conservation as an approach to product development (notably the electric car) but this soon petered out.

Japanese executives, recalling that period, talk about it as a period of recession malaise (*fukeiki byoo*), when meetings increased in number and length in the search for new ideas, uncertainty and lack of decisiveness was prevalent, and marketing risks seemed intolerably high. Product development and marketing departments operated as though they were worlds apart, failing to co-operate with or stimulate one another. Sales departments, exposed to demands for new products from the trade, and sensitive to any competitive initiative, continually complained about the lack of new products. Corporate staff, in turn, complained about the decline in the performance of the sales staff, who, it was often said, were knowing less but pretending more, asking fewer questions and giving less market feedback. (This recession malaise still provides a good description of the situation today inside those companies who are struggling to meet competition or develop new products.)

From this experience, major companies created the guidelines they needed for effective new product/new business development. The products had to be 'genuine ones'. They had to be 'serious' (*majime*), meeting needs more effectively than anything else, with real functional improvements, not tarted-up versions of existing products. Production, technology and marketing had to work closely together. And, not least, the reflection and mulling-over of ideas from the Japanese past culminated in a guideline which was to prove a true inspiration—'small is beautiful!'—and lead to the *keihaku tansho* philosophy (discussed below) of the present day.

SUCCESSFUL ADAPTATION OF FOREIGN PRODUCTS

The successful adaptation of foreign products to Japanese tastes now has a long history. Among food products, Coca-Cola, Nescafé Instant Coffee and McDonald's hamburgers are some that are famous for having changed the product formula to suit the Japanese. Smaller makers have been successful as well. A tiny Belgian maker of biscuits, De Strooper—employing only twenty people—exports a specially adapted range of biscuits to Japan as 'The Pride of Belgium'. The Great Australian Pie Company changed their export product by lowering salt content and making the product smaller. It gained very rapid acceptance as a fast food among young Japanese. The American chain of cookie shops, Mrs Fields, have interestingly done the same kind of thing—that is, lower sugar content and reduce cookie size—although they found that the larger, sweeter American version, sold side by side with the Japanese, did outsell it for a time ('A sweet opportunity', 1987).

Adapting Foreign Products to the High End of the Market

Looking at other products that have pursued high-price high-quality strategies, Levi's chose the high end of the Japanese market to position its jeans, pricing them 20 per cent above regular Japanese-made brands. This gives Levi's an almost luxury product image as a high-quality American original that no Japanese maker could claim.

Haagen Daz Japan, an ice cream joint venture between Pillsbury of the USA and Japanese whisky distiller Suntory, has established a strong market position by selling what is now perceived as a super-premium ice cream. According to Tamio Yamamoto, their marketing director (Chandler, 1986), a super-premium ice cream has a lower air content and a creamier taste, and is made from natural ingredients only. Consequently, or perhaps in addition, Haagen Daz in Japan sells for almost twice as much as other ice creams. In upper-class areas of Tokyo, Haagen Daz has put some nearby Baskin & Robbins stores out of business, for the very reason of its superior positioning.

Hewlett Packard, in a joint venture with Yokogawa Denki Seisaku to sell electronic measuring instruments in Japan, has maintained high product quality and adamantly refused to offer discounts. None the less it has achieved annual growth of more than 20 per cent for the last twelve years.

Gadelius K K, a Swedish importer of high-tech machines located in Tokyo, has relied on high quality and high price to make impressive inroads into the supposedly impregnable Japanese robotics market. They were so successful that a factory was established in Japan in 1984, to produce 1000 robots annually.

SHOULD EVERY PRODUCT BE ADAPTED?

Not every product needs adaptation. One of the hit products in Japan in 1988–90, and the best-selling confectionery (first time ever for a foreign product), has been Snickers candy bars from Mars Inc., the world's largest chocolate manufacturer. The famous Hershey Bar and Hershey Kisses have been steady sellers in Japan, as have the European products of Jacobs Suchard. While it did not begin to be widely accepted in Japan until the mid 1980s, Perrier mineral water imported 15,000 kilolitres in 1989, fifteen times as much as in 1985. In 1990 Perrier had 65 per cent of the Japanese imported water market, in conjunction with its sister product Volvic (which now sells well in Japan as an ideal mixer for whisky) ('Perrier Japon: a sparkling success', 1990). None of these products seems to have been specially adapted for Japan.

As we will see later when we talk about the segmentation of the Japanese market (chapter 8), Japan's customers have diverse and increasingly sophisticated tastes, meaning that opportunities for new products are constantly emerging, and that generally valid generalizations about taste preferences—such as that Japanese consumers prefer less sweet or less salty foods/beverages—may not always need to be followed. Moreover, standardized consumption habits need not last forever. Not so long ago the standard Japanese breakfast was rice, a raw egg, fish and pickles. While this is still eaten, today many eat scrambled eggs, toast and coffee. Almost every Japanese remembers the time, not so long ago, when no one ate or knew about mayonnaise, tomato ketchup, french fries, hash browns, imported chocolate, pizza, American hamburgers or Australian meat pies; not long since they would not walk the street eating food or drinking a Coke.

WHY DO FOREIGN PRODUCTS FAIL IN JAPAN?

New products fail in Japan for a variety of reasons, but especially important reasons are the lack of difference in product performance compared to brands already on the market, or lack of a dramatic difference (from the consumer's viewpoint). Put another way, products fail because they are not parity breakers—they are seen as merely on a par with existing products, so no reason to try or buy is offered. How is it that businesses can make such elementary mistakes, especially in a market as challenging and costly to enter as Japan?

In the electronics field, Professor Kenichi Ito, a well-known Japanese inventor and professor of electronic engineering, has been a devastating critic of the poor quality of American electronic equipment. He cites the poor quality of American-made integrated circuits, a low safety coefficent and disregard of climatic variations in product design.

What is little known is that Japanese importers of American-made electronic products are kept busy sending their maintenance people around to fix things up . . . some importers, it is said, reserve a tenth of their overhead for maintenance alone . . .

In contrast [Ito explains for Japanese edification] Americans take [product breakdowns] more philosophically. A breakdown . . . is a breakdown. If something is breakable, then there is bound to be a breakdown. In Japan [however], when faced with a complaint about a faulty product, companies apologize profusely and offer to fix it. (Ito, 1985)

In the consumer product area, studies indicate that failure to undertake or follow the findings of research into consumer attitudes to or acceptance of the new product is by far the single biggest factor contributing to failure, followed by defects in the product, which is obviously related to lack of research. These can include leather products that discolour, garments or other sewn products that are stitched irregularly, wines with visible sediment or printing that has the slightest shear. When you reflect on how challenging the Japanese market is, it is hard to resist the question: how could people be so shortsighted or dogmatic as to launch the product as is?

James A. Lee (Terpstra, 1987) gives one answer. He says that the 'root cause of most international business problems overseas is' what he calls 'the self-reference criterion' or SRC. This means 'the unconscious reference to one's own cultural values' when faced with decisions about doing business in a foreign environment.

When the American Barbie doll was introduced into Japan, it did not sell, in spite of being a best-seller in the USA. Mattel Toys, in frustration, sold the manufacturing licence to Takara, a Japanese toy and doll specialist maker. It didn't take Takara long to find out that Japanese women found the Barbie doll's legs too long and chest too large. These modifications made, plus changing eye colour from blue to brown, Barbie doll quickly became a best-seller in Japan as well.

When Cadbury management refused to accept research findings showing that Japanese consumers did not like the high milk fat content of their Dairy Milk Chocolate bar and went ahead with its introduction in Japan, only to have it fail, they were surely demonstrating the SRC at work.

In contrast, when the French dairy food giant Danone took twelve months to modify and retest its range of yogurts and dairy desserts repeatedly until it had achieved formulations in line with Japanese consumer tastes, they were surely demonstrating adaptive intelligence of a high order at work. Today, Danone's joint venture with Ajinomoto is thriving; that of Cadbury with Kanebo long since a thing of the past.

OTHER DIMENSIONS OF DIFFERENCE

Salt and sweetness taste preferences and preference for smaller-sized servings are just some of the very large number of potential differences that foreign products may have to adjust to in Japan. Japanese body dimensions are quite different from those of Western people. Limbs are shorter relative to trunk or backbone length. Children's heads are quite large. Feet, hands and heads are generally smaller and narrower. Suits, jackets, shoes, gloves and headwear for Westerners (save those which are size-adjustable, or 'free size') are not suitable for the Japanese. Change in the Japanese physique continues, but for most Westerners in Japan it is impossible to get gloves to fit; men's socks and shoes in larger sizes are available only in restricted variety in a few large department stores in Tokyo. Safety helmets from the West do not fit the Japanese and have to be redesigned.

Climatic conditions in Japan surprise many foreigners. Winter is cold and very dry, like much of North America. Static electricity is a problem, skin dries and chapsticks for dry lips are commonly used. Summer is exceptionally humid, with mildew and mould a serious problem in the maintenance of clothing, motors, storerooms and other places where goods are stored. Consequently, food importers have to guard their products against these extremes, while wooden products have to be well seasoned to prevent cracking.

The four seasons in Japan are very distinct, and the Japanese are accustomed to changing their wardrobes four times a year with great precision on the same days each year, meaning that there are restricted periods in which seasonal articles can be sold.

SPACE AND REDUCTIONISM IN JAPAN

The Japanese have long been regarded as masters of the miniature, and their standard complaint to foreigners is how small and crowded Japan is. In many ways, however, crowding has been a deliberate choice they have made, not just in this century, but over the past thousand years or so (Lee, 1984). The folding fan is a Japanese invention, dating perhaps from the third century, and in many ways it symbolizes what the Japanese have done ever since: created objects which fold up, collapse, shrink and become more convenient to use or store while being novel and surprising.

The sliding paper-covered doors (called *fusuma*) within Japanese houses can be slid away out of sight or removed as well as being used to create a wall between rooms. Japanese traditional rice-paper lanterns, unlike the Chinese lantern from which they derive and closely resemble, differ in one important way: they fold up. The *bento* or lunch box, of which today there are thousands of varieties, dates from the sixteenth century, and is nothing but the contents of a food tray bearing a complete meal reduced to fit into a box.

In modern times, products originally created somewhere else, but miniaturized or 'reduced' in Japan, are legion: the folding umbrella, the transistor, miniature cameras, radios, office machines, wristwatch TV, radio-controlled toy cars, Walkman stereo radios, instant noodles, capsule hotels, high-rise parking towers for small lots, double-decker garages, compact carwash units (taking up no more than 360 square feet), compact triple-decker clothes hangers with accessory hooks, Team Demi desk sets containing seven stationery gadget items in a pocket-sized plastic case, multi product vending machines (e.g. cigarettes and beer), mini beer cans, co-ordinated stationery sets, mini cars, and so on and so on.

Reductionism of this kind reflects a longstanding Japanese tradition of packing things together, a remarkable sense of order which perhaps the *bento* typifies, but which extends also to the way things are offered. For instance, you can order complete meal sets in many restaurants. These are called *teishoku*, meaning fixed or settled meals. Travel packages fall into the same class.

If you as a foreigner, as a product designer perhaps, want to get under the skin of reductionism in Japan, you should live there, preferably in a small apartment with *tatami* mats on the floor. Japanese *tatami* rooms can be thought of as modular (the mat size is standardized wherever you go), multifunctional and so compacted. They usually have little or no furniture. By night you sleep on *futon* (mattresses) rolled out on the *tatami*. When you wake in the morning, you fold up the bedding and store it away behind sliding doors. During the day, you sit on the *tatami*. That is a type of reductionism as well, because your legs fold up under your body, and the amount of space you occupy in the room is much less than half what you would occupy if sitting on a chair. When you travel by train to work, you will probably stand in a carriage which is largely designed to contain as many standing people as possible—seats are few.

The congested nature of urban living in Japan also makes many Western products unsuitable. Examples are: large cars, large furniture, appliances with noisy motors (that would disturb the neighbours), merchandise in large cans or bottles (which don't suit small families) and, incongruously, wallets that are not large enough to carry large Japanese bills. Measurements also should be indicated in yards and inches, nor should electrical appliances have voltage ratings inappropriate to Japan.

Keihaku Tansho

Keihaku tansho is a portmanteau term meaning 'light—thin—short—small'. It represents a philosophy that the Japanese have today about what makes for a successful product. Strictly speaking, the elements that make for new product success are more complex than this but, as one Japanese commentator has explained, 'It is a guideline, a philosophy'. It seems to give some non-physical dimension to the new products pouring out of Japan today, a kind of Japaneseness that, as the previous paragraphs demonstrate, actually has its roots deep in Japanese history and tradition. David Kilburn (1986) has pointed out what are some examples of *keihaku tansho* for the Japanese:

> To Japanese perceptions, *kei* or 'light' qualities are found in small cars, polyester suits, family bicycles, duvets and Mild Seven (a cigarette). Unscented cosmetics, solar calculators, disk cameras, and low salt/fat/calorie foods have *haku* or thin qualities. *Tan* or 'short' products include mini-lipsticks, mini-umbrellas, convenience foods and delivery services. *Sho* or 'small' is typified by headphone stereos, liquid crystal TVs, draught beer and minicompos.

Two new products, which typify so much the reductionism philosophy of the Japanese, caught my eye during 1989. One, from Seiko Epson, is a *karaoke* (Japanese sing-along) set, complete with mike and speaker. You are probably familiar with *karaoke* sets which are about the size of a stereo set. This one is different. It is the size of your hand! The other product interested me because I am a scuba diver who, like others, has been turned off the sport because of the cumbersome nature of the equipment. Manufactured by Nippon Sanso KK, it is a very small and light (1.8 kg, or 500 grams submerged) breathing apparatus that dispenses with oxygen tanks. Called 'eOBA' (enriched Oxygen Breathing Apparatus), it removes the CO_2 from the air exhaled by the user, adds oxygen to the air and recycles it for breathing. Underwater breathing becomes as natural as normal breathing ('New simple and light equipment for underwater strolls', 1988). We can only wonder about what miracles of *keihaku tansho* will be produced in Japan during the 1990s.

CASE STUDY 5-1: EELS FROM TAIWAN

Key Points

- Opportunities for huge sales to Japan exist in many areas because of centralized buying.
- Japanese buyers need to be meticulous in their demands because of the standards expected by Japanese consumers.

Japanese people have been fond of *unagi*, or eel, for many years. It is found in other countries but nowhere else is it as popular as in Japan. Therefore, Japan is a rather large market for those in the eel business. Ten years ago local production accounted for 70 per cent of all eels consumed in Japan, but that figure has gradually fallen to 40 per cent. The other 60 per cent is imported from China and Taiwan.

Mr Yoshihara is the man responsible for importing eels from Taiwan. When asked last year by Otori Bussan to represent its interests in Taiwan he agreed to do it and established his own company, Toshin Co. Ltd, just for that purpose. After meetings with their supplier in Taiwan, Bohman Co. Ltd, over several months, the two sides finally sat down and negotiated an agreement for the export and sale of eels to Japan. His job now is to fly to Taiwan monthly to arrange for each sale and shipment, and then he sells the eels to Otori Bussan when they reach Japan.

Background

Mr Yoshihara became interested in the eel importing business ten years ago when he was asked by a friend in Yoneuchi Bussan to join them in the eel business. The firm was doing poorly at that time due to a high death rate of eels during shipment and stiff competition from Otori Bussan, the only other Japanese firm importing eels from Taiwan. Mr Yoshihara declined the offer because he felt that the cut-throat competition was too extreme for either company to fare well. Instead, he began researching the eel industry and the consumption patterns of the Japanese while keeping an eye on the situation between the two firms.

Last year when Yoneuchi merged into Otori so that they became the sole purchaser of eels for Japan, Mr Yoshihara decided the time was right and accepted their offer. Behind him he had their confidence, an extensive knowledge of the field, investor support and the strong economic position of Japan, so he felt sure of success.

Preparation

After the decision was made to enter the field, Mr Yoshihara's work really began. First, he located investors for his new company, most of whom were business contacts and associates. Once they were found he had to arrange for a letter of credit from a bank. He also worked out average eel consumption and seasonal fluctuations. During this period he often flew to Taiwan to discuss business matters, eel-raising methods, improved shipping methods and so on. Finally, after two or three months of such preparation, both sides were ready to negotiate an agreement.

Negotiations

In the summer of 1985, the two sides met to reach agreement. Mr Yoshihara and two investors flew to Taiwan and met three men representing Bohman Co. Ltd and the eel grower. Both sides were ready to do business so they sat down and worked through the agenda. All discussions were in Japanese and there were never any problems in communicating. The topics discussed were as follows:

Eel Care. This was the most important topic for the Toshin side. Eel-raising is a very specialized industry and care in the past had not been good enough. The quality of the eels had improved over the years but was still not comparable with that in Japan, so he outlined how they could work towards improving quality. Also, the death rate in the past had been too high so better care had to be taken in shipping them. For example, Bohman had to agree to make the growers keep the eels in clear, clean water for the few days before they were shipped to help reduce the number of deaths. Mr Yoshihara would make on-site inspections during his monthly visit to insure that procedures were being complied with. Also, since eels will fall asleep below 15°C, special care of the temperature had to be taken.

Quantity. Mr Yoshihara gave them an outline of average consumption and asked if supply could be changed seasonally to satisfy demand. Bohman agreed to it, and the exact quantity would be determined each month at their meetings after consultations with both Bohman and Otori.

Transport. The eels would be shipped by air because of their perishability. Also, all forms must list 'Japanese Airport' as the port of entry to allow for some flexibility in receiving ports according to availability of air cargo space (because if it were written as 'Japan Airport ' the eels *must* be received at Narita).

Price. Both sides haggled over the price but it ended up as a pure compromise. Mr Yoshihara felt it was the only real concession he gave because, if he received his ideal price, the eel growers could not afford to stay in business. Bohman required payment in American dollars. It was decided that the yen price would stay roughly the same but the price in dollars would change if there was a fluctuation in the yen–dollar exchange rate.

Toshin would make payment in dollars through a telegraphic transfer on receipt of the eels. However, Bohman required a letter of credit each month to ensure guaranteed payment even in the case of a default by Toshin.

Capital plan. Bohman wanted to see Toshin's capital plan to find out how the company planned to finance its purchases. As a result, Toshin showed its line of investors and their assets.

Tariff. The tariff on eels imported to Japan is 5 per cent, in order to protect the local eel industry. Bohman wanted it reduced if possible, but Toshin was helpless and the situation has not changed yet.

Resolution

After all areas were discussed and agreed on, a contract was drawn up and signed and is in effect today. No problems occurred during the negotiations, which were actually just clarification of many things they had already discussed. Both were well prepared and ready to do business, and the Taiwan side was willing to give in to the demands on eel care because they realized that it was essential to conducting business with Toshin.

Evaluation

Both sides were pleased with the agreement and the feeling was, and is, mutually friendly and co-operative. The only thing Mr Yoshihara said he would do differently if done all over again would be to discuss more specifics of eel care and include them in the contract before discussing prices. He did not feel that the difference in cultures affected the negotiations, especially since the man he dealt with speaks Japanese as well as being a native speaker. The only difference that he has to keep in mind is that Saturday is not a working day in Taiwan.

Current Situation

Business is continuing as usual with the monthly meetings but two issues may change things in the future. First, the eel growers are interested in raising things other than eels, such as black tigers (shrimp). Their profit margins would be much higher for black tigers than for eels. Mr Yoshihara is not interested in black tigers because he feels they will not sell in Japan so he has to figure out how to keep them interested in raising eels. Another area where they need motivation is in quality. The quality of the eels from Taiwan is still not as good as those raised in Japan so locally produced eels are favoured. He feels that if the Taiwanese could increase the quality to equal Japan's, theirs would then become the favoured eel and increase their market share.

CASE STUDY 5-2: LEGO IN JAPAN

Key Points

- A large initial investment is critical to success.
- Do not expect instant success. You must persevere.
- Adapt! That means the product should fit the Japanese consumer.

Nihon Lego K K is the Japanese sales company of Interlego, the world's largest toymaker. Although Lego toys had been sold in Japan since 1962, the wholly-owned subsidiary, Nihon Lego, was not established until 1978, and a very large investment (reputedly eight figures in US dollars) was needed before the company came into the black around 1983. Moreover, this performance, since maintained, occurred in the midst of the Japanese toy industry suffering under seige from the arrival of advanced video games.

Looking back on their experience, Nihon Lego executives emphasized that the large initial investment was the key to prosperity in Japan. Their eyes were on long-term profit, not instant success, so they committed themselves to 'really understand Japan, to do their homework thoroughly'. In adapting Lego to Japanese customers, reports Daniel Masler, Nihon Lego ensured that boxes containing a given product should be readable by Japanese customers, and goods should be immediately available. Variations in quality can make an immense difference to sales. 'Even a slightly damaged package will be returned, and if you disagree, you are out of business'.

CASE STUDY 5-3: DOING WHAT YOU DO BEST: THE UNILEVER SUCCESS STORY

Key Points

- Unilever originally entered Japan in a joint venture with Hohnen Oils, but switched to a totally-owned subsidiary within a few years.
- The Unilever global philosophy of marketing management and brand-name marketing guides their activities in Japan, in particular giving them scope to create products especially for Japan or to adapt global products to the local market.
- Marketing planning and new product development in Japan is undertaken by local teams of both Western and Japanese marketing people within Nippon Lever.
- The development of new products for Japan has stemmed from their consistent policy of developing consumer insights and 'touch and feel' for consumer tastes and preferences, then fitting new product ideas to identified market opportunities.

Unilever is one of the ten largest companies in the world, best known for its line of toilet products, but also a major force in food and confectionery. It has been involved in most foreign markets since the 1930s, either through exporting or through wholly-owned subsidiaries, because this is the only way to create what they call 'Unileverization' within each subisidiary. Their philosophy stems from long experience in overseas marketing and has several facets. One, the company always tries to keep a low profile. A low-profile local company, they have learnt, encounters fewer problems when dealing with governments or consumers. Two, the company is highly brand-name-oriented, and would be rather known for its prestigious brand names and their quality than for the power of the company name. Third, given 100 per cent ownership, Unilever is able to create a special atmosphere within each of its companies that fosters the internationalization of each individual employee's outlook. They especially emphasize the development of basic knowledge and skills in marketing, believing that once these basics have been mastered, they can be applied anywhere in the world.

However, Unilever's entry into the Japanese market did not follow its customary practice. Restrictions on the formation of wholly-owned companies in the late 1960s led them into the Hohnen joint venture. As soon as they were able to buy Hohnen out, they began the process of full Unileverization, importing twenty or more foreign executives and specialists, instituting a powerful new product development program, and vesting most corporate decision-making in local hands. This did not mean full control in every respect, but when it comes to marketing and product adaptation, Nippon Lever has complete autonomy, within corporate guidelines. These guidelines provide Nippon Lever with a core description of their brands (for instance, Lux toilet soap) and how they should be presented to the consumer. This helps ensure that the high product image is maintained all over the world. For instance, the core description for Lux may be something like: 'So good for your face that it is used by beautiful women all over the world'. But, as their marketing strategy specialist has pointed out, after that Nippon Lever is free to adapt the product and message to the country.

'The perfume we use in Japan is unique,' says Roger Brookin, marketing strategist with Nippon Lever. 'Japanese dislike using highly perfumed products on their skin. The packaging, formulation and lather are unique as well. In order to elicit the right emotion from our [Japanese] customer, we also adapt marketing communications to local needs.

'In Japan, we offer six varieties of Lux because of a unique characteristic of the market: the strong emphasis on gift-giving. Some 70 per cent of Japanese homes never buy soap. In fact each home has on average forty bars of toilet soap stashed away—the world's highest inventory. This is because in summer and at New Year people give each other gifts. According to custom, these gifts must be relatively acceptable to everyone in the family, without having too much individuality. That describes Lux rather well.'

Lux is only one of many successful Unilever products in Japan. Others include margarines, shampoos and other personal care products, and frozen and snack foods. Some recent other successes include achieving market leadership in Japan with their Timotei range of hair shampoos, market leadership with their Fish Oh Finger! range of fish fingers, a continuing strong share of the margarine market with their Rama brand, and many successes with their brands and varieties of frozen confectioneries.

They look not for rapid expansion but for market share maintenance and the exploitation of gaps in each market. This search is undertaken by teams of both Western and Japanese executives, and very heavy investments are made in market research. This includes basic, exploratory research into Japanese consumer tastes, colour preferences, attitudes and lifestyle. This culturally attuned information provides them with the sensitivity, the 'touch and feel', needed to keep on designing and modifying Unilever products successfully for Japan.

CASE STUDY 5-4: HOW UNILEVER'S GLOBAL COMPETITORS HAVE FARED IN JAPAN

Key Points

- In contrast to Unilever, its two major global competitors, Proctor & Gamble and Colgate-Palmolive, have had many difficulties and failures in Japan.
- Failure to have on-the-spot marketing decision-making, especially for new product development, means serious insensitivity to rapidly changing markets.

In most respects, Unilever's two biggest competitors, Proctor & Gamble and Colgate-Palmolive, differ markedly in the way they have tried to market in Japan. They have made decisions about Japanese products at their head office in the USA rather than in Japan. Proctor & Gamble have made much heavier investment, but their mistakes are many. Take their toilet soap Camay, which is in direct competition to Unilever's Lux. It has never been modified for Japan and is exactly the same product as that sold in the rest of the world. No 'touchy feely' product adaptation for P&G, it seems. They were the losers, for both brands started out in the mid 1970s from the same level of sales in the Japanese market, with Lux pulling away to market leadership and Camay remaining a minor brand.

Since entering the Japanese market in 1973, some analysts have estimated P&G losses at a quarter of a billion or more US dollars. For instance, in the late 1970s their Bonus and Cheer laundry detergents held 15 per cent of the Japanese market. Cheer, with 10 per cent of the market, did well at first by discounting its price, but this eventually eroded the reputation of the product among smaller supermarkets, who were responsible for 30 per cent of total sales. They were making less money on them, so they switched to other brands.

Colgate-Palmolive did almost the same with Colgate toothpaste as P&G did with Cheer. Colgate achieved a remarkable 12 per cent share of the Greater Tokyo toothpaste market, only to lose it by price discounting that impacted negatively both on wholesalers and on retailers. Both companies were given good advice to stay away from their extreme form of discounting. Neither apparently listened.

As an example of failure to be sensitive to the environment, P&G blundered in not introducing a phosphate-free detergent in the late 1970s. Japanese mass media and consumer groups were expressing outrage at the pollution, with phosphate-rich detergents, of the nation's largest freshwater lake, Lake Biwa, and Japanese companies were quick to introduce phosphate-free detergents. P& G, in spite of having such a product already on the market in the USA, did not introduce one in Japan until two years later.

Also, P&G had been damaged by advertising approaches which emanated essentially from their United States head office.

In the late seventies Japanese housewives voted Cheer commercials as the least liked on Japanese TV because they were repulsed by a hard sell that stressed product benefits and user testimonials. Bad advertisements were even more devastating for Camay soap. In one commercial in the late 1970s, a man meeting a woman for the first time immediately compares her skin to that of a porcelain doll . . . the Japanese were insulted.

'For a Japanese man to say something like that to a Japanese woman means he's either unsophisticated or rude,' says an adman who worked on the P&G account in Japan . . . The Japanese ad executive warned that women would find the commercial offensive, but 'P&G just wouldn't listen'. (Tanzer, 1986).

The biggest failure and blow to P&G's corporate pride, however was the loss of its 90 per cent share of the disposable diaper (nappy) market held by its Pampers brand. P&G had introduced the product into Japan in 1978, and built and educated the market. In 1981, with P&G holding 90 per cent of the market, a small Japanese sanitary napkin maker, Unicharm, entered the market with a new and better nappy, and by 1985 the Pampers share had fallen to just 5%.

CASE STUDY 5-5: WAITING FOR A TACO BREAK

Key Points

- Lawyer Kent Gilbert sensed an opportunity for Mexican tacos in Japan, and was responsible for bringing together the key people in a joint venture: the United States franchise owner, a major Japanese company as venture capitalist and facilitator of introductions and connections in Japan, and himself as organizer and entrepreneur.
- Some Westerners have masterful talents at matching Japanese negotiators on their home ground.
- Entrepreneurs without knowledge of Japan and the Japanese can benefit from trusting the judgements and insights of a Japan specialist.
- This case also illustrates points about searching for and evaluating the right Japanese partner.

Aoyama Agency was established in 1984 by Mr Kent Gilbert, a bilingual lawyer who also happens to be a national television 'talent' in Japan. The agency handles a variety of business, including promotions and consulting. For some time Mr Gilbert had been watching the fast-food market in Japan and waiting for a Mexican fast-food chain to make its entrance into this market. Mr Gilbert felt strongly about being the first to introduce a concept in a market where the first would always be no. 1. Since Mr Gilbert is a TV celebrity in Japan, he felt that his image would help promote business. In early 1985, he approached Taco Bell USA in order to discuss franchise rights. According to Mr Gilbert, he decided not to do business with Taco Bell mainly for three reasons:

1 Pepsi Cola owned Taco Bell and, according to Mr Gilbert, 'Pepsi is a dismal failure in Japan because they only hold 4 per cent of the cola market in Japan which tells me that their marketing strategies are weak.'
2 Pepsi Cola did not think that Mexican food would appeal to the Japanese, and
3 Pepsi Cola could not offer Mr Gilbert the franchise rights to Taco Bell in Japan because another existing franchise wanted to open up a test store.

Then Mr Gilbert decided to approach the second biggest Mexican food franchise in the United States, TacoTime International, which had 270 stores in North America.

On 21 September, 1985 Mr Gilbert sent a business proposal along with his résumé to Mr Fraederick, president of TacoTime International in Oregon, USA. On 27 October, 1985 Mr Gilbert received a vague letter from Mr Jam Azumano of K-Pac, another Oregon-based company owned by Mr Fraederick. From his letter, Mr Gilbert assumed that Mr Fraederick had not even read his proposal. On 25 December, 1985 Mr Gilbert sent another letter to Mr Fraederick stating the terms of their proposed relationship. The negotiation continued slowly through correspondence and fax until Mr

Fraederick visited Japan in March 1986. According to Mr Gilbert, the franchise rights agreement was satisfactory to both parties but the cost was far too high; the figure desired by TacoTime International was seven digits (in US dollars). Since he could not afford that, though he was convinced tacos would be a winner in Japan, he purchased the option rights from TacoTime International and started looking for a financial backer, a partner in a joint ventureship. Part of Mr Gilbert's initial problem was to weed out the companies he could tie up with. Some had a lot of real estate available—which can be a very difficult problem in Tokyo—but Gilbert did not think he and his staff could have got along well with their officers.

Another Japanese company was interested, but did not like the way Gilbert drew up his franchise rights agreement, nor were they willing to agree on the share split that Gilbert wanted. He would not settle for less than a 50–50 split. Although this company was very interested in Mr Gilbert's concept, they could not agree on the share.

Gilbert changed his strategy and decided to use a different approach with Nissan Corp. During their first meeting on 28 December, 1986 he concentrated on selling the concept of Mexican fast food in Japan to middle executives first. This worked; he was able to sell the concept to the lower executives, who in turn sold it to Nissan's top executives. Following this, Gilbert had a market survey done, and this found, as he expected, that the Japanese would eat tacos. 'We fed the product to lots of different people', he said, 'and they seemed to like it.'

With these findings in hand, Gilbert made a second presentation to the top executives of Nissan and this deepened their interest in the potential joint ventureship. Before Nissan would finalize their agreement, however, they wanted some changes in the franchise rights agreement. Their main concern was the clause which stated that TacoTime Japan would be required to open a hundred stores in Japan in the first five years. 'Nissan wanted to evade this risk since we did not feel confident about doing it,' said Mr Kaneko for Nissan Corp.

Final negotiations between, Nissan, TacoTime International and Gilbert took place in Tokyo in late January 1987. Representing TacoTime International was Mr Fraedericks. Since he was president and owner of TacoTime International and he had developed a trusting relationship with Gilbert, he felt confident in coming to Japan alone. By this time Gilbert 'had already renewed his option agreement with TacoTime International and this was costing him money out of his own pocket'. Luckily the negotiotions were completed and agreements were made on the day that his option agreement renewal ran out. TacoTime officially began its operations on 23 April, 1987.

Planning and Preparation on Each Side

With Mr Gilbert's experience and knowledge, he was able to draw up his proposal for the franchise rights fairly. In his opinion, if a proposal is one-sided, then the other side will sift through every sentence looking for things to argue about. It was obvious to that point that TacoTime International was asking for more than Nissan and Gilbert were willing to pay.

'The Nissan team and Mr Fraederick', Gilbert said, 'seemed to get along real well. The men on the Nissan team seemed to enjoy using their English, plus they felt that it was the American way to be very friendly up front. Yet when the negotiations actually began, the Japanese on the Nissan team still assumed that they were negotiating in the American way and thus began their counter offer at a ridiculously low price (low-balling) and putting themselves in for a heated debate.'

As the negotiations stalled on this point, Gilbert realized that he was 'running out of time and money'. He had to make Nissan and Mr Fraederick reach an agreement. Soon the negotiations were in Japanese only since it was easier for everyone concerned, but during the moments of offers and counter-offers Gilbert translated for Mr Fraederick. The key issues that were discussed included whether TacoTime Japan would develop company-owned stores or franchise. There was a lower financial risk with a franchise. Above all Nissan wanted to make some revisions to the Master Franchise Agreement because, at this time, TacoTime was not assuming any risk. Yet Nissan was not willing to assume all of the risk. Another key issue was what governing law would apply. TacoTime International wanted Oregon law to apply and of course Nissan felt that, since the franchises were to be in Japan, Japanese laws should be used. The most important issue was the pre-conditions for the payment.

At the end of the first day of negotiations, only the pre-conditions of issue were left to be resolved. Back in Gilbert's office, the two Americans discussed the day's negotiations. Gilbert recalls, 'Mr Fraederick was upset at all the time that it was taking to get through each issue. I assured him that Nissan was very interested yet it was the Japanese way to do things slower than we're accustomed to in the West . . . I myself felt that Nissan was being too unrealistic and even I couldn't agree with their proposals.' Later that evening they finally reached an agreement with TacoTime International taking some of the financial risk, softening its stand on payment pre-conditions and reducing its asking price from a seven- to a five-digit US dollar figure. Gilbert convinced Fraederick that he would be able to persuade Nissan to agree to their new proposal. Gilbert decided that it would be strategically advantageous to let Nissan have some time to relax. Thus he made up excuses like: 'Mr Fraederick needs to discuss some of these things with his people in the corporate office. Let's give him a couple of days.' After this two-day break, the negotiations resumed and the outstanding issues were amicably resolved.

Post-negotiation

TacoTime Japan opened the first three Tokyo stores within nine months of reaching agreement, in spite of the large difficulties of finding sites in Tokyo. However, Nissan's connections, plus the findings of traffic flow surveys in prime areas, helped to identify main-street locations acceptable to them.

6 Distribution Strategies for Japan

Whatever the complaints about the difficulty of entering the Japanese market, or the complexity of the distribution system, one thing is certain today. Foreign products and imports, services and technology, are welcome and needed as never before. They have become a life-support system for Japan's enormous economic success at every level of Japanese government and business: in policy-making, retailing, wholesaling, manufacturing, and in the daily lives of consumers. But this does not mean, it hardly needs saying, that the job of distributing your product is any easier. Of course, when you are selling directly—without intermediaries—to the Japanese customer, the issues of how to enter, or the problems of seemingly tangled and complex channels, hardly exist.

On the other hand, when the channels you must use are long, with many intermediaries between you and the end customer, you will unquestionably find many of Japan's distribution practices to be complex, difficult to understand, and hard for any newcomer—foreign or Japanese—to gain acceptance.

DISTRIBUTION CHANNELS

Most consumer goods channels have three different kinds of wholesalers. Each specializes in serving retail outlets of different sizes and, therefore, different order quantities. Some wholesalers, acting as the manufacturer's agent, also specialize in serving other wholesalers. Bigger wholesalers break lots to meet smaller orders from the smallest wholesalers who never buy directly from the manufacturer. Consequently, the same goods tend to be sold and resold through different wholesalers, so much so that the turnover of the wholesale sector is five to six times that of the retail sector. According to the Economic Planning Agency, the distribution costs of products that flow through these long channels are dominated and inflated by operating and promotion costs, rather than by physical distribution costs (which account for most of the costs for products moving through short channels).

One important reason for this tiered structure is the degree of fragmentation of the retail industry. There are about 1,620,000 stores in Japan, or 132 per 10,000 people, and 437,000 wholesalers (36 per 10,000 people), figures double or more those of almost every other country. This fragmented scatter of stores means that most of the stores are very small, with one or two employees only, undercapitalized, often located in backstreets or difficult-of-access places, and ordering only small quantities from wholesalers at any one time.

In a way, these small stores represent yesterday's Japan, when large retailers were very few in number. In the post-war period, as larger retailers appeared on the scene, small retailers were threatened, and this lead to the enactment of the 'Large Retail Store Law', designed to protect the small stores by restricting the construction of large-scale retail businesses. What this law has done, over the last forty years, is to inhibit the growth of the retailing sector, which did not seem to the Japanese Government too high a price to pay to protect the livelihood of one million small shopkeepers and their families.

In today's affluent Japan, however, these shops are increasingly threatened by dramatic changes in the structure of distribution, as well as by changes in the law scheduled for 1993. The newer channels, especially chains with their centralized purchasing, computerized operations and professional merchandising, will probably overwhelm the small storekeepers eventually. More and more of them are joining with voluntary chains, or going out of business as these newer outlets—convenience and discount stores, mini-supermarkets, telephone and mail order, direct marketing, door-to-door selling—bite into local business life. 'Mom and Dad' stores will continue to be protected by law until 1993 at the earliest, but the surge of change in other areas will make them slowly redundant.

CHANGES IN THE 1980s

In particular, the dynamic changes of the 1980s saw a significant change in membership of the traditional channels as new companies replaced old, as newer types of retail outlets emerged and grew. The more traditional outlets, shopping centres, general merchandise stores and department stores, in that order, dominated retail sales during the first half of the 1980s, but newer types have since grown lustily. Voluntary retail chains showed remarkable growth and now rival shopping centres. By 1987–8 they had outstripped department stores and general merchandise stores in total sales, with a growth rate nearly double that of the other large types. Convenience stores and franchise chains, which jointly now have higher sales than department stores, grew very rapidly during the 1980s, at rates averaging up to 20 per cent each year. Although much smaller, door-to-door sales and the mail order business have also grown at about equivalent rates. The prognosis for the 1990s is that these newer types of retail businesses will eventually outstrip the more traditional outlets.

All this change is of critical importance to many foreign manufacturers, especially those targetting products to the affluent younger consumer segments patronizing the newer outlets: students, working women, singles, etc. In attempting to penetrate a market as large and as complex as Japan, the foreign business ought to think in terms of market segments—Who are you aiming your product at? What particular channels give best access to those customers?—rather than in terms of national distribution. In fact, even among those foreign products which have been outstandingly successful and become household words in Japan, only a handful—such as Coca-Cola, Nescafé, Snickers and Schick blades—have the market power to develop and profit from total national distribution. So usually you should put the picture of a huge, complicated national market aside, and focus instead on what can be achieved by using just one or a few distributors, who could be retail chains or specialist wholesalers.

Restriction to a few regions, often just Tokyo and its environs (which delivers thirty million of the most affluent Japanese), is also sensible and even unavoidable, because of cost factors. And this might still be putting too ambitious a slant on things. In the opening stages of setting up a new foreign product, just securing one department store chain as a (non-exclusive) distributor, or one convenience store chain customer, will be occasion for jubilation. Never mind the dazzling prospects of 125 million Japanese hopelessly addicted to your product.

CHOOSING YOUR DISTRIBUTOR

If you accept this picture of a target market within a market, of an enticing niche appropriate for your product, the discovery of the right partner or distributor is one important decision. Another is whether you should have an exclusive distributor. The case in favour is probably well known, but there is something to be said for non-exclusive relationships, as Mr Makio Matsusaka, vice-chairman of Pfizer MSP Inc., Tokyo, has said:

> In my own experience and opinion, the best strategy . . . is to use a couple of trading companies or wholesalers as agents or distributors, but not to give exclusivity to any one company and not to give exclusivity to the total number of companies. In other words, in Japan, in principle, if we designate three trading companies as our agents, there is an understanding between the supplier and the three agents that the supplier will not designate any company afterwards, unless there is a very strong and very good reason for it. It is only an exception that they could add any other new company as an agent . . .
>
> Now . . . the action I did take for many foreign companies was [just this]—to start with, but [also] maintain . . . direct sales whenever customers request to buy direct from us. But . . . we do not take any action on our own to try to make increases in direct access, but try to entertain [sic] their position as our agents . . . this is the very best arrangement in Japan. In other words, the majority of the sales should be made through agents, but we have flexibility and have reserved the right to make direct sales. (Matsusaka, 1986)

Matsusaka points also to savings in staff through employing multiple agents. He might have added that this method also gives access to a far greater number of clients—especially from within the non-overlapping trading spheres of each of the trading companies—than is conceivable working through one distributor or trying to sell direct. On the other hand, not all products would be suitable for this arrangement.

Thinking of the Japanese market in one or other of these simplified ways—either as a consumer segment accessible by segment-specific retail outlets, or as a set of wholesalers or trading companies who provide access to mutually exclusive segments—eliminates much of the apparent complexity of Japan. It reduces the problem to a few questions like:

- What retail chains provide good access to a good portion of our target segment?
- Can/should we approach them direct? or:
- What wholesalers or trading companies specialize in serving the types of outlets that attract our target customers?

Not only is the Japanese market already highly segmented, but also the question of how it will further segment is a continuing issue for everyone in Japanese marketing and distribution. Therefore you can be sure that Japanese retailers are already well aware of whom they serve and what the opportunities are for products like yours, before you ever sit down to talk to them. If they do not display immediate interest, you are probably with the wrong people.

SOME SPECIAL CHARACTERISTICS OF DISTRIBUTION IN JAPAN

Import-oriented, import-hungry Japan is already a reality, but there are many problems to be faced, due to some of the unusual or unique features of distribution. These include the following:
- tiered channel structure
- housewife shopping patterns
- consignment sales and stock return practices
- the Japanese rebate system
- skewed structure and regional markets
- buyer-seller relationships
- margins and pricing
- rationalization of distribution.

Tiered Channel Structure

I have already described some features of the tiered channel structure, the most important of which is the three kinds of wholesalers. Primary wholesalers, who are very large, tend to specialize in one area only, or even to be contracted to one brand or maker only, and buy in very large quantities. Their customers, in turn, are very large organizations which buy in large quantities only—especially major chains (department stores, voluntary chains, convenience store chains), institutional buyers and secondary wholesalers.

While having primary wholesalers supporting your product is essential to success in Japan, the secondary wholesalers, who service medium-sized chains and retailers, are essential to the diffusion of the product. One of their most important types of customers is the tertiary wholesaler, whose responsibility it is to provide product stock and support to the one million or more small 'Mum and Dad' retailers throughout Japan. In fact, you might well call them 'Mum and Dad' wholesalers, for they too are small and undercapitalized, offering a personalized but ultimately costly service to nearby small retailers who can afford to carry little stock, and need to be able to get deliveries quickly, as they need it (making it a simplified form of the just-in-time system practised by major retailers as well as being used in manufacturing). A telephone order to the local tertiary wholesaler will soon see a boy on a bicycle or scooter winding his way through narrow streets with two bottles of this, or a broken lot of that, delivered within the hour or sooner.

Those narrow, winding streets, and the inaccessibility of so many of the 'Mum and Dad' stores to large delivery trucks, are the reasons why the logistics of delivery are handled the way they are in Japan, why distribution costs are at their highest at the end of this long, tiered distribution channel, one reason why retail prices are so often unreasonably high for foreign products. So, costly it is, but boys on bicycles are simply the best way to get the product through to one million or more little stores.

Consumer Shopping Patterns

One of the reasons for the continuance of many small local specialized retailers is the pattern of daily shopping for fresh items (common in other Asian countries as well). Japanese housewives still tend to shop daily for items that will be consumed fresh that day. Driving to the supermarket is still not customary as most people live within walking distance of stores offering these daily requirements.

The consistent preference for fresh foods has also meant that smaller stores, rather than large department stores or supermarkets, have had the skills necessary to buy, handle and sell the important fresh fish, vegetables and fruits that the Japanese prefer.

Skewed Structure and Regional Markets

Turning again to the number of retail outlets, 1.6 million, it is surprising to discover that only around 2000 of these employ a hundred or more employees, and that they generate more sales than do all the Mum and Dad shops combined. This is a typical skewed market—1 per cent of stores account for 27 per cent of all retail sales, while 60 per cent (close to a million stores) account for only 14 per cent of total retail sales. The number of neighbourhood Mum and Dad stores will inevitably decline, as discussed earlier, through the impact of better-managed small chain outlets. They are also being affected by soaring land prices and increasing rents.

Regionally, there are differences within Japan. Forty-five per cent of the population lives in just three metropolitan areas: Tokyo, Osaka and Nagoya. In total, these areas account for 50 per cent of all wholesalers, who in turn account for 70 per cent of all wholesale sales. Tokyo wholesalers alone account for 42 per cent of national sales, making it the wholesale centre of Japan. Although there are only 41 per cent of all retailers in the three areas, those retailers account for 46 per cent of national retail sales. Population pressure and high land prices make car-oriented shopping centre developments, on a Western scale, difficult in much of these three regions. In regional urban areas, however car-oriented lifestyles are well developed, and supermarkets and shopping centres have large parking areas for car-culture consumers.

Consignment Sales and Stock Return Practices

The system of consignment with payment only when goods have been sold has been practised in Japan since the seventeenth century. Return of unsold goods is acceptable and commonplace, usually based on a prior agreement. Consignment sales are practised with some new products, thus eliminating risk for retailers, while major department stores sell many products on a consignment basis. Returns with full credit are also practised in the fashion and clothing, stationery, over-the-counter drugs, publishing and seasonal products fields. Cheese and margarine are returnable, and butter can be returned to be exchanged for cheese or margarine. Wine is returnable if affected by exposure to sunlight. Pharmaceutical drugs, cameras and knitwear, among others, are sold to retailers on a 'partial payment system'—adjustment comes later when the products have been sold. Whatever the form of the partial or complete consignment system used, the cost to the retailer is lower margins on the products sold.

Consignment sales, together with just-in-time delivery and inventory minimization, are important ways of enhancing profitability in the Japanese retail sector. The retail giant Ito-Yokado depends heavily on wholesalers because of its detailed stock control system (Industrial Groupings in Japan, 1988). Another giant chain, Jusco, 'will not allow its stores to store merchandise in their yards'. On the other hand, Daiei, the biggest retailer in Japan, is gradually to 'take over the physical distribution presently undertaken by wholesalers, to purchase merchandise at lower prices' (Industrial Groupings in Japan, 1988).

The Japanese Rebate System

Japan has an ancient but continuing practice of giving congratulatory monies (*o iwai*) as favours on special occasions—weddings, birth of male children, mourning, completion of a new building, at year-end and so on. In business, *o iwai* were given by wholesalers and retailers to one another. In contemporary Japan, *o iwai* continues to be practised, privately and in business, and the system of rebates is clearly recognized as stemming from the ancient *o iwai* system. Consequently, there is a strong feeling in business that rebates are means of signifying respect and gratitude for others.

Rebates differ from margins because they are incentives aimed at promoting or retaining business, over and above margins. Nor are they necessarily monetary. For example, rebates are given for achieving sales targets, gaining new business or customers, clearing excessive inventories, early ordering, on-time account payment, maintaining the fixed retail price and not returning goods (*Distribution Systems in Japan*, 1985). Then there are rebates which are closer to the *o iwai*, such as those at year-end to express gratitude for the year's effort, the so-called 'madam rebate' for female store managers to express thanks for cooperation, and those given to express thanks for obtaining display space in a retail outlet.

Non-monetary 'rebates' can include: theatre tickets, travel vouchers (sometimes for overseas trips), golf vouchers, shopping or book vouchers, and goods of all kinds such as golf equipment, alcohol, food parcels, facial tissues, toilet paper, towels, chinaware or writing equipment.

From being a favour freely given or not given, the rebate in today's Japan has become a fixed cost for the giver, a vested interest and part of the deal, for the recipient, so that the original meaning of 'gift' has virtually disappeared. Only in individual consumer transactions does the *o iwai* concept still exist, where it is usually called *saabisu* (from 'service'). *Saabisu* means something given to you, the customer, as a result of ordering or buying. It may be a discount, a gift of extra products or another product, free delivery or installation or gift wrapping. Smaller local stores use *saabisu* effectively in competing with giant competitors.

Buyer–Seller Relationships

A Japanese medical researcher friend spent three years in a West German hospital some years ago. Talking about his experience there, he remarked that the biggest difference and shock for him was in the service given by German pharmaceutical companies to the hospital. In Japan, he said, major pharmaceutical companies kept a representative more or less full time at leading hospitals, ready to resupply drugs with same-day delivery, or whatever was requested. The West German situation was almost a complete contrast. No representatives were at the hospitals, and calls were rare. If you ran out of a certain drug, you had to telephone the maker and place an order, which might take a week to fill. It was, to the Japanese mind, a very cold and rationalistic environment.

I remembered what he said when I read a research report (Campbell, 1985) on differences between the Japanese and Germans in the way buyer–seller relationships in the packaging industry were handled. The findings were consistent with my friend's comments, and with my own views on the differences *generally* between Western countries and Japan in the way buyers and sellers relate to each other.

Compared with Germany, Japan has:

- A more competitive business environment.
- A more harmonious, trusting social system.
- A more dynamic technical environment—industry is younger, climatic conditions are different and consumers set high standards.
- Fewer takeovers between suppliers.
- More stability in buyer–seller relationships, little or no poaching of staff *between* supplier companies, continuity of service to customers irrespective of who the sales representative is. In contrast, German customers often changed suppliers when representatives—or buyers—moved on.
- Sales departments are organized around customers, to deal with all their packaging needs. The Germans tended to offer sales teams for each type of packaging application.
- In Japan, when there are negotiations over price increases, the customer receives detailed justification of labour costs, raw material cost increases and changes in overheads. This does not occur in Germany.
- More frequent personal calls on the customer.
- More frequent after-hours entertainment of customers. In Germany, many buyers do not wish to be entertained.
- Fewer formal agreements, and greater trust and commitment.

The lessons to be drawn about dealing effectively with Japanese customers, and about the changes we need to make in the way we think about business and about relations with customers, are, I think, self-evident.

Margins and Pricing

Potential exporters and marketers to the Japanese market must make decisions on trade margins and end price. These need to be at the same level as competing products. In general, margin level depends on the types of services rendered by wholesalers and retailers, and on the amount of risk they have to accept in handling the product. As well, in Japan, a special point is that wholesalers often receive a premium for their special ties to the retail sector. Japanese retailers tend to be very dependent on wholesalers, who provide credit and risk-free consignment sales. Examples of margin levels for some foreign goods are given in Table 6.1.

Table 6.1: Margin levels of foreign goods

	Producers	Prices (Yen) Wholesalers	Retailers
Cosmetics	55	70	100
Electrical appliances	70	78	100
Sporting goods	60	70	100
Furniture	52	65	100
Carpeting	45	65	100

Source: *Distribution Systems in Japan* (Business Intercommunications Inc., Tokyo, 1985).

While there has been a sharp increase in the purchasing of high-priced goods by Japanese consumers, the middle ground, as it were, has been considerably weakened, as consumers and the competitive distribution sector all push for goods to be sold as cheaply as possible.

As elsewhere, psychological pricing is widespread in Japan. Deluxe or luxury goods are thought to require a price as much as 30 per cent above middle-ground products, in order to be perceived as high-quality. Pricing in the important gift market involves some psychology also. Gift prices are standardized in Japan, but if a gift is not appropriately priced, the buyer may lose face in offering it as a gift.

Vending machine sales are also of great importance in Japan. Some products, such as cigarettes, derive more than half their sales from the machines. Coca-Cola and other vending machine operators have held

the price of a can to ¥100—that is, one coin—for many years. Cigarettes, priced at ¥200, required exactly two coins for a long time. When
the price increased to ¥220 for domestic brands, the foreign brands,
priced at ¥250, began to take off, since both domestic and foreign now
required *three* coins.

In the confectionery market, the question is usually: should it be
¥60 or ¥100? At ¥60, the product would be perceived as targeted
towards children. At ¥100, it would seeem like an adult product. ¥100
is suitable for vending machines, but inside the supermarket, the psychologically right price is not 99c, as it might be in the USA, but 98c.
In general, the psychologically reduced price in Japan ends with
eights rather than nines.

CASE STUDY 6-1: REEBOK IN JAPAN

Key Point

- Despite market leadership, Reebok faces a dynamic and highly competitive, highly segmented market, which demands continuing innovation in
product and distribution strategies (Uchimura, 1989).

Reebok athletic shoes have enjoyed great popularity with young Japanese,
and they are leaders in the intensely competitive Japanese market. Reebok
Japan Inc. only began business in 1986, when it sold 360,000 pairs of shoes,
and sales grew quickly to 1.2 million by 1989. However, even in this short
time, its share of the aerobics and fitness shoe segment dwindled from a high
of 70 per cent in 1986 to less than 40 per cent in 1990, with further severe
competition anticipated.

To cope with this, Reebok has developed strategies and products specifically for the Japanese market. In the USA, Reebok shoes were targeted at
health-conscious working women, who switched dramatically from high
heels to Reeboks for commuting, changing into dress shoes at the office.
While this was out of the question for stylish young women in Japan, Reebok
Japan set out to strengthen their product's image among the young. The number of outlets was reduced to 600 and they were concentrated in chic, high-
class areas mainly in Tokyo. Next, they are planning to introduce Reebok
shoes specifically for every age group.

'We want people to grow up with Reeboks,' says Mr Tetsuo Mochida,
president of Reebok Japan ('Reebok gets a foothold in Japan', 1989). In 1989,
they began to market sports shoes for children, and new ERS (energy return
system) shoes for adults. The number of outlets has now been increased again
progressively, up to a thousand, to match their new emphasis on all life
stages, and especially the development of new market niches such as the
over-40 market. In future developments, Mr Mochida is contemplating
Reebok direct retail outlets in fashionable Tokyo shopping districts, and the
use of the now well-established brand name on upmarket clothing and
luggage.

CASE STUDY 6-2: SONY-PRUDENTIAL LIFE INSURANCE

Key Points

- Changes in laws were negotiated to enable this new type of venture to be established.
- An entirely new type of insurance sales representative was introduced, in the face of seemingly intractable tradition.

Sony-Prudential Life Insurance is one of the best-performing members of the Prudential group in the world, but when the joint venture idea was first suggested to Sony's Akio Morita, Japanese law prohibited the formation of joint ventures in the life insurance business. In order to move the idea ahead then, Mr Morita himself had to go cap-in-hand to the Japanese Ministry of Finance and request its consideration of a change in the law to permit the venture to be formed. Although negotiations with the Ministry were to take eight months before being successful, it is very likely that without the initial solicitation by someone as powerful and respected as him, the Ministry would have refused the request. As it was, the Ministry made things very difficult for the negotiating team. It was only when the negotiation team leadership was handed over to the Prudential executive that the Ministry changed to a more co-operative. less authoritarian stance, the law was rewritten, and passage through the Diet was facilitated by the Ministry.

A second challenging but innovative aspect of the formation of this joint venture was the Prudential desire to establish a distribution channel new to Japan. Initially, the joint venture formation team looked into the idea of selling insurance through authorized Sony retailers throughout Japan. Research, however, indicated that this would not be well received, and that it would not give sufficient market penetration. This idea was then put aside, and the idea of direct sales representatives looked into.

At that time in Japan, all life insurance had been sold by women, usually housewives working part-time. Prudential strongly resisted this, demanding that men only be employed. Fortunately, the concept of male salesreps was readily accepted by the Sony people (after all, they had had no previous experience in the business). And they added one further new factor: employing the men full-time, an idea which initially was almost unthinkable to the Prudential side, accustomed to having commission-only salesreps in other countries. Sony pointed out the problems that would be involved both in getting people to work in this way in Japan and the problems of motivating people through the use of individual sales commissions. (Although one or two companies do use commission-only remuneration in Japan, most attempts to introduce the method have failed badly—NCR is a notable example.)

CASE STUDY 6-3: HOW WELLA DEALT WITH JAPANESE DISTRIBUTORS

Key points

- Wella built its distribution strategies for Japan on its international sales strength which was non-existent in Japan.
- By understanding the situation and needs of cosmetics wholesalers, Wella was able to develop a strategy that actually supported and strengthened the wholesalers.
- The Wella strategy of satisfying wholesaler needs is one available to any foreign firm within Japan.

Wella Cosmetics Japan is a subsidiary of Wella A G, headquartered in Germany. The parent company is one of the largest manufacturers of cosmetics worldwide. It employs 750 people, five of whom are foreign nationals. It has two markets, the retail market which includes department stores, high-class supermarkets, pharmacies and cosmetics shops, and the professional market which consists mainly of beauty parlours and barbershops.

What was Wella's strategy for successful entry into the Japanese market? The key was to find something that the Japanese did not have. Top management started by defining possible areas where they might find a plus-alpha. There were three areas of possibility: product (including price), image and sales know-how. Examination and comparison revealed that sales know-how offered an excellent opportunity to make quick gains early and establish a market position.

At the time of Wella's entrance—the late 1960s–early 1970s—two main features of Wella's international sales know-how were non-existent in the Japanese market. Analysis by headquarters staff indicated that these two techniques could probably be implemented in Japan.

The professional hair-care product market consists of about 310,000 outlets, of which 150,000 are barbershops and the remainder beauty parlours. The typical beauty parlour operator in Japan is a married women whose husband brings home the main income for the family. The shops are quite small with only one or two chairs and any help is usually part-time and low paid. Because the shops are small, average revenue is low. The result is that beauty parlour operators do not want to pay for the more expensive brands like Wella. In fact, in some shops it is not uncommon to purchase the expensive brands once and then refill the bottles with a lower-priced competitor's product. It was within this context that Wella attempted to offer its special sales know-how.

The professional shampoo, rinse and treatment product is normally packaged in a 1000 ml or 500 ml bottle. This product is usually placed, for convenience in usage, within the direct line of sight of the customer. It was very easy, then, for the beauty parlour operator to persuade the customer that 'using the same shampoo and rinse at home that we use in the shop will be much better for your hair'. Wella packaged the professional product in a retail-size 200 ml bottle and arranged to have it placed near the cash register for a simple point-of-purchase sale. The strategy worked effectively for three reasons: (1) it was a simple and innovative way for beauty parlour operators to increase revenues; (2) it was, similarly, a simple way for wholesalers to increase revenues; and (3) it did not directly challenge domestic makers. Wella, in essence, told wholesalers that they had a new product (line of products in professional- and consumer-size). This approach appealed to wholesalers who did not feel that they were handling just another line of hair-care items. It enabled Wella to grab a large share of the market before competitors could respond with a similar strategy.

A similar approach of capitalizing on sales know-how for that something extra was used in entering the retail market. Until the early 1970s hair-care products, with the exception of dandruff removers which were sold in drug-stores, were of the toiletry variety. They were cheap, packaged like dish soap and placed on the same shelf as bath soap. Wella came in with a much higher-priced product, packaged it like a cosmetic in a nice box and added an expensive perfume to the solution. The difference was so great that it was then possible to persuade cosmetics stores and department stores to carry it with other cosmetic items rather than with toiletries. The move once again resulted in a quick grab of market share before competitors could respond. And one dividend has been a company image of creativity and innovation in the cosmetics industry.

In both instances Wella endeavoured to create an image in the wholesalers' minds of 'new' business. The products were really not that different from what was being offered. The difference was in the sales technique, which created an impression of new business, essential if Wella was to break into the distribution system.

Company Policy

The basic company policy at Wella focused on two areas: product image and company image. The product image is European. This was done to trade on the slight, though still present, prejudice towards foreign products that Japanese consumers have. The company image is Japanese. This was done to gain acceptance from the job market, distribution system, government ministries and Japanese Wella employees.

The European product image was established in a number of different ways. All product names are either German or English with the name never being printed in Japanese *kana*. All advertising models are European, often blonde. All user instructions are in two languages, either German or English and Japanese. New product demonstration seminars or training seminars are done with foreign hairdressers brought over from the United States or Europe. The seminar is first done in the foreign language with the foreign hairdresser and then repeated with Japanese hairdressers. Advertising is done jointly with other German companies, such Mercedes-Benz, Lufthansa or Porsche, whose company products will be used in the background to maintain the foreign image.

A Japanese company image is necessary for three reasons. First, recruiting is very difficult for foreign firms in Japan. By creating a Japanese company image the problem of recruiting is lessened because the company is 'not so foreign'. Second, distributors have a preference for doing business with a Japanese company. While consumers may want to buy foreign products, wholesalers do not want to carry them. They do not trust foreign companies and are a shade xenophobic. A Japanese company image overcomes some of these prejudices. Third, the Ministry of Health and Welfare is more co-operative with Japanese companies. It is easier to work with them for approval on new products or restriction on the importation of United States Wella products (which are lower-priced) if they view Wella as being Japanese.

The Japanese company image was established by doing the same things that a Japanese company does. The president of Wella is Japanese. This enables the company to send a Japanese manager to weddings and other important social functions where everyone can see that the company is run by Japanese. The chairman of the company is a German and, in reality, he is really in charge. The official language of the company is Japanese. Whenever documents are drawn up in two languages the Japanese copy is labelled the translation. All meetings in the company are conducted in Japanese. Foreign executives must either speak Japanese or use an interpreter. The personnel manager is Japanese. Though it is not possible to get top college graduates, Wella still will hire twenty to thirty college graduates per year and careers follow the same pattern as Japanese companies. Banking arrangements are set up in similar Japanese fashion with Mitsubishi Bank being Wella's major bank and major banking shareholder. Mitsubishi presently holds 5.5 per cent stock in Wella, followed by Fuji which holds 4.5 per cent. This allows Wella to imply, if the subject should arise, that they are part of the Mitsubishi Group or the Fuji Group.

Beneath all of this the company is still very German and very foreign in Japan. Recognizing this, the foreign staff still rely heavily on their foreign sales know-how which has worked quite well so far. In recruiting, too, it is necessary to offer something extra to attract good people. Wella offers an employee shareholder fund, offering employees up to 8.9 per cent interest in the company.

Controlling the Distributor

Wella operates through four different distribution channels, each with its own characteristics:
1   Wella's sales force
2   big wholesalers
3   small, family-owned wholesalers
4   local, joint venture wholesale companies.
This case study will focus mainly on the professional hair care distribution system.

In the professional market the wholesalers are all small, family operations. Wella uses 150 wholesalers whose sales range from about ¥300,000,000 to under ¥200,000,000 per year. These wholesalers service about 57,000 B&B (beauty and barber) shops of which 27,000 are barbershops and 30,000 are beauty parlours.

Wholesalers have three big worries. First, they are worried that they will be crowded out by other wholesalers or that their market will fade out. They are afraid that B&B shops will be supplied by cosmetics shop or drugstore wholesalers. They are afraid of the cash-and-carry beauty market.

Second, they are afraid that the manufacturer will set up its own distribution system. Many companies do so after establishing strong demand for their product among the retailers. Foreign firms are notorious for attempting this manoeuvre.

Third, they are afraid of their top salesman. The top salesman is usually underpaid and overworked. Most successful wholesalers have a key person who is responsible for most of the sales. Wholesalers are concerned about top salesmen leaving and setting up their own companies, taking their accounts with them.

Wella tried to solve these problems for wholesalers so that wholesalers would develop some loyalty towards Wella and would want to work hard selling Wella products.

Problem no. 1 was solved by trying to make the B&B shops more profitable and at the same time more dependent on the wholesaler. This was done by making the B&B shop not just a service business but a service and sales business. The approach mentioned previously of marketing consumer-size products for point-of-purchase sales was used for this purpose.

In addition, Wella tried to make the B&B operator a better professional through the wholesaler. It did so by setting up eight training centres and employing sixty technicians who instruct in colouring, winding, cutting and hairstyle trends. Tickets for attending these seminars were made available to the B&B operators *only* through wholesalers. To be of value to the B&B operators and to wholesalers it was necessary to make the training seminars very expensive. Naturally, wholesalers had no desire to pay for these seminars, so Wella would set prices and then provide ways for wholesalers to get tickets to the seminar without paying for them. For example, wholesalers would be told of a seminar and that they could get so many tickets free if they ordered so much merchandise. As the seminars were very popular with the B&B operators this helped to make the wholesalers' customers dependent on them which helped to give them a feeling of security and allay fears about inroads being made by other distributors.

The second worry of wholesalers is more difficult to resolve. Wella has no desire to try to handle distribution to 57,000 outlets, let alone trying to grow and service the 310,000 B&B nationwide. Even so, it does no good to tell wholesalers this because they would never believe it. Instead, it is necessary to try to prove it by strengthening Wella's ties to the wholesalers.

Wella tried a number of different approaches. It invited three major wholesalers to become members of the board. It gave shares to and circulates shareholders' notices to all the major wholesalers (about thirty). It established a 'go to Wella Germany' scholarship program for the sons of wholesalers. The sons can go and study language and spend some time in the head office learning about the business. It employed sons of shareholders in its sales force. All of these activities made it different from its domestic competitors, who do not do any of these things, and developed the wholesalers' trust in Wella.

For the third worry, which concerns the spinning off of the top salesmen and most valuable accounts, Wella has tried four approaches. It began by offering benefits to the wholesalers' employees that only a large company can afford to offer. The intention here was to make the present position of top salesmen more comfortable so that they would feel less inclined to set up on their own. There has been some difficulty here with the Ministry of Finance, but certain benefits have been allowed. At the moment Wella is trying to work out a pension plan for wholesaler employees. This was followed up by conducting seminars for wholesalers on how to manage the business better, providing technical help and encouraging them to set up their own shareholding plan for their employees. Wella also offered its assistance in recruiting. By using the Wella name some wholesalers were able to attract better employees. The fourth and most recent approach has been to set up prefectural sales companies. In this arrangement wholesalers own two-thirds of the stock and Wella owns the remainder. Wholesalers then offer participation in this sales company to the top salesmen. The approach adds a measure of stability to the top salesman's future. The reason for this is that most wholesalers intend to turn the business over to their sons, leaving little future for the top salesmen. These measures allow the salesmen more participation and a feeling of greater security.

Within the typical small wholesaler organization there are four key people, any one of whom can influence the entire operation. The relationship somewhat resembles a diamond.

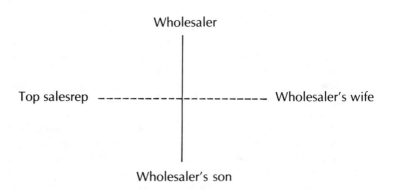

Because the relationships among the four parties are very complex and at times somewhat volatile, Wella requires that monthly reports be made on each one of the parties. These reports allow Wella to pinpoint the problems and deal with them in a way which will protect Wella's interests. Moreover, Wella has specific strategies for courting each one of the parties to ensure greater devotion to Wella.

1   *Wholesaler.* The wholesaler is not really the decision-maker in the group. However, he usually holds the keys to the client relationship. Consequently, he spends a lot of time with the client outside business. For this person Wella holds golf tournaments, provides trips to foreign countries (a recent Wella wholesaler trip to South America on a Concorde SST established a new record in mah-jong playing at a speed of Mach 2) and extends invitations to board meetings.

2   *Top salesmen.* The top salesman is usually the true businessman. He is keenly aware of the business side of the operation. Wella uses what it calls the 'Harvard Approach'. The top salesman is invited to attend seminars on marketing and management at Wella's expense, which gives a feeling of being manager of the operation and appeals to his image of himself.

3   *Wholesaler's wife.* The wife is usually an assistant in the business and, of course, influences her husband's behaviour. In order to curry favour with the wife Wella holds special events such as concerts and fashion shows. Wives always receive tickets for the best seats in the house. On their birthdays wives receive a birthday card and a present from Wella. None of these things are being done by competitors.

4   *Wholesaler's son.* The relationship between the father and son is usually rocky. Wella tries to provide opportunities for the son without making them appear as gifts from his father. The son is given the opportunity to travel overseas to one of Wella's other offices. The most popular is England. Trips for sons are never allowed to overlap with the head office trips of their fathers. Wella also offers to hire sons who are not interested in wholesaling.

Conclusion

The Wella strategy of defining the needs of wholesalers and determining how those needs can best be satisfied through the manufacturer–wholesaler relationship is one that any foreign firm working within the Japanese distribution system can use. Two points are worthy of reiteration.

First, bring 'new' business to wholesalers. At Wella this is defined as business resulting from introducing new sales techniques or sales know-how to an established market. The conception of new business will provide wholesalers with a rationale for carrying the product. Without this conception the foreign firm is consigned to the fate of being treated like any other manufacturer with the same product. In fact, it is worse off due to the somewhat lower position that it occupies as a foreign firm.

Second, determine what wholesalers need and want and then develop a course of action designed to meet those needs and wants through handling the foreign firm's products. By so doing the foreign firm can command the loyalty of wholesalers and demonstrate clearly the benefits that they receive by handling the foreign firm's products.

7 Communicating with Japanese Customers

One of the biggest questions for foreign marketers is how to communicate persuasively with Japanese customers—in advertising, selling or promotion. Should you understand the media available to you, rely on advertising agents or researchers or consultants, or take heed of what has succeeded for others? The key to successful marketing communications will not be found in studying any of these but rather lies in genuinely understanding who your target customers are, what drives them and why Japanese marketing people choose to communicate with them in the often strange (to us) ways that they do.

This chapter looks at Japanese customer behaviour and the segmentation of customers. The emphasis is on developing a deeper understanding of communication in Japan, first by discussing three basic propositions which are equally relevant whether you communicate with the Japanese face to face or through the mass media. They are: one, reserved introverts demand a different approach, two, the customer is really king, and three, style and manners still really maketh the man.

RESERVED INTROVERTS DEMAND A DIFFERENT APPROACH

People in Japan take a long time to warm up to others and much longer to feel that they can trust them. Meetings with strangers are not especially welcome in Japan; many remember the old feudal proverb: *Hito o mitara dorobo to omoe* ('when you see a stranger, assume that he is a thief'). In presentations or lectures, audience and speaker alike expect the presenter to take a low key self-deprecating approach in the beginning to build the lecture around illustrations, case studies and anecdotes, rather than systematic explanations of principles or points. Whenever strangers are together, the formality of 'self introductions' (*jiko shokai*) by each individual is culturally required. It aims to break a little of the ice of social distance, awkwardness and suspicion that Japanese invariably suffer in novel social situations.

Even so, the Japanese take much longer (sometimes 'forever'!) to relax with newly met people. It is correct to say that the Japanese believe it is proper behaviour for them to be reserved, sceptical and even suspicious of people or things they do not know about, Japanese or foreign. Most Japanese know intuitively that they are, as a people, somewhat on the shy and introverted side—and this shows in their behaviour towards each other. When the relationship is not intimate, they do not crowd each other, keeping respectful physical distances, giving one another time to answer, cultivating light, even inconsequential, conversation, avoiding anything 'heavy', not exercising social pressure or hard selling, but allowing others space to make up their own minds in their own time.

Housewives out shopping for perishable foods expect to take their time with any purchase, to eye and appraise the produce coolly and sceptically. They will spend a great deal of time on evaluation and appraisal, look over each offering carefully, scrutinizing it carefully in the best light, to determine from its appearance how fresh it is, what cut it is, before choosing. Watch a Japanese business group appraise and reappraise a proposal for a new product or service—expect everyone in the group to behave about as impulsively as their mothers do when buying fish! Few executives make impulsive, hurried choices in Japan. Bureaucratic needs for proper procedures and decisions by consensus are usual in most organizations. Personal or corporate needs to avoid or eliminate the risks of product failure or wasting money have to be satisfied.

Richard Bush puts it this way:

> In Japan today you will face what is the most discriminating shopper in the world . . . For instance, if your goods fall into the soft line category, Mrs Ito will undoubtedly examine the garment carefully. She will check the stitching, the seams and the label. She will look for loose threads, flaws in the material. If the garment doesn't measure up to what she is used to buying . . . she will reject it . . . If your goods fall into the industrial supply category, they will be subjected to very critical testing on an ongoing basis to be sure that they meet all the specifications that were set forth. (Bush, 1981)

THE CUSTOMER REALLY IS KING

Japan is still a marketplace where the customer is king. Japanese customers feel it is their right to be treated as the central figure in any transaction, to receive careful, respectful service. In the West, while many countries are moving to a pragmatic economic philosophy of user pays—for extra services over and above some basic package—and so starting to lend a little arrogance and coldness to the way suppliers deal with customers face to face, Japan remains squarely in a supplier pays mode. Sellers are expected always to go whatever extra mile is required to ensure that customers are satisfied and that the product or service is giving the performance promised (see also March, 1983). So the Japanese version of 'customer is king' means that sellers or suppliers accept that theirs is the subordinate, service-oriented role in the transaction. (A probably rare exception would be instances of mammoth companies selling to small buyers, or under conditions of a seller's market.)

STYLE AND MANNERS MAKE THE MAN

Style and presentation, one's appearance to others, count enormously in how Japanese evaluate each other. This is a complex issue, one that goes close to the heart of what marketing communications are all about in Japan. Let me first quote a variety of specialists on Japanese advertising, especially television commercials.

Bernard Barber, the executive vice-president of McCann-Erickson-Hakuhodo, one of the largest joint venture advertising agencies in Tokyo, has this to say: 'Japanese advertising usually doesn't explain things [or] present facts', says Barber (1987). It doesn't usually give reasons why. Often it doesn't even state a basic consumer benefit . . .' Barber argued that Japanese advertisers believe the emotional aspects of commercial messages are more persuasive than facts or information.

David Kilburn, the Tokyo correspondent for *Advertising Age* magazine, says: 'The Japanese approach is more indirect, more of a "soft sell". In Japan, as elsewhere, advertising works on both rational and emotional levels, but in Japan the emotional dimension is relatively more important than in many other countries' (Brookin *et al.*, 1986).

Kazumasa Nagai, president of Nippon Design Centre, says that communication in Japan does not focus on logical conviction or argument: the important aspects are sensitivity and feeling. These differences he attributes to the homogeneity of the Japanese—they are all the product of the same education system, speak the same language and share the same culture.

Again, Tamotsu Kishii, the international division creative director of Dentsu Inc., Japan's largest advertising agency, says:

> It is more important to evoke a sense of sympathy which seems to provide a link of fellow-feeling between the consumer and the advertiser . . . In order to make commercials that appeal to the sensitivities of the Japanese people, it is more important to devise ways to increase their interest in the product and to heighten the image of the enterprise than to use a lot of words to explain the 'superiority of the product'. (Schmidt et al., 1986)

Kishii was obviously contrasting Japanese with American or European ('use a lot of words') commercials. George Fields, the author and advertising research specialist, has this to say :

> When a Western businessman enters his hotel room and turns the switch of his TV and watches the Japanese commercials, he invariably complains that they seem heavy in mood . . . [and] often difficult to understand what they were selling . . . On the other hand, the Japanese complaint on returning from the US was the heavy verbiage in the US commercials . . . how could the viewer, they asked, stand being talked at so incessantly? (Fields, 1982)

Fields went on to identify some of the special characteristics of Japanese commercials which, in spite of not making 'much sense to Westerners' were both of high interest and high effectiveness. These contained 'strong (non-verbal) visual symbols which were highly relevant to the product.' And in reflecting on what substituted for the Western emphasis on the verbal, Fields (1982) concluded that 'style and manner of presentation is an important part of [Japanese] communication' which means a greater tilt to the non-verbal.

There is hardly an avenue of life in Japan where style and manner of presentation are not important. The formalities of meetings, the exchange of business cards and the manner of presenting them, the agreement on what is appropriate dress for different occasions, or what is appropriate behaviour for people of different ages, how you behave as a superior or as a subordinate, the niceties of a refined and complex etiquette, the sophisticated arts of packaging or the manner of serving food or drink, the style and manner of presenting gifts to others, of writing letters in particular styles for particular occasions, the use of seasonal symbols in decoration, in dress, in gift-giving—the list is nearly endless. The following of the right form is an important way to ensure that others appreciate your worth, sincerity, delicacy and sensitivity. Ultimately, your worthiness as an individual or corporation will be judged by the quality of your presentation.

Manner and presentation are critical factors in a society as formal as Japan—because mostly what you see is appearance, the formal face, the words and behaviour appropriate to an occasion, the calculated presentation, and never the unvarnished thing, product or person, in itself. The rules and etiquette of Japanese presentation are so numerous and complex that they offer a rich and special vocabulary of manner by which to communicate to others. It is moreover a vocabulary of manner that is almost entirely unknown to non-Japanese. No wonder that visiting American businessmen should, in George Fields' story, be so baffled by what they see on the television screen.

MOOD ADVERTISING AND THE VOCABULARY OF MANNERS

It can be no surprise that advertising, which is a practical art concerned with making good impressions on others, should draw on this vocabulary of manner in Japan. Could Japanese advertisers do otherwise? Yes, often they can and do—new products that require consumer education, or those for which consumers demand a lot of information before making brand choices, differ little from the West in style of print advertisements. The evident difference in approach is mainly to be found in television commercials. TV in Japan, however, has some characteristics that contribute to this difference. Whereas in the USA, nine out of ten commercials are 30 seconds long, in Japan eight out of ten are 15 seconds or less long. This shortness is the main reason for the Japanese tendency to try for impact by doing *something* different, via mood, emotion, humour or shock, rather than to attempt rational, factual communication.

The best television advertising in Japan, for a variety of reasons, tackles the task of creating interest in and good attitudes towards products, via mood approaches that fit with the culture's preferences for making good (first) impressions. The print media, retail outlets and printed matter are set the tasks of being educational and informative. Good impressions are made non-verbally, however, not by reciting what the company or product does that is better than anyone else. Such claims, since they can convey an attitude of egotism, can be tricky in Japanese and must be handled carefully.

One partial exception is the increase in the use on daytime television of more informative, directly persuasive commercials, directed towards stay-at-home housewives. Given that the products are relatively low-priced ones (and so not unduly risky purchases), part of the success of this approach lies in the audience's acceptance of the program and its individual presenters, many of whom have huge followings and even fan clubs. Their credibility and familiarity, as in other countries, produce good impressions and a sense that risk is low because a trusted person is vouching for the product. Testimonial advertising, using folk heroes of all kinds—sportsmen, writers, composers, artists and so on, as well as Hollywood stars—is commonplace in Japan. Another factor is that the housewives who make up this audience constitute just one of the many market segments. They are professional shoppers, if you like, but they are also less sophisticated than the audiences that Japanese admen have in mind when they create the mood commercials much discussed by foreign observers.

I wrote earlier about the Japanese suspicion of verbosity, and the cultural injunction to understand others intuitively. Most Japanese indeed believe, as their most famous novelist, Natsume Soseki, wrote, that 'reasoning leads to social discord'. On the other hand, the Japanese are also inhibited from free expression of their ideas and feelings by the heavy emphasis on form and formality. Ordinarily, you would expect that people so constrained would become bored quickly—and so they do. But logical argument or reasoning do not offer an escape route. So this leaves three other routes: (1) for the more sophisticated, the use (in place of reasoning) of suggestion, indirect expression and the cultivation of feelings; (2) the use of humour, which has universal appeal; or (3) for the less sophisticated, games and pastimes, especially spectacles and events, that serve to enrich dull lives or kill time.

First, about the use of the language of suggestion in Japanese advertising. Suggestion is highly developed and highly regarded among the Japanese. They are proud that their culture has raised suggestion and indirect communication to the form of high art. Many educated Japanese sincerely believe that language is relatively unimportant for interpersonal understanding. Many things about others can be understood without direct enquiry: people emit (*hassan suru*) their true character non-verbally, and the observer's reading of a person's psychological emissions has an aesthetic quality to it, as in the visual appreciation of a work of art. It is as a consequence of these attitudes that much television advertising in Japan treats Japanese viewers in a very respectful way by *not* using verbal persuasion or argument—which is not highly regarded, in any case by—presenting something for them to interpret aesthetically, using the cultural vocabulary of presentation and manner. In other words, they are saying: 'We recognize that you are sensitive and refined people. Therefore, rather than insult you with words, we present something that may be worthy of your refined perceptions.' In passing, this will also demonstrate how refined and sophisticated the advertiser is.

The best contemporary example by far of how to appeal to Japanese aesthetic sensitivities is the television commercials of Parco, the most *avant-garde* commercial–cultural complex in Japan. The Parco complex in Tokyo houses up-market fashion boutiques, specialty shops, bookshops, theatres and cinemas, gourmet restaurants and art galleries. For the sophisticated, everything you might want for a full day's shopping and day-out is to be found under one roof. Parco have pioneered a new style of mystifying advertising which has since been imitated by many others. In the 1970s, they were the first to use black models from Africa and India in their native cultural environments. Many of the early slogans were powerful in their directness and unexpectedness: 'Men! Be beautiful for women'; 'Girls! Be ambitious' (an inversion of the nineteenth century expression 'Boys! Be ambitious!' which is well known in Japan); 'Don't stare at the nude—be nude!', etc. More recent commercials include one where a hauntingly beautiful African tribal woman breastfeeds her baby. The headline reads: 'My Dear Superstar'. In another, a slightly overweight Westerner wearing a cowboy hat and a benign expression is surrounded by Japanese schoolchildren dressed in gym clothes. The voice-over intones: 'Hunter, traveller'. In another commercial, the American movie star Faye Dunaway, clad in an exotic robe designed by a top Japanese designer, plays the part of a Bodhisattva, about to enter Nirvana.

There is no clue as to what is being sold. This is, mystifyingly to non-Japanese minds perhaps, merely part of a grand design, according to Tsuji Masuda, head of the Parco complex.

'When you see a Parco advertisement, you can't understand it,' says Masuda. 'You have to look at our advertisements as a whole and then you'll see what we're about. Our advertising is obviously aimed at the younger generation. Actually, the young people have made an adjective out of Parco—*parco teki*, meaning "something quirky and difficult to understand".' (Robledo-Hara, 1986)

For all its quirkiness, I regard Parco as in the grand tradition of indirect communication in Japan, as it targets and capitalizes on the sensitivities and impressionability of its target market of young, single, well-educated and affluent Tokyo women. One student of Parco commented acutely on the appeal of the female models in Parco ads:

These women [models] were spontaneous, sensual and unyielding and totally at odds with the Japanese equation of femininity with obedience. Images were intended to reflect, and hopefully accelerate, changes in society . . . Parco ads rather cleverly appealed to women's growing sense of themselves as being cultured, independent and glamorous, and provided the place to indulge these fantasies. (Golden, 1986).

HUMOUR IN JAPANESE ADVERTISING BY ROGER S. MARCH

Despite their reputation for seriousness and unsmiling faces, Mr and Mrs Sato of Tokyo enjoy a good laugh just as much as your next-door neighbours. Humour is apparent in most walks of Japanese life. In Japanese advertising, as Bernard Barber (1987) reminds us, 'humour comes in a very broad range from slapstick to subtle.' In fact, so many Japanese commercials rely on humour for their pitch that you might wonder if the Japanese had any time to do anything but laugh.

The favourite humorous devices are puns, because of the large number of homonyms in the language; slapstick, which draws on a very old tradition of popular entertainment; and the absurd, which is also quintessentially Japanese. Also increasingly there have been commercials that make gentle fun of foreigners speaking heavily accented but quaint Japanese.

Here are some examples of recent humorous commercials in Japan: A man is drinking a nightcap when his wife suddenly grabs hold of his necktie and twists it, shouting angrily: 'I think you've had enough!' He gives her a surly look. Then they notice that their children are aiming a video camera at them from the next room. Suddenly, they compose their faces into forced but comic smiles and, like so many Japanese when they have their photos taken, make the V sign with their fingers. This is a widely used commercial for Panasonic video cameras. It says little about the product or its special features, but research has shown that its humour appeals greatly to the Japanese, who retain a positive image of the product and brand from the commercial.

A plain middle-aged spinster goes to a film-processing counter and asks the assistant to process some film. 'I'd like you to make them as beautiful as possible,' she says. The shop assistant replies matter-of-factly, 'Well, beautiful people appear beautiful, and . . . ' Her voice trails away. Crestfallen, the spinster says, 'And the not so beautiful appear not so . . . .' 'That's right', chirps the assistant brightly.

A young girl with a squeaky voice, dressed in extremely bright-coloured clothing, dances happily around a large, equally colourful statue of a racoon, a beloved animal in Japan associated with business success. The only voice-over comes at the end: 'Sumitomo Metals, a major Japanese steel company!'

A monkey listens blissfully to a Walkman he is wearing. Production values are everything here.

This last one is an example of a pun. A health drink commercial places a well-known comedian in a number of situations, where each time a little cedar tree appears in front of him. The pun is on the words for 'cedar' and 'too much', both of which are *sugi* in Japanese. In each situation the following words are voiced: *hataraki sugi* meaning 'working too much', or (fantastically) 'a working cedar tree'; *asobi sugi*, meaning 'playing too much', or 'playful cedar tree, and *nomi sugi*, meaning 'drink too much', or 'the drinking cedar tree'. Very cute and well done!

Trends in advertising humour are difficult to gauge. Some humorous ads are so good that people look forward to the next issue or broadcast just for the ad. A job-placement magazine in Japan, called *Do-Da*, is running a series of commercials which are always amusing and a subject of everyday workplace conversation. Personalities are also in demand. A very talented stage comedian has a series for a petrol company. He drives up to a service station, and while the attendant fills his tank, carries on a conversation with himself. He talks about his golf swing and about taking his kids to the soccer game, and is surprised when the attendant has already filled the tank and even cleaned the windows.

Spectacle and fantasy are also commonplace in Japan, and often border on humour. Isuzu Gemini fascinates, and creates amazement with two cars roaring down the Champs-Elysees each on two wheels at 45 degrees.

The Japanese have learnt how to shock in the paltry 15 seconds at their disposal, and there's many a Spielbergian fantasy to be seen in Japanese advertising: monsters, science fiction machines, scenes from outer space, the imagined presence of Darth Vader and his gang. A crying cartoon penguin was the central character of Japan's most successful beer advertising campaign in the late 1980s.

ADVERTISING APPEALS IN JAPAN

Appeals that do Not Work

Cultural differences mean that many advertising appeals, which we might think are universal, turn out to be only relevant in our own culture. Here are some examples that do not work in Japan:

'Less work for mother . . .' This doesn't work because mothers are still proud full-time housewives in Japan, who have ample time to do whatever chores are needed.

'Free . . . this $5.99 book . . . no strings attached.' This would arouse suspicions about the quality of the main product, and a sense that there must be a trick in this somewhere.

'10 per cent off—if you act now!' Quality is the most important consideration for most Japanese. This appeal would translate as high pressure selling, to which they would immediately react negatively.

'Be an individual! Stand out from the crowd . . .' The Japanese do not want to stand out from the crowd. At best, they will want to look generally like others, conformist in style, with individuality coming from minor accessories or co-ordinating.

'Be the first in your street to . . .' No, thank you. The risk is too great for most Japanese.

'Do it yourself this weekend, and save!' Home handyman is not a role for which most Japanese husbands have the time or inclination. The typical pattern is for the housewife to call in a tradesman, without bothering her husband at all.

'Eliminate pimples/get rid of bad breath/kill nasty germs.' The Japanese do not like to have their attention drawn directly to their personal defects. Positive themes are preferable.

Other types of appeal that do not work in Japan include: appeals to the young that feature roughing it, wild parties or dishevelled appearance, anything that seems to poke fun at any groups, older people acting in a youthful way or wives as Western-type hostesses.

Appeals that Work

In addition to the use of humour and spectacle, here are some other appeals that work.

'Our company's long tradition . . .' This is an important element in building trust in the marketplace.

'Reliability guaranteed . . .' Risk reduction, and the assurance of speedy after-sales service and minimum of product downtime is most important.

'This is the era for this product . . .' The Japanese accept that timing is important, and are ready to buy products that seem right for the age.

SOME CRITICISMS OF ADVERTISING IN JAPAN

Norman McMaster, president of J. Walter Thompson Japan, has been an outspoken critic of what he calls the 'qualitative underdevelopment' of Japanese advertising. He says:

> Given the importance, even the dominance of the media [broking] function, it's not surprising that the large Japanese agencies paid very little attention to the content of the advertising they gave to the client . . .
>
> . . . Japanese agencies do not see themselves as the architects of the client's advertising . . . rather they see themselves as the client's general contractor . . . This abdication of the creative function has resulted in the failure in many Japanese agencies to develop, within their own creative and account management departments, a strong body of knowledge on what constitutes good and bad advertising. (McMaster, 1985)

A study group of American marketers in Japan a few years ago also reported caustically: 'Another major difference that must be recognized in Japanese advertising is the "style over substance" idea. This is especially acute in TV advertising. Basically "style over substance" concerns the use of unrelated things (images, props) as opposed to the central idea of the product. For example, when the Japanese have no central idea, they typically introduce a top forties song, or a personable Westerner, and let the camera roll "creatively".'

Clearly, if these comments are correct, foreign advertisers need to have a clear idea of the creative abilities of their Japanese advertising agency, whatever the medium they are creating for.

8 Consumer Behaviour and Market Segmentation

If you could travel back to the Japan of 1960, what sort of consumers would you expect to find? You could expect to find a people far from affluent, with the majority barely a decade away from impoverished agricultural origins. Their standard of living would not have equalled that of today's Malaysians. Money was short, everyone practised frugality and 'waste not, want not'. Old things were treasured, nothing was discarded. Backyards often looked like junkyards, old lumber cheek by jowl with used cracked tiles, old bricks, indeed anything that could possibly be used again. Housewives religiously stored cartons, boxes and wrapping paper.

The usual household menu was still close to the traditional agrarian one—rice-based, with pickled, boiled or sautéd vegetables and dried fish or tofu for protein. Left-over food was never thrown away, and even grains of rice were kept for the following meal. Saving money through meticulous household management was a top priority for most housewives. Many housewives kept a detailed household journal, the *kakeibo*, of every daily expenditure, no matter how minor.

The mood was hard work, improvement of livelihood, no frivolity in the pursuit of long-term goals of occupational success and saving for retirement. Young men studied hard and strove to realize the cultural ideal of young manhood—a hard-working, taciturn personality indifferent to his appearance. He shaved with a blunt safety razor blade and lathered with common soap in front of a minute, unlit mirror. She wore neat but somewhat drab, plain clothes, avoided wearing jewellery or accessories, was maternal and nurturant, and cultivated an appearance of innocent, giggling empty-headedness. This was unthreatening and pleased Japanese men, reared as they were to act as the undisputed and autocratic masters (*teishu kampaku*) of their households.

They were poor but proud, serious-minded and contemptuous of frivolity or game-playing. They married for life, and secretly felt superior to the divorce-ridden Americans and others. They could not afford and had no time for the good life, although they could sample it through their unique Japanese philosophy of the 'one really splendid thing' (*itten gooka shugi*).

Under this philosophy, though you had to live in mean circumstances, you permitted yourself one sumptuous luxury—perhaps a prestigious car, to be parked ostentatiously outside the door of your one-room apartment, or the largest, grandest colour television receiver, an imported Savile Row business suit, or a gold cigarette case, for instance.

They had one other guiding philosophy to keep them sane under the pressures of work and the struggle to survive. This was a 'letting go' philosophy, variously called *bureiko* (roughly, 'hanging loose') or *hame o hazusu* (literally, 'removing the panelling'); either way, it meant using rare occasions to let it all hang out, to relax completely. This is also akin to the well-used proverb: 'Scratch off shame when travelling' (*tabi no haji wa kaki sute*), which was virtually a licence for many Japanese men to play up without shame or embarrassment when away from home.

Let thirty years fly by, and you find an amazingly changed society. Young men and women of today have little in common with their counterparts of thirty years earlier (see also Toshizumi, 1985). They are permissive, hedonistic and affluent. Heterosexual relationships are more knowing, more casual. Today, it is all right to be fashion-conscious. Even young men are wearing cosmetics. Jewellery and accessories are also 'in' for young men and women. So are sophisticated cosmetics. Deodorants, for instance, were unheard of in 1960, and would have been regarded as wasteful luxuries then. Now they are necessities.

Old things no longer clutter the home. To waste and discard is now good, positively satisfying. Now it is proper to junk possessions, even if still usable, to make way for the latest high-tech miracle; or to discard furniture just a few years old when one moves to a new apartment, and creates a new decor and lifestyle. (In fact, young foreign students living in Tokyo have discovered that they can completely furnish their apartments, in a matter of weeks, with what rich Japanese junk—TVs, stereos, washing machines, all in working order, beds, wardrobes, chests of drawers, cooking utensils, even working personal computers!)

Signs are even emerging of an alternative, anti-possessions style among the some of the young and innovative Japanese young men. This involves owning nothing but one's clothes, renting or leasing everything else and spending one's money on the real essentials—clothes, travel, food and entertainment.

Consumption is 'in' for these affluent young adults. They spend freely on overseas travel and personal cultivation—meaning arts and crafts classes, aerobics, English conversation, jazz or ballet dancing, piano and so on. Instead of the long-term focus on owning your own home and doing without for many years to achieve it, they demand pleasures they can enjoy now. Instead of hard work and the drive to escape poverty, today's main motivations are either personal cultivation (which has no obvious economic pay-off), or being rich (the English word is used often, rolled around the tongue with evident sensuous pleasure), making a lot of money and having a distinct status as someone wealthy. For many, being rich (or living as though one were rich) is a major preoccupation. If you are rich, then you can create a more distinct identity for yourself in Japan's mass society, and escape from the boredom, mediocrity, and piercing sense of being just another face in the crowd that are the lot of so many. The Japanese young rich represent a major world market for luxury goods by Hermes, Cartier, Dior and so on.

> They want expensive but discreet jewellery, clothing and accessories which are the insignia of their club . . . [says Bernard Cendron, of Les Must de Cartier in Tokyo] They do not like flashy fashion or big logos, and wear their status symbols with a serious chic . . . The items they buy must be 'in fashion' but must also be recognised as *durable* fashion, not tied to seasonal fashion. (Cendron, 1986)

In *New Rich*, Kazuhiro Ono describes a pyramid of wealthy classes in Japan: on top the super rich, a group of 200,000 households; then some 2,000,000 households who earn between ¥8 and 20 million a year; and a further 20 million whom he calls the 'pretend rich', not rich, but who behave as though they were. Their tastes are for the very best in everything ('one really splendid thing-ism' again!), from yachts in the harbour to second houses in the mountains. This picture of the distribution of wealth in Japan, whatever its limitations as statistically reliable, paints a believable picture of the changes being wrought in Japanese society.

Today's young know nothing of 1960. The world they live in is complex, exciting, affluent, stylish, innovative, enormously abundant in ideas and information, terribly aware of its mental processes, dreams and obsessions, of its image and how it appears to others, of its need to be constantly on the move (off with the old and on with the new), and of its opportunity to be able actually to try and make dreams and possibilities into realities.

Unlike their parents, today's young adults have grown to adulthood in an affluent society which they take for granted, where there is so much less stress or social pressure on them than was true for their parents. They expect to marry at a later age, and to marry for love, not in an arranged match. Parental pressure to marry at a certain age, or for family reasons, is far weaker than in the past. Their relationships with one another as unmarrieds are far longer than they were in the past, both more romantically and more pragmatically inclined, and style, fashion and dining-out, in places that young women feel are romantic, are central to much of young adult life. They are more self-confident and visit foreign countries unconcernedly, feeling much more at home in the world, helped by a disposable income their parents could not have dreamt of.

OH, TO BE FASHIONABLE AND RICH!

In this young world of today, brand names and style are of absolute importance (as they are, with different nuances, among the young in other countries today). It is the philosophy of owning one really excellent thing suddenly gone crazy.

Young, rich Tokyo men- about- town must have a VAN jacket; yes, and a BMW and a top-of-the-range Toyota 4WD (the idea of borrowing Dad's Mercedes Benz is 'gross' to the real rich); there are weekends in Hawaii or Saipan, holidays abroad of course, and a sizeable bank account for playing the stockmarket or other money-making activities.

Tokyo *ojoosama* (young ladies from well-to-do families) must have a cute little new car for the weekends, a pedigreed French poodle, a stylish wardrobe with pieces from Jun Ashida and Hanae Mori and company, not to mention an extraordinary collection of stunning formal kimono easily worth ten or fifteen million yen or more. Health-and culture-conscious, she may spend up to ¥100,000 a month on aerobics, scuba diving or jazz ballet classes, flower arrangement, the tea ceremony, pottery or oil painting classes, in addition to weekend shopping with her equally affluent girlfriends in Aoyama Doori or Jiyuga Oka or, for slumming, Roppongi or Shinjuku.

They will enjoy most or all of their income (daddy and mummy will not ask for board—and the boys may live in subsidized company dormitories), feel free of old-time community pressures on behaviour (especially true for the young ladies), and marry later. The girls in particular may change jobs frequently, or work only as temporaries when they need to rebuild their savings. The young men, once at work, devote much time to learning how to make a fortune and read many of the dozen or so popular magazines devoted to finance. Articles such as 'How to marry a rich girl', or 'How to get the 5 million yen you need to get married' are widely read. They assiduously play money games and talk money, worrying their elders with their crass materialism.

Men or women, Tokyo's young adults are much more assertive, speak up more than their parents did, prefer friends or home to the boss and his cronies at their office. They are shocking Japanese and foreign shopkeepers alike with their tenacious bargaining, whether for electrical appliances at Akihabara or in duty free shops around the world. Tiffany's in New York have been unable to resist rich jean-clad Japanese young ladies from invading their sacred halls and demanding discounts! They have become keen comparative shoppers at home; men might visit five or six stores just to compare colours, styles and prices for polo shirts.

High price is no longer always the indicator of high quality. A store that asks for the standard or fixed retail price, as many department stores do, will today be shrugged off and lose business. The young today want to know where and for how much their friends bought products, and vie with each other to buy at the keenest price. Nothing could be a greater contrast to their forebears in 1960, who meekly paid whatever prices stores at home and abroad asked of them.

Not every young Japanese is rich, nor does everyone have the kind of lifestyle described above, but it is important to understand the rich because they are now trendsetters in a society that has long been famous for its herd-like, follower qualities. Moreover, it is the young people of Tokyo who are leading the way in creating new lifestyles. What is adopted in Tokyo today, it is said, will be adopted in the rest of the country tomorrow.

Listen to the phrases that young Tokyoites use about their self-conscious age, and you can understand much of the era. Many of them call this era *kokoro no jidai*, that is, 'the era of the mind' and say it represents a trend 'from things to the mind' (*mono kara kokoro e*). In their world, unlike that of their parents, it is healthy to be playful and to experiment with one's own mind. Their interest in mental games, fantasy, meditation, mysticism and the occult go along with more overt and materialistic activities—such as being conspicuously rich, eating fish wrapped in gold leaf, drinking *sake* with gold flakes in it, receiving a massage using gold flakes (to keep the skin smooth, someone has convinced them)—as being very different ways to strive to discover who one truly is, to strive to plumb one's identity (again the English word is used evocatively by the Japanese). The days of arduous striving for long-term goals seem but memories in this new age of speedy satisfaction and its 'many really excellent things-isms'.

If the rich can escape into realizing their consuming fantasies, the never-to-be-rich, under greater pressure to earn money and survive in often boring jobs and obligation-ridden family relationships, make do with down-market outlets for undischarged tensions and an aimless search for boredom-relief. There is the cult game *pachinko*, where stainless-steel balls catapult endlessly down an upright pinball machine. This is an easy, approved time-killer for millions. There are cartoon books of all kinds, which young adults consume voraciously. And for almost everyone but especially young ladies, there is cutesy-cutesy: cute toys, porcelain ducks, penguins, and piglets, and Hello Kitty telephones and socks and stationery.

TRADITION IN A NEW ERA

Still, we are not looking at Westernization, although some do call what is happening de-Asianization. Much that is traditional remains, albeit in a form adapted to the new era. The emphasis on the indirect, as I pointed out in the last chapter when discussing Parco advertising, is based on a traditional cultural preference for stating things indirectly (*enkyoku hyoogen*), which is regarded as one element of personal elegance among most Japanese. They have been raised to appreciate hints, not direct statements, soft approaches, not hard sell.

Indeed, this is built into the language. Rather than make demands or give orders to equals, the approved mode of expression is: 'If you do such and such, how would that be?' (*nani nani shitara ikaga deshooka?*)'; or 'Would it not be good to do such and such?' (*nani nani shitara yoroshii dewa nai deshooka?*) as a softer expression than 'I think you ought to do/think something'.

The emphasis on improving oneself is ancient, with deep roots in

the Confucian past, even if young Tokyoites see it in much more hedonistic terms than Confucius might ever have done. (A current trendy
expression of this in Tokyo is *wanranku ue*, meaning 'one rank up'.)
Then there is the emphasis on privacy. The Japanese have always been,
as individuals, very private people, not revealing themselves to any
save a few intimates—or not at all. Unlike the West, the Japanese concept of utopia is quintessentially a private domain—a small hut deep
in the mountains, perhaps with a pond and a moon-viewing platform,
only to be reached by a narrow, steep and winding path. That house
somewhere in the mountains is on the shopping list of so many
middle-aged Japanese.

THE NEW LOGIC OF JAPAN'S YOUNG GENERATIONS

In their emphasis on style, elegance of appearance and meticulous attention to detail, the Japanese draw on behaviour and values in their
culture going back a thousand years or more, and perhaps most characterized by the *samurai* of the Middle Ages. A *samurai* would not face
an enemy in battle until he had removed his overnight beard, polished
his shaven head and dressed in his finest armour. But the young Japanese are no longer *samurai*, or even *samurai* offspring, in any mean-
ingful sense (though their parents could have been).

To go deeper into who they are, we are lucky to be able to draw on
the results of quite ground-breaking research done by Hakuhodo Inc.,
one of Japan's largest advertising agencies (Maruyama, 1985). In one
publication they describe the main orientation of young Japanese as
'the switchboard approach' to life. This puts the individual in the
position of being the autonomous designer of his or her own lifestyle,
having free access to multiple paths or multiple social roles. Looked at
from the viewpoint of older Japanese, these youngsters appear unpre-
dictable, unreliable, inconsistant and illogical. From the individual's
viewpoint, there is the danger of serious identity confusion from
having so many choices, so the task is to find a mixing strategy, or at
least a withdrawal or avoidance strategy, to minimize overload problems. Hakuhodo identified a varity of alternative strategies used by
Japanese youngsters. I will discuss the six most interesting ones.

Summit Strategies

These young consumers are concerned with being the best one can be
(meaning reaching a summit) in physical, economic, cultural, intellec-

tual or sensory fields. Physical summits can be achieved by plastic surgery, or body-building, or wearing a wig, or even a perfect suntan (despised by older Japanese). Cultural summits include becoming an expert in some esoteric field of knowledge—the occult, ancient myths, computer science.

Hakuhodo states that those choosing summit strategies prefer to buy packaged systems—hair transplants, sports equipment, specific models of machines, etc.—and buy on the basis of quality and personal preference rather than price.

Maniac Strategies

These are counter-strategies to counter identity diffusion or confusion. They include 'doing something seriously because it is fun', 'pursuing some interesting subject with great seriousness', or to discovering fun in something outdated or conventional or unexpected, such as farming, taking slow trains instead of express trains or owning no possessions.

Scanning Strategies

These include 'the wish for metamorphosis', such as becoming a film star or hero, or some unusual person; avoiding deep involvement in any relationship; hiding one's true skill by pretending to be unskilled, only at some time to give a surprise peformance and command instant respect from others.

All of these have precedents in Japanese traditional culture. The metamorphosis wish is related to Japanese longstanding interest in supernormal powers, while the pretence of lacking skill is a perverse reaction to traditional pressures for modesty and lack of ostentation.

These strategies are typical among opinion-follower types of people, who could be attracted to product advertisements that include the use of contradiction, or are inconspicuously positioned.

Handling Strategies

Handling strategies include 'taking initiatives', 'acting in anticipation of something', 'taking care of' and 'fixing up', but exclude any connotation of manipulating other people. The purpose of these strategies is to develop automatic response patterns for all social situations so that there is no intellectual or emotional involvement. Such situations include dating, sex and interactions with parents or superiors. Users of these strategies are said to keep themselves continuously up to date through specialized magazines, such as those dealing with finance, securities transactions, etc. They show preferences also for home delivery services, and 'arhythmic' fashions—that is, those featuring discordant or mismatched items, antique fashion, etc.

Restatement Strategies

There are both positive and negative restatement strategies. Positive ones include: revivalism, finding new applications for traditional systems and methods; endurance, keeping at tasks however difficult or impossible they may appear; outspokenness, which includes deliberate exhibitionism in perverse contravention of traditional values; and nostalgia or the cultivation of 'retro' values and products, such as music, books or decorations.

Negative strategies include: argument deflection and question begging, common among teenagers still at school, and fixing by 'bribery', which may include monetary gifts as well as favours.

The Safe Niche Strategies

Softening of personal tastes and values, and a generally spineless approach to life, are typical here. The researchers claim that these people are frequent consumers of crêpes, soft ice cream, hamburgers and other 'invertebrate' foods. Psychologically they are seen as being disappointed in their own abilities. These strategies free them from anxiety and give them emotional detachment. Their Freudian wish is to return to the womb, so they prefer types of merchandise that provide physical warmth, such as down-filled clothes and disposable belly-heaters.

Without accepting the categories or their labels uncritically, my personal view is that these strategies reflect many aspects of traditional Japanese national personality, especially single-minded absorption, avoidance and retreat strategies, and the various perverse reactions and behavioural patterns. Anyone who has lived intimately with the Japanese will recognize these immediately. The suggestions made about product preferences and types of advertising likely to appeal to groups, all from Hakuhodo, are in my view, all sound and deserve consideration.

OTHER RECENT FINDINGS

In the most recent research (cited by Maruyama, 1985), Hakuhodo has pointed to further new developments in the behaviour of young Japanese consumers, including:

- Accelerated programmed learning, by speeding up VTR playback speeds to acquire more information in the same time; self-programming of video games; faster absorption of the logic of video games from foreign countries; more private creation of music by sound synthesizers.
- New trends in dress and emphasis on appearance. Some young Japanese feel they are supposed to make efforts to translate their inner self into the outward appearance.
- Group-oriented individualism. Each peer group member, often an only child, strives to be recognized by others in the group for the special skills he or she can contribute to the group, so that there is no absolute pecking order in the group. (My personal experience suggests that this is widespread in Japan today among schoolchildren.) Although this is inconsistent with contemporary bureaucratic decision-making style, it is entirely compatible with more ancient Japanese concepts of having mutually beneficial combinations making up an effective and harmonious whole.
- Young consumers are beginning to avoid known shops and products. Once stores become widely publicized, they lose their attractiveness for many young people. Consequently, some companies are directing limited edition strategies at youngsters: baking only a limited number of cakes each day or producing only a limited number of special styles or designs. Some chain stores now have their branches look like non-chain members. Possession is becoming less important. Cars or VTRs are no longer status symbols—in fact, rental cars for special occasions usually suffice. Even children are wearing more secondhand school clothing today.
- The established orthodoxy is disappearing in a special way. Fewer of the best students are going to the nation's no. 1 university, Tokyo. People from less prestigious backgrounds are becoming prominent and successful. Values about what makes for success in business are rapidly changing, with women achieving entrepreneurial success.
- 'Breeding' or 'incubation' is an increasingly seminal concept in today's Japan. The works of artists yet to be successful are invested in. Venture capital is being invested in new, apparently risky businesses.

As Maruyama (1985) has pointed out, these findings demonstrate huge shifts in consumption behaviour, which may not have emerged yet in other advanced countries. Moreover, he observes, there seems to be evidence of a move away from what he calls H-type logic—characterized by deductive, sequential, competitive, categorical modes of thought—towards G-type, which are interactive, pattern-generating, looping and iterative rather than deductive, co-operative and contextually sensitive. For foreign marketers and product designers, there are clear signs of the direction in which Japan's most dynamic market segments, teenagers and young adults in Tokyo, are heading, and of the potential opportunities to design products more specifically for them which are increasingly individualistic in their appeal. It means being on the spot and always up to date with what is happening in the dazzling city of Tokyo.

THE SEGMENTATION OF SOME JAPANESE MARKETS

Another way to look at what is happening to Japanese consumers is to study some of the market segmentation research undertaken during the 1980s.

To give more focus to the Japanese studies, I will first compare the Japanese studies with three market segmentation studies I collected in the 1980s for the USA and Australia (March, 1990). Consider first one study from newspaper-funded research in each country, which tends to use lifestyle questions only. The segments are listed in their order of size in each case.

USA Lifestyle Segments

1 Female segments
   - old-fashioned traditionalists
   - chic suburbanites (upper-middle-class women who are community leaders)
   - contented housewives (house-proud)
   - militant mothers, strongly feminist, resent their home role
   - elegant socialites, concerned with fashion and a stylish lifestyle.
2 Male segments
   - traditional family men (the biggest male segment)
   - self-made men (small business entrepreneurs)
   - professionals, upwardly mobile
   - blue-collar workers frustrated with life and their jobs
   - retiring homebodies.

Australian Lifestyle Segments

Whereas the American segments fell rather neatly into five male and five female segments, sex associations were not mentioned in the Australian study. The main segments were:

- traditional attitudes and values
- upwardly mobile people
- hedonistic experience-seekers
- socially unconcerned
- home-and hobbies-oriented
- sports-involved
- the Good Life—parties, wine with meals, trying new foods.

Japanese Lifestyle Segments

The Japanese segments also failed to discriminate between the sexes. Here the main segments were:

- tradition-oriented—living in traditional housing with *tatami* rooms, socializing Japanese-style, eating traditional food.
- disciplined/moralistic orientation—focus on children's education, avoid frivolous socializing such as parties, drinking alcohol or gambling.
- Westernized and outgoing—interested in food, cooking, fashion, trends, wine, etc.
- counterculture orientation—uncomfortable with traditional values and mainstream society; focus on mobile, outdoor life; younger, non-family people.
- active hedonists—focus on cheerful socializing with others. TV and mass culture orientation.
- do-nothings—no interests, avoid socializing; closed and defensive people.

COMPARISON OF THE THREE LIFESTYLE STUDIES

Granted the differences in technique and data collection between the three countries, there are clear similarities between the two Western countries and provocative contrasts of both with Japan. In the two Western countries, there are segments revealing social concern, community involvement and upward social mobility that do not appear in Japan. Rather, what we know about Japan is that social concerns tend to focus on specific issues, not principles or orientations, that community involvement tends to be lower among the Japanese, who are locked into long-term commitments to exclusive institutions such as companies and schools. These commitments tend to be antagonistic to the very Western idea of social mobility.

In each country, segments reflecting attachment to traditional values are sizeable, and probably indicate a central tendency of all societies. In the Japanese case, however, it is likely that attachment to tradition is very deliberate in the face of competing non-native styles. What we have in Japan is a prominent 'Westernized' segment, which may play an innovator or tastemaker role in Japanese society for new products and behaviour. It is a segment showing interest in Western wine and cooking, and so seems open to the whole area of modern or Westernized living.

There is a fascinating contrast between Japan and the two Western countries when we look at segments that are critical or hostile to society. In the two Western countries, these segments comprised people who were disillusioned, frustrated or cynical about society. There was no such segment in Japan, merely a counterculture segment that was avoiding rather than hostile or critical.

Again, there were upwardly mobile segments in the West, whereas the closest we find in Japan is a segment that has 'disciplined and moralistic attitudes', which offer a different perspective on achievement motivation. This segment also reflects a deeper traditionalism than that of the main segment, which has a superficial tradition-bound quality and is probably connected to the oft-observed grim determination of many Japanese parents to see that their children have the very best education as the basis for a successful life.

Common to the three societies, however, is a strong hedonistic attitude to life. This is particularly strong in Japan, where the level of nightlife dining and drinking out of home by men is high. In an unpublished study of the hedonism of Japanese men, four lifestyle segments were identified, all about the same size. One was a well-educated, consciously upwardly mobile group of elite businessmen and government employees. Exuding the easy arrogance of those conscious of having proved their superiority, they were the most socially confident group, interested in male fashion and sports. A second group, in contrast, was personally insecure, its members tending to be followers of others in their social life. The third group was the most mainstream of all, most average in their social behaviour, showing keen interest in everyday affairs, avid readers of weekly magazines. The final group was the least responsive to news and trends, prudent to an extreme about their social behaviour, and representing perhaps the tendency of many Japanese to avoid losing face. This gave their hedonism a certain cautious and mechanical air.

JAPANESE MARKET SEGMENTS RELATED TO FOOD

A number of major segmentation studies of food purchasing and consumption were undertaken in Japan during the 1980s (see, for example, Nippon Information Service, 1981; Nippon Marketing Systems, 1988), the results of which I will present in a generalized way. Generally, segments are large in number and no one, save the first, is especially dominant. The main ones identified are:

1 *Food enjoyment orientation*: interest in trying new recipes, in new tastes, in spending money on food. The dominance of this segment suggests that increasing affluence and education are motivating an ever-wider interest in the good life.
2 *Simplicity and convenience orientation*: here the focus is on the use of canned, dehydrated and frozen foods, and speed in preparation.
3 *Health orientation*: these housewives show concern about the extent to which foods contain fats, sugar and salt, and they monitor their family's intake. They are also interested in health foods and sensitive to the presence of additives.
4 *Family-oriented segment*: the husband serves as the primary reference for the housewife, who searches for cooking ideas that will please him.

Other segments of interest in these studies include those concerned with 'mood eating' (that is, making the environment of eating attractive), those who eat out a great deal, those who are shopping-oriented and those with special interests such as baking cakes or making Chinese food.

LIFESTYLES OF JAPANESE TEENAGERS

In 1987 Marplan Japan undertook in-depth interviews with 1000 teenagers. The results (Wilk, 1987) revealed the following six psychographic types:

1 *The Naives* (20 per cent of the sample). These are mostly very young teens who just want to please their parents.
2 *The Drifters* (9 per cent of the sample). Educational achievement is the key to success in Japan, and these young teenagers have already

slipped through society's cracks by failing at school. Such disenfranchised youths are prime targets for motorcycle and car purchases.

3 *The Leaders* (13 per cent of the sample). Good backgrounds produce these trendsetters; their fathers tend to be corporate managers. Mostly older boys, these future business leaders have a more pronounced social consciousness than they did in 1978.

4 *The Independents* (15 per cent of the sample). These teens think for themselves. It runs in the family, since their parents are independent and rather well-off. The mothers are the best educated of any segment, while the fathers are professionals. More girls than boys fall into this category.

5 *The Followers* (36 per cent of the sample). More girls than boys fall into this group. They do whatever the leaders do, a few steps behind. They are future housewives and office workers.

6 *The Strivers* (7 per cent of the sample). These are tommorow's entrepreneurs. They are similar to the leaders, but their families are less wealthy. They work hard, with management positions a preferred future goal. They love adventure and risk-taking.

CONCLUSIONS

Japan emerges from this research as a steadily differentiating consumer society. It is stable, hedonistic, differentiated sharply along occupational and educational lines, is open to new ideas from abroad, and puts paid to the idea that the Japanese are homogeneous. Rather, it seems certain that the Japanese consumer market will continue to segment further, that more and more market niche opportunities will emerge.

Part 4

DOING
BUSINESS
WITH THE
JAPANESE
ABROAD

9 Japanese Customers Abroad

Think of the Japanese economy of the 1990s as an enormous centrifuge, sucking in products and services from all over the world to satisfy its affluent and sophisticated customers, and spinning off investment in subsidiaries abroad, whose appetites for local services, staff, products and components are going to grow out of sight by the end of the decade. Indeed, this is the decade of the globalization of the Japanese firm.

As I have indicated elsewhere in this book, major Japanese enterprises have set their sights increasingly on manufacturing overseas, as well as sourcing overseas the raw materials (especially parts and components) that they need. Honda Accord is already a prime example. The most popular car in the United States, it was manufactured largely in the USA with parts coming from Japan, Brazil, France, the USA and other countries.

Apart from the USA, Japan's main target for investment related to globalization is Asia, and no one in Tokyo believes that the flow of investment into Asia from Japan is going to change. According to the *Sydney Morning Herald* of 21 April 1990, Takaki Saito, general manager of the Asia and Oceania Department at Marubeni Corporation, says:

> Japan's role will be providing capital, technology, management and know-how. ASEAN nations and later West Asia will produce textiles, light industry and machinery and NICs [newly industrializing countries] higher-technology items . . . Over the next decade, India and Bangladesh would be recipients of investment, with Thailand and Malaysia becoming NICs and the existing NICs becoming similar to Japan, which will mean become [*sic*] an ever-growing market for their goods.

A major consequence of this, for so many countries (as I said in the introduction), is that the Japanese are and will be increasingly abroad—buying, selling, manufacturing, investing, employing (as well as consuming and holidaying).

Japanese customers abroad come in a variety of guises: those who have been able to acquire permanent resident status in another country; those with work visas who will spend a limited number of years there representing their company; tourists and other temporary visitors; Japanese from Japan who have come expressly to buy materials, goods or services, or to set up agreements or new ventures. Japanese business people have a variety of missions abroad: to set up and manage joint ventures, to invest venture capital, to manage existing Japanese businesses, to undertake or supervise research and development, to license or acquire licences for new technology, or to manage mergers and acquisitions on behalf of their corporate headquarters. These people are also followed by employees of service industries such as banks, shipping, transport and insurance companies, securities firms and other investment businesses. Japanese professionals are also abroad working for local branches of international law, accounting and consulting firms as specialists handling Japanese business matters. Then there are Japanese who have emigrated, especially to advanced countries like the USA, Australia and Canada, who set up their own businesses, usually with the aim of serving local expatriate Japanese in one way or another. All of these Japanese, plus local people who have special relationships with Japanese companies or individuals—such as lawyers, accountants, bankers or traders—become members of the local interpersonal networks of friendship, information and influence that assume importance for expatriate Japanese in learning about the local business environment and the quality of its members.

To understand Japanese customers abroad, however, first understand them at home. Without any such understanding, you might get by in simple one-on-one relationships, such as serving Japanese customers in a store or being a tour guide. But when you contemplate a long-term corporate relationship you will benefit greatly from much general and specific knowledge and understanding. Generally, you will need to understand Japanese business values and style, and approaches to decision-making, and the buying situation.

Most Japanese companies regard sales growth, not profitability, as the no. 1 target for overseas subsidiaries or joint ventures. If the bottom line is the absolute god for American companies, with profitability almost expected from day 1, for Tokyo the god is the largest possible market share, without making a loss. Of course, in the long term the Japanese are in no doubt about the connection between market share and profit. As one Japanese manager overseas told me, 'The manufacturer who has the largest share makes the biggest profit. He can dictate the market and force others to follow.' The Citizen company has this written into its corporate philosophy: 'Our key goals are to become no. 1 in all we do, and increase market share in all products.' In the National Panasonic group, part of the founder's credo is: 'Profits should not be a reflection of corporate greed, but a vote of confidence from society that what is offered by the firm is valued.' What Canon calls its 'international creed' says that it aims to serve society and help build a better world. From such philosophical backgrounds, the Japanese have come to make the emphasis on growth central to the business life of all their overseas subsidiaries and joint ventures.

Without this knowledge of the Japanese customers' attitudes and values, mistakes and missed opportunities are virtually certain (see also Lorence, 1987; McPherson, 1987). For instance, failure to develop and pursue a clear strategy in the relationship, based on your reading of their needs and your own requirements, will surely find you floundering early in discussions, as they demonstrate by their questions and approach just how focused they are on what they want to achieve and how they propose to get it. From a different perspective, failure to understand the Japanese expectation and demand for initial contacts to be devoted to building the human relationship will probably create stress.

Again, there is a big contrast in decision-making style. Many Western executives and entrepreneurs trust in their 'gut' reactions to proposals. In contrast, the Japanese undertake such exhaustive analysis that it is easy to understand why Japan is sometimes called the land of a thousand feasibility studies. More specifically, failure to recognize the value of providing them with detailed information in the Japanese language will in most cases mean failure to communicate all the points you want to make. If this seems to contradict my earlier comments on the Japanese, the explanation lies in the different context. The Japanese are thorough and analytical in planning, intuitive and tactical in new product marketing. Westerners are much less thorough in planning, much more thorough and systematic in new product marketing.

Specific knowledge is also important—of the company, its particular personality and culture, its policies, priorities, goals and needs, as well as about the individuals you will deal with. Virtually every company of substance in Japan today is heavily involved in business diversification, searching for new business opportunities abroad as well as at home. Why are they talking to you? How does this discussion fit into the overall corporate strategies of the company? Is what they are proposing to do in your country something they have already attempted elsewhere? How well did that succeed? How high is the priority of establishing this business in your country, compared with other countries?

These are questions that ought to be asked and answered. Outside the EEC and a few major regions of the USA, local businesses will always be tempted to exaggerate the importance to the Japanese of their pending or existing relationship, fail to see it (as the Japanese will) within the context of their overall corporate goals and of their total activities abroad. Given our understandable local vision, it is easy to fail to appreciate that, in the total scheme of things for major Japanese corporations, we can be very small beer indeed.

Information on all these questions you will probably be able to get from your contacts and the answers should help you to be clear about how serious they are in their discussions with you, how important this activity is in the total corporate context. It is well to keep in mind that many of the Japanese expatriate managers you meet in your country, while spending much of their time on managing existing enterprises, will almost certainly have missions to search out new business opportunities, or handle special projects, as well. Direct questions about *all* their activities will probably be answered, and will help you get a better perspective on what the company is up to in your country.

JAPANESE PERCEPTIONS OF THE FOREIGN ENVIRONMENT

Knowing what the Japanese really think about your country and its businesses can be useful to you as well, if often a little hard to take. One English manager expressed surprise on a trip to Japan that the Japanese were so prepared to tell him highly confidential details about their future plans. On his return to London, he asked the local Japanese manager of their branch why there would have been this frankness. 'The reason he would have felt comfortable', the Japanese replied, 'was that he is convinced that no British company would ever be able to compete with them in this field.'

The other questions you ought to have answers to, then, can include: How do the Japanese evaluate businesses in your country or view your home business environment? How do they evaluate its opportunities, quality of personnel and potential partners? What feasibility studies have they done, and what conclusions have they drawn? Are they in your country to acquire existing companies, to go into partnership with locals or perhaps another Japanese company? Are they there mainly to procure components or product for direct exporting back to Japan?

Of all foreign countries, the one of most interest to Japanese businesses and executives has long been the United States of America. Even today, they see it as a great nation, but in decline, and now profoundly different from the one they learnt to respect and emulate after World War II. The Japanese see American complaints about Japanese trade practices and about the burdens of paying for Japanese defense as yet other symptoms of decline. Americans are not unaware of this. In the *New York Times* of 20 August 1989 former trade negotiator Clyde Prestowitz acknowledged that: 'Most Japanese feel that the US is a cry-baby nation and that it can't handle its own problems'. Public opinion polls in Japan also suggest that the constant stream of complaints from the USA is draining the huge reservoir of Japanese affection for the US. Japanese executives working in the US or dealing with Americans privately have mixed views of their American counterparts, and usually very qualified opinions of the quality of American products, services and personnel. They know that these negative opinions are also shared by many Americans.

Joseph M. Sakach Jr, executive vice-president of Borg-Warner Chemicals Inc., wrote a highly critical article in 1987 that reflects the tide of self-criticism mounting in the US (and most other Western economies). Entitled 'Can we compete? Selling to Japan here at home', the article warned that: 'US domestic marketers who don't think they need to understand Japan's culture are in for a suprise'. He explains: 'Gaining business from those new companies is not the same as gaining business from American manufacturers. At Borg-Warner Chemicals, many of our field sales and marketing people are sometimes baffled. Top, seasoned salespeople scratch their heads.' Sakach sees most of the problems as due to differences in communications or human relations style. Americans do not practice business in a way that the Japanese find comfortable. Among the things that Americans need to do are the following:

- Put more emphasis on the human relationship, less on money.
- Give intensive cultural training to employees with contact with non-United States companies.
- Include language skills, and world travel and experience in the criteria for personnel hiring.
- Ensure that key employees who work with Japanese companies have experience working in other business cultures (Sakach, 1987).

There is an equal lack of confidence in dealing with Japanese companies on their home ground in other countries. Anthony Surtees is chief executive officer of a successful Sydney-based executive search and consulting firm that specializes in Japan-related areas and is now a 50–50 joint venture with a blue-chip Japanese company. He voices observations very similar to those of Sakach.

'Basically, few Australians have any concept of how to design and manage their relationships with Japanese customers. They think everything can be done in top gear from the start, but the truth is that you must start in *low* gear—very quiet, low profile, with no extravagant claims, concentrating on doing every job perfectly, fixing problems as soon as they arise without quibbling. This is the only way to be accepted by Japanese customers. Only when this was achieved did I try to move into second gear, which was to offer more complex and sophisticated products.

'One of the spin-offs of this approach is the recommendations that satisfied Japanese clients make to other Japanese. The word of mouth networks among expatriate Japanese are very important. New expatriates come into foreign countries having no local knowledge at all. So they need advice from the old hands. I'm not saying that somehow one can manipulate these networks. You can't. But you should recognize that they exist—it makes you realize how tangible a thing your business reputation is.

'Another problem is that Australian business still has little conception of how to communicate with Japanese customers. In my business, I surrounded myself with bilingual Western female managers from the beginning. They have been excellent communicators with the Japanese. They listen better than men, they follow instructions better, and Japanese customers feel more comfortable with them. This has made nonsense of the often-heard belief that the Japanese do not accept women in business.

'One other problem to mention is how to present yourself to the Japanese. No matter how fluent a Japanese manager's English seems, he will appreciate receiving materials in Japanese as well. We always present proposals in both languages, our newsletter is bilingual, and we are about to install a special telephone number which will handle Japanese language only.' (Surtees pers. comm.)

In major cities around the world, including Los Angeles, New York, Boston, Frankfurt, London, Sydney, Hong Kong, Delhi, Cairo, Singapore and Seattle, Japanese business communities are now large and linked by complex networks. Service businesses devoted to such Japanese communities in these and many other cities can employ many thousands. There are said to be more than 60,000 Japanese living in the New York metropolitan area, for instance. The Japanese American *Yellow Pages* covering New York, New Jersey and Connecticut is well over 300 pages, has more than 200 advertisers and indexes such esoteric categories as abacus schools, box lunches (*bento*), Japanese calligraphy, culture centres and dance, the games of *go* and *shogi*, kimono, *koto, sumie* and Noh drama classes, and *shiatsu* practitioners. There are ten Japanese typesetting and printing businesses in New York City alone. The Japanese international retailer Yaohan announced plans to open an up-market Japanese-style hotel (*ryokan*) in New York City by late 1992, complete with *tatami* (woven mat) rooms, *yukata* (sleeping kimono) supplied and huge communal baths. In fact, New York has been called 'the 24th ward', says Daniel Burstein (1989), 'a tongue-in-cheek reference to the fact that Tokyo has 23 wards'. When the tourist season is on, up to two-thirds of Tiffany's customers are Japanese (Mitsukoshi owns 14 per cent of Tiffany's, and the Tokyo store recently became a major stockholder in Bloomingdales).

The number of Japanese-owned factories in the US increased from 886 in 1988 to 1,100 in 1989, according to MITI, and the total number of Americans working for Japanese companies exceeds 200,000. In New York City alone, 50,000 Americans work for Japanese companies. Japanese security houses have significant investments in major Wall Street firms. New York State has twenty-seven substantial, Japanese-owned manufacturing facilities, while more than 200 members of the Japanese Chamber of Commerce in New York cite manufacturing as their principal activity.

Japan Societies in all of these cities produce magazines and business listings in bilingual editions. For instance, the Japan Society of Boston produces a sixty page *Guide to Japan in New England* that functions like a yellow pages telephone book. Japan's economic penetration of the USA is perhaps even better witnessed by the Japan-related networks

in the small north-western city of Portland, Orgeon, which, in addition
to Japan-related societies and groups, has seven Japanese restaurants,
four specialist Japanese translation companies and more than forty subsidiaries of Japanese manufacturing, shipping and trading companies.
The commercial importance of the hundreds of expatriate families, as
well as tourists, is attested to by the many Japanese-language signs
('we speak Japanese', 'welcome!' etc.) already widespread in Portland.

JAPANESE REMOTENESS FROM THEIR HOST COUNTRY

Notwithstanding Japanese interest in doing business abroad and being
good corporate citizens, as individuals the Japanese have a poor reputation among foreigners and other Japanese because of a widespread
failure to settle into the host country. In many discussions I have had
with Japanese managers abroad, I have been told how much they
wished they could spend more time socializing with the locals. But
there are always so many calls on their time: 'Golf matches with other
Japanese, a constant stream of visitors, customers from Tokyo who
must always be looked after, in the evenings and also at weekends . . .
and then there is just the need to sleep!' Japanese managers abroad
are sometimes so tired from their long hours that they spend the entire
Saturday in bed—just as they do in Tokyo!

> We Japanese need to learn more about what American and European and
> Asian people are doing and thinking in their own countries. [says Makio
> Matsusaka, vice-chairman of Pfizer Japan] Most of the highly qualified
> Japanese people stationed in foreign countries working for Japanese com-
> panies go to the office every day, even on Saturdays, and watch the tel-
> exes come in from head office and decide what kind of response to send
> back immediately. But they do not pay attention to what they could con-
> tribute to the society in which they are living at the time. (Matsusaka,
> 1986b)

EXAMPLES OF JAPANESE JOINT VENTURES ABROAD

Paul McSweeney is an Australian lawyer heading the Hong Kong office
of Baker & McKenzie, and a specialist in Japanese–Hong Kong joint
ventures. According to McSweeney, Hong Kong has special appeal to
those seeking to understand the way Japanese companies go about setting up joint ventures abroad, because it is so often the first investment
abroad that a Japanese company will make. Compared to Western
countries, 'Hong Kong is a relatively familiar cultural environment', he

says (McSweeney, 1989). 'So the amount of investment there is quite astounding . . . a lot of it is joint venture and partnership . . .'

McSweeney gives examples of joint ventures entered into by Japanese in Hong Kong:

> The first one in the service industry is a joint venture food manufacturer. The HK side held 51 per cent and the Japanese side held 49 per cent. The Japanese introduced technology and know-how in relation to the production of food. The local partner was able to give information on the local market, locations and the tastes of the local market . . . there was mutual benefit. The parties were introduced to each other by the Japanese bank of which they had both been customers . . .
>
> A second was a joint venture for equipment leasing between an office equipment supplier which was also a distributor for many Japanese office equipment manufacturers, together with a Japanese leasing company . . . the Japanese introduced leasing know-how and Japanese customers. On the HK side there was an introduction of local market knowledge, a local customer base and credit assessment expertise. These parties were put together by a Japanese trading company . . .
>
> Another was a joint venture for coach tours in the service industry between a small bus company and a Japanese tourist agency . . . the Japanese ended up with 85 per cent of the venture. The background to the relationship was that there was an existing contractual relationship where the HK side was a sub-contractor for the Japanese tourist company . . .
>
> [Finally] a joint venture was concluded with a HK distributor of Japanese telecommunications equipment . . . to manufacture, distribute and assemble telecommunications equipment. It was a 50–50 one [which] grew out of the existing trading relationship. (McSweeney, 1989)

In reflecting on his experience, McSweeney (1989) had these points to make: every Japanese supplier or buyer should be considered and treated as a potential joint venture partner, for you never know when opportunities are going to arise. Keep your mind as well on opportunities for import replacement or exports to third countries, not just on exports to Japan. Finally, keep in touch with Japanese trading companies. They have a huge client base of potential partners, and are increasingly being involved in foreign merger and acquisition activities, he concluded. McSweeney's experience and comments seem pertinent to most other countries as well, not just Hong Kong.

CASE STUDY 9-1: BUYING HOT SAILS FOR JAPAN

Key Points
- Not every buying negotiation with Japanese has to be businesslike.
- Some Japanese buyers have more in common with 'subculture' foreigners than they do with Japanese businessmen.

Hot Sails, Maui, is a very popular manufacturer of sails for sailboats and windsurfing boards. Its logo is a red circle on a white flag, with the company name written across the circle. Anyone who has spent time on Hawaiian beaches has probably noticed them.

When Kenji Tanabe starting windsurfing in Japan, most of the equipment was made in Japan. It was made by people who had been to the US for a vacation and, then, on return to Japan, they decided they could make windsurfers from memory. The quality was not very good at first, but as time went by, it slowly improved. Tanabe decided that since all the famous windsurfers were from foreign countries, Japanese windsurfers would want to use the same equipment, because they are so fashion-conscious. Several years ago, he decided it was time that he acted on his ideas.

Because windsurfing is a relatively new sport, the equipment is rapidly evolving, to keep up with new developments in style and technique. There are literally hundreds of small board and sail manufacturers, much like the early days of any fledgling industry. Every famous windsurfer started his own little shop, using his expertise to change the design slightly in an attempt to maximize a certain aspect of performance. But most of this activity was taking place in Hawaii, California, and Hoodriver, Oregon. Later, lots of developments came from Australia, too. Japanese equipment was slowly falling behind, so imports of windsurfing equipment rose, but because so few people windsurfed in Japan, it was not a spectacular increase.

Tanabe, among others, recognized an increase in demand on the horizon, and decided to make some contact with foreign windsurfing manufacturers.

How the Negotiation was Initiated

Tanabe had long been familiar with the names of various companies through previous trips to Hawaii, and advertisements in a windsurfing magazine he sometimes read. He decided he would go to the American Embassy first, and ask for help in contacting windsurfing equipment manufacturers. They were not very helpful; all they could tell him was to contact the Chamber of Commerce of the state with which he wanted to do business. He was very frustrated, he had expected to get more help, but they did not take windsurf boards very seriously. So he decided to write a letter himself to Hot Sails, Maui. He got their address from an advertisement in a windsurfing magazine called *High Wind*.

Very soon, a reply came from Hot Sails, Maui, thanking him for his interest in their company and products, and asking him whether a meeting in Tokyo or Maui would be preferable to him. Since he was planning a vacation in Hawaii in the near future, and because he liked the beaches of Maui better than Tokyo Bay, he decided on Maui. In his reply he said that he had purchased a ticket to Hawaii, and he told them when he would arrive and leave Hawaii. They wrote back and told him that they had arranged a place for him to stay, at no cost to him. A meeting was set to take place in Maui, and he was happy.

Planning and Preparation

He began checking very closely on the reputation of all windsurfing equipment manufacturers, not just Hot Sails, Maui, by reading everything he could in windsurfing magazines. He read not only the advertisements but also the articles about competitions. From those articles, he gained valuable information about who was using what equipment, and why. He already knew the basics of windsurfing equipment, but he was learning about who was popular with the experts. He was very impressed with the reputation of Hot Sails, Maui, and he was sure that new Japanese windsurfers would be, too.

As he was packing for his trip, he was careful not to take any T-shirts that advertised any equipment manufacturer, American or Japanese. It just didn't seem right. He wasn't worried about any differences between them because he had had a lot of contact with foreigners before, and he was confident that he could get along with anyone, even in English.

Opening Moves

When Tanabe arrived at the airport two representatives of Hot Sails, Maui, met him. They took him to a condominium where he was to stay for the next twelve days. After dropping off his bags, they went to dinner and stayed out drinking all night. The next day, after breakfast, they went windsurfing. They talked no business the first day, they just enjoyed the Hawaiian sun and surf and girls. Late that afternoon, the president joined them. The four of them stayed out late drinking again.

On the third day, they went to the Hot Sails factory. Tanabe was able to see all their different products, and examine the quality. He was impressed with the products, and the fact that he was dealing with the person who could make decisions.

On the fourth day, while on the beach, Tanabe and the president began talking about a deal. It was very relaxed and low pressure. Tanabe liked the Hawaiian style of doing business. Hot Sails, Maui, has a policy of being flexible in their dealings with customers. Usually the contract looks nothing like an American contract. The contract was to determine who had what responsibilities, instead of specific prices and quantities.

Complications and Problems

The main complication was to determine who could afford to pay for what percentage of the shipping costs. There was no problem with language because Tanabe speaks English like an Hawaiian. Also, both parties were more concerned with creating a friendship than a strict business relationship, governed by rules.

After taking two days to enjoy his vacation time, he felt he was ready to close the deal. The people from Hot Sails, Maui, were in no hurry; they would adjust to Tanabe. When they started to negotiate about shipping costs, Tanabe immediately said he could pay them. He said this with confidence because he knew he could sell the sails for such a high price in Tokyo that it would more than cover the extra cost. The prices of the sails were not set, because the price varies according to the type of sail, which are constantly being adapted to new situations.

Compared with most other negotiations, this almost seems not to be negotiation. But it is. The personal styles of the parties involved are the major factors determining the character of this negotiation. Each side negotiated from a position of friendship, so they were concerned with the other side being able to do well enough to survive and continue doing business together.

CASE STUDY 9-2: TOLERATING EACH OTHER

Key Points

- National shared experience in dealing with the Japanese can affect the way business is conducted.
- Sometimes the wrong people may be in charge of negotiations with the Japanese.
- More emphasis may need to be placed on good interpersonal skills and friendship in dealings which have an historically difficult background.

Australia is one of the major suppliers of commodities, including iron ore, copper, coal, bauxite, wool, wheat, sugar, beef and many others, to Japan. Some of the contracts for the supply of these are renegotiated every year, and much the same people will face each other. In many cases, human relations between the two sides are only superficially cordial, with a strong concealed vein of antagonism and mutual criticism.

On the Japanese side, most buying is centralized, with all the buyers grouping together and appointing one central buying committee to negotiate with the Australians. On the Australian side, individual companies usually negotiate with the Japanese. This is one of the first facts that the Japanese are critical of in the Australian approach.

According to the head of one of the biggest Japanese buying teams, 'Australia is rich in natural resources, and there is the so-called "natural resources nationalism"—they are proud of their natural resources and the fact that they are supplying them to other countries. They seem to feel that it is a sin to sell them at low prices . . .'

He goes on: 'Because Australia is located in the Southern Hemisphere and is far from other countries geographically, it seems they are not good at co-operating with other countries. Accordingly, their first demanding price always ignores the business and marketing conditions of other countries . . . Australian negotiators do not compromise easily, so negotiations with them have always taken time . . .'

To some Japanese buyers, the Australians are the most difficult people they have to deal with. Away from business, many Japanese find them 'nice and friendly', and in some cases feel more affinity with them than with any other people. But in business, they complain of their stubbornness and dogmatism, and their casual, unprepared approach to business meetings.

On the Australian side, we do know that Australian businesses feel they have long been victimized by Japan and its economy. Japan is seen as a much bigger, threatening country than it does to the Japanese themselves, while its social and economic structure and business practices seem inexplicable to most Australians. At the same time, they greatly fear what might happen to Australia if it were to lose Japan as a major buyer. Not surprisingly, then, it is much more difficult to get anyone to say anything directly or concretely about the Japanese. Understandably, I suppose, Australian sellers, with a long history of difficulties in dealing with the Japanese, do not want publicly to say anything that would create further trouble between them and their biggest customers by far. The problem is probably chronic, for the Australians have been complaining about how unfairly they have been treated by Japanese commodity buyers since the late 1960s, and there have been some notorious cases, such as a sugar dispute in 1976–7, which many Australians are convinced showed the Japanese up as 'not men of their word', as 'contract breakers'. Consequently the Japanese commercial reputation in Australia is a mixed one.

Memories are long, and Australians are cautious and often defensive in dealings with the Japanese. In some cases, they may be justified. One senior Australian negotiator, in what I took as an uncustomary moment of frankness, did tell me of the way in which he had been personally abused and threatened across the negotiating table by the Japanese side for his refusal to accept their price offering after a long and particularly bitter period of price dispute. In another, less open discussion, a commodities negotiator in Australia, particularly fearful that I might disclose damaging testimony about his real views of the Japanese, and unforthcoming about his obviously extensive and colourful experience with Japanese buyers, still said enough to indicate that he felt distant from, hostile to and condescending towards the Japanese.

'We cultivate our Japanese opponents, but do not necessarily have warm feelings for them,' he said in unmistakably icy tones. He went on pedantically: 'Fundamentally, they are not good negotiators. Nor are they well organized as a team. The lead negotiator does not have the personality needed to impose his will on the group as a whole.' This sounded very plausible, in any case, if the lead buyer is responsible to a large number of otherwise competitive companies for negotiating policy.

Interpersonal relationships between the members of both countries seem fairly evidently strained, and this has to be attributed in part to the personalities on each side, and their relative ineptitude in interpersonal relationships. This is an inference on my part, of course, for a great deal is hidden. If we trust the views of Japanese concerning Australian businessmen, one source of the problem lies in their lack of certain skills (as mentioned earlier), suggesting that more care needs to be taken in the appointment of people to deal with Japanese buyers on the part of medium-sized foreign enterprises, not merely in Australia, but also in most countries wanting to do business with Japan.

10 Developing Foreign Staff to Handle Japanese Customers Abroad

In this final chapter, I will look at the opportunities and challenges in developing local staff to deal with Japanese customers abroad in a variety of roles and at every level.

A wide range of local or third-country people could have contact with Japanese on business. We have to assume that most of these people generally know little or nothing about Japan, and that their talents and motivations for serving Japanese customers vary enormously. How do you establish good policies and practices for dealing effectively with the Japanese when the staff, including the managers, are ignorant of their Japanese customers? Experience suggests that the starting point should not be what you know about Japan and the Japanese, but the approach your management has to customer service and to employing the best people for the job. Your approach and philosophy are the leadership direction you give to staff. If you are unduly bottom-line oriented, and that translates into a dry, rationalistic business style, your chances of succeeding with the Japanese may not be as high as they ought to be. If, however, you have both the right service philosophy and the right staff, training will pay off quickly in good business dealings with the Japanese.

THE RIGHT SERVICE PHILOSOPHY

Japanese Tourists
It is essential that you understand what service Japanese tourists are accustomed to receiving, what their expectations are. They come from a highly customer-oriented society, in many ways almost the antithesis

of the user-pays rationalism being espoused in some Western countries today. They are accustomed to buying the best of everything. As tourists abroad, they expect and are looking for authentic experiences, for friendly contact with authentic local people, and for a chance to purchase gifts for friends back home which are unusual, high quality and nicely packaged.

The only real way for a manager or policy-maker (in the hospitality and tourist industries) to gain a genuine understanding of these matters is to spend some time in Japan, observing how the Japanese treat their customers—especially in department stores, restaurants, luxury goods shops and boutiques, hotels and especially in *ryokan* (Japanese traditional inns)—the best of these still set the standard of service excellence in Japan. Managers in other industries will learn a great deal about how customers are serviced by Japanese sellers.

If much of it is beyond your comprehension, or if it is something which cannot for legal or cultural reasons be introduced into your own country, you should at least let the spirit that informs their approach leave its mark on you. You don't have to become Japanese—and if you are in tourism that is the last thing that Japanese customers want—but friendly, interested and willing-always-to-be-at-service attitudes are essential, and you should be able to communicate them to your staff back home.

Second, keep yourself informed about Japan. What are the current issues in society and in your particular industry? Understand what engages the attention of your target market. Young tourists are interested in fashion, (Japanese) show business and movies, and sport. They like to learn when they travel as well as have fun. What can you tell them about your country or district (or even about yourself) that will be fascinating to them? They like to enjoy themselves in a modest, convivial, good-natured, un-rowdy way. Understand what they like to eat and drink in Japan. What are their perceptions of your country? What do they want to do while there? Think about how you can help them to achieve some of their holiday goals.

Third, understand something of their values and psychology. Much of chapter 8 was devoted to describing young consumers in Japan today and this should help you to understand their needs and interests even when abroad. Understand that they are the first generation in Japan who have been exhorted to be 'international people' (*kokusaijin*) and who have had the self-confidence to dare to feel comfortable with foreigners, especially with Westerners. They are encouraged by the social climate in Japan to think of themselves as international, to cultivate international understanding (*kokusaikan*), and even to think of their overseas travel as being a good investment for their future career. Even their overseas honeymoon (perhaps five days in Hawaii or Australia) will be seen as having some market value in making them a little more international. There are opportunities here to serve this need by providing more enriching experiences abroad that they will value as enhancing their international sense. Making personal friends out of foreigners is certainly one important such activity. After all, in Japan, while they do have friends—from school and university days, and from the office—a foreign friend offers to supply colour and stimulation lacking in Japan's controlled and busy society.

The Japanese are well known as a polite and co-operative people, excelling at team work, who are also intensely competitive. There is in fact a well-known expression in Japanese, *sessa takuma*, which means 'living and working together in friendly rivalry.' The Japanese understand this in practice, and are very accustomed to good-natured group competition. Indeed, there is a huge variety of games that the Japanese play which are readily adaptable to foreign settings, with locals as friendly opponents.

Fourth, recognize that the Japanese are generally on the shy and introverted side. Even among young Japanese, many do not know how to relax and enjoy themselves, while most of the older Japanese men are excruciatingly shy. What will you do to make them feel more at home and not embarrass or offend them? They need more psychological space, cannot and will not be pushed into 'fun' activities, although they can be amenable to non-threatening activities—such as simple sports, tours with some educational bias or interesting shopping tours—that are explained and organized in advance. Both younger and older Japanese women are rather more sociable, the older ones more maternal in orientation, with a better idea of how to relax and enjoy themselves. They also have more romantic notions of Western society and Western people than their male counterparts, and this can be a key to helping them have memorable experiences while holidaying.

Japanese Executives

Japanese executives in your country will usually be there on a three- to four-year contract. During that time they will work hard, and many will be glad to get back to Japan and the security of the home office again. While overseas, they will probably feel insecure with the locals.

Their polite behaviour will be good enough, but if they do not know the language well enough to make friends with locals, you will probably find them melting into the background on social occasions, and generally spending their spare time with other Japanese or in the office, or attending to the needs of visitors—customers as well as corporate heavies and specialists—from Japan. It is not necessarily a happy life, but if you can empathize with his particular situation, who knows what might be possible?

For the younger men—under say 35—it is a posting for them on the way up in the organization. In major companies, it will be necessary experience in the process of becoming better and more internationalized managers. For the man older than this, it will often be the case that he has been given a rank—such as local company director, regional general manager or president—that suggests he is an important man in the head office in Japan. This is not always the case. Many men with impressive titles overseas revert to modest-titles and nondescript office surroundings when they return home.

Nonetheless, their titles require them to be given full respect. Remember that the Japanese is playing the role appropriate to his position. If he becomes local president, you can expect him to behave in ways quite different from those he used when he was in a more subordinate role.

If there are times when you need a friend at court back in the Japanese head office, it is well to develop them well in advance. The former resident in your country may not have the power or prestige to do you much good once he returns home.

At home or abroad, a Japanese executive will feel most comfortable with you if you have been introduced to him. Try for this. But it need not be the head of the company—in fact, chairmen, presidents and senior vice-presidents of Japanese companies at home have largely ceremonial duties, and even abroad they delegate most decision-making to middle managers.

There are many tricky aspects of Japanese business behaviour. Business cards are extremely important to the Japanese, and should be used and handled with the same respect that the Japanese accord them. Meeting behaviour can be subtly different from that of other countries, especially in the early stages of a relationship, when the emphasis is on building the personal relationship, and discussion of hard issues is subordinate. This is one of many very hard lessons to learn. Others include interpreting the true meaning of Japanese indirect communications, using informal channels when negotiations seem to have reached an impasse, etc. There is much to commend your retaining the services of a bicultural, bilingual consultant who knows your business well—either your compatriot or a Japanese may do.

As I have said frequently in this book, soften your sales approach to the Japanese! It is easy to distress and overwhelm them with heavy attempts at persuasion and demands for immediate decisions—with the high probability of losing the business for all time to boot. In Japan, salespeople act with humility and patience. They concentrate on serving the customer.

Associated with our sometimes insensitive tendency to push others can be an insensitivity to a Japanese loss of face. You should never, however tempted, try to put him in a position where he is shown not to know something, or where he has to admit failure. Rather, the sales representative's role at home or abroad is to personalize the customer–salesrep relationship—make friends of customers, help them, support them far beyond the limits of any 'user pays' philosophy.

Japanese customers abroad want and expect this as they do in Japan. The Japanese head of the Japan Service Section of an English merchant bank commissioned an executive search firm to find him a Japanese assistant. The required qualities, in addition to an excellent education and good English, were: must be golf player, willing to caddy and chauffeur for his boss at any time, including weekends! Nothing less than this would do him—but it is significant that he asked for a Japanese national as assistant. Clearly he recognized that asking for these extracurricular favours would only work with a Japanese. So the moral for foreign salespeople is to search for some middle ground of service, to search for that little extra that may not match the level of friendly service given in Japan, but should put you well ahead of your local competitors.

Old Japan hands offer two connected pieces of sage advice about dealing with the Japanese: Say little! Don't panic! As Mark Zimmerman (1985) said, the wise foreigner lets the Japanese do the talking—however long the silent gaps in the meeting. When things seem to go wrong, don't go to pieces believing the deal is sunk. Understand that their system takes a lot of co-operation and organization, which means time. If you panic, or lose your patience, you might lose everything when you are on the very threshold of success. Trust in part to the creative process on the Japanese side, and in part to your own unflappable belief in your offering and your sincerity. Ask the Japanese to advise you what should be done. Often it is simply enough to wait —though that may be the most difficult thing of all.

THE RIGHT STAFF

What sort of staff do you need for contact with and sales to Japanese customers in a business that earns much of its profits from them? In most countries, the trend to increased sales to the Japanese has been gradual for most companies, and sales people have the time to discover that some of them have a natural affinity with the Japanese, finding them exceedingly easy to deal with, while others either learn slowly by trial and error how to handle the Japanese, or never feel happy with them. Other businesses, for example on-shore duty-free stores, have learnt that people with Japan affinity, plus a courteous manner in the Japanese style, are critical, especially for handling tour groups. Another important lesson is that even Japanese living and travelling abroad, who want to work as counter staff in stores, do not necessarily have the right level of Japan affinity (put another way, some of these Japanese staff do not like to serve other Japanese, and they show it). In any case, everyone acknowledges that dealing with the Japanese is different.

On the face of it, the ideal people to deal with the Japanese are the first type, those who feel some comforting affinity with and interest in them. At least some of the people in your country who feel this kind of affinity have knowledge of Japan and may have been there, while a few of them may have lived there and learnt to speak the language. So it is an attractive idea to think of your ideal sales and contact staff as all having this kind of affinity, sensitivity to and interest in the Japanese: and I want to follow up this idea further a little later.

First, however, a caveat. There is an interesting and very successful gift shop in San Francisco which, in addition to over-the-counter sales, has a thriving mail order and catalogue business. The target market for this mail/catalogue business is Japanese residents of northern California, and the business opportunity that the shop has capitalized on is the twice-yearly Japanese custom of gift-giving. The Japanese customers are offered a comprehensive range of luxury and high-quality American and European-made gifts, suitable for giving to other Japanese.

This is now a very successful business, but it is not a business noted for its Japan affinity or sensitivity. None of its staff speak Japanese, few feel any special affinity with the Japanese, while the manager sees him-self primarily as a smart merchant of high-quality goods. The human tone of the business is dry and practical. Most Japanese customers come to the store to see the goods advertized in mailings and cata-logues, but they are not treated differently.

Therefore, when I write about the value of using staff who have Japan-affinity, I am thinking most of all about those businesses where a close human relationship over time is capable of being built up with Japanese customers. Businesses such as duty-free shops where customers come cold to the store (unlike the Californian gift store) and a relationship or warm human contact can be built quickly by the cour-teous service orientation of the counter staff also seem appropriate, but other types of business could prove my affinity idea wrong.

BEING OF SERVICE—THE JAPANESE WAY

Throughout the book, I have been at pains to stress the central role of service in the Japanese customer–seller relationship. To non-Japanese, some of it must have seemed overly obsequious, simply not the sort of behaviour for anyone with pride. But let me look more closely now at Japanese-style service, and then you can decide what is feasible for you and your staff.

Customer service, along with product quality and after-sales service, are the triple pillars of marketing and selling in Japan. 'The customer is king' is enshrined in adages, and repeated daily in ten thousand business places when bosses give early morning pep talks (*choorei*) to their staff. Service behaviour conventions are well established and well learnt by customer-contact people. These can be singled out.

When the customer enters your establishment, every staff member nearby will greet the customer with a standardized call of 'Welcome!' (*irasshai mase*). In popular restaurants and other bustling places this will be in a loud vigorous tone, which becomes moderated and more dec-orous as the status of the establishment increases. When the customer receives her/his ordered goods, and when the customer is leaving, with or without having made a purchase, there will be a chorus of '*arigatoo gozai masu*' ('thank you very much') from all nearby staff. This expres-sion of gratitude will have the same vigour whatever the status of the establishment.

When the sales representative visits the customer's office, with the situation reversed, the salesrep will still frequently receive the same treatment as customers, unless he is already accepted as a part of the customer organization. If he does not have specific business to discuss, his visit may take the form of a 'just dropped in to see how you all are' (*Go kigen ukagai*) visit. He will stick strictly to small talk, make polite enquiries of recent events, common friends and golf experiences, and will not attempt to talk business unless the customer initiates it. At the end he may say, 'If I can be of assistance in any way, please don't hesitate to call me' (*Moshi o tetsudai dekiru koto ga arimasu to zehi o yobi kudasai mase*).

If the salesrep is accepted as a part of the buyer's organization, he will be happy to offer his services on each call for whatever might have to be done. If stock has to be moved, he might roll up his sleeves and help out. Salesreps representing wholesalers or manufacturers will often attend to customers in retail stores if other retail sales personnel are busy, and will join in the same calls of welcome and thanks to customers as they come and go. At stocktaking or store remodelling time, usually undertaken on the one day of the week when the shop is closed, some salesreps will offer their services—even if it also happens to be their weekly day off.

The Japanese salesrep's behaviour is designed to create a web of obligation and dependence. As soon as a customer enters a retail store, the calls of welcome start that process of dependence. The helping-out activities serve the same function. Bernard Cendron, of Les Must de Cartier in Tokyo, has this to say about service in the sale of luxury items in Japan:

> Service is extremely important in the sale of brand items. The style and behaviour of shop assistants in boutiques or at brand counters (in department stores) are important elements in the creation of the atmosphere of luxury and exclusivity which is designed to predispose consumers towards paying premium prices for costly merchandise. It is important that sales assistants are properly groomed and trained to meet the demands of a discerning and often difficult clientele . . . to be better seduced into purchasing merchandise, the consumer must penetrate the 'territory' of the brand, which has to be physically delineated within a department store or retail outlet. Once the customer is inside 'brand territory', it is easier for a sales assistant to persuade him to purchase something. (Cendron, 1986)

The 'Sensitivity' Aspect of Service

Sales and service people in Japan learn to anticipate the needs and demands of customers as much as they can. This is true everywhere in

Japanese society, and is something that the Japanese are accustomed to and expect. As Kiyomi Sugahara, president of Jetour Inc., puts it to Western service and sales personnel: 'Don't wait until you are asked something by the Japanese customer. Go one step ahead, by anticipating the logical sequence of their wants, and, at just the right moment, offer that which is wanted' (Sugahara, 1988).

The 'Saabisu' Aspect of Service

What the Japanese call service (*saabisu*) refers only to tangible premiums, special gifts, free delivery or installation, or discounts off the regular price. A drug store may include as *saabisu* complimentary sample packs of vitamins with small purchases, while larger ones may have the total price rounded out to the lowest hundred, or a larger free product included. If you buy big ticket items, such as furniture or appliances, you may receive *saabisu* without asking: such as a 10 per cent discount, or free delivery or installation, or all three. Conclude a exclusive contract with a real estate agent to sell your house or flat, and you may receive, as I did, a free battery-operated razor and a telephone card—total value ¥3000. When I renewed the insurance on my car in Japan, the agent gave me a set of towels—value ¥800. For an investment in a bank fixed deposit, I received an elegant set of handtowels, worth perhaps ¥1000. The custom of *saabisu* thus runs very deep in Japan. The rebate system, described in chapter 6, is best seen as another version of *saabisu*.

Abroad, Japanese tourists already receive some *saabisu* of different kinds: free refreshments in stores, courtesy bus or taxi coupons from their hotel to special stores, video explanations of quality goods for sale without sales pressure, discounts for 'window shoppers', etc. There are opportunities for the extension of *saabisu* to Japanese-corporate customers as well, working on the model of what is done in Japan.

The Courtesy Aspect of Service

Japanese customers, but notably tourists, can expect some or all of the following, depending on the situation:
- Friendly greetings, a modest bow, willingness to assist immediately.
- No hard sell.
- Even if they titter or laugh, don't laugh back.
- Clean clothing and immaculate appearance.
- Know your product and company thoroughly.
- Avoid giving your own opinion.

- See that everything they use or see (counters, glassware, briefcases, etc.) is spotlessly clean.
- Rather than describe a route or point out a place, take them there yourself.
- Wrap things carefully, or present things that are immaculately wrapped or packaged.
- Be considerate and gracious at all times, no matter how trying the customer. Avoid doing anything which puts the customer in a bad light.
- Speak slowly and clearly. Avoid slang or local idiom.

The following service mistakes with the Japanese may be close to unforgivable:

- Embarrassing comments about their appearance or clothing.
- Throwing things—change, cards, booklets—to them.
- Being offhand or indifferent to the customer.
- Being impatient, nervous or otherwise not totally focused on the customer.

PREPARING FOR JAPANESE CUSTOMERS

Tourists

Points to be careful of include:

Food preparation. Most Japanese tourists are more content with familiar than exotic food. Moreover tour group parties tend to order the same items from the menu. The reason is that, feeling uncertain, they tend to go along with the order placed by some key person whose judgement they trust.

Food presentation is important to the Japanese. They are used to less quantity than Westerners, and to more white space of the plate showing. Thus a 300-gram steak is not valuable for its size but for the way it is prepared and presented. Buffet meals are especially acceptable to them, enabling trial of a wide variety of local dishes. Soya sauce should always be made available, even with fish dishes, with optional sauces also available. Rice should be steamed in the style they are accustomed to eat at home.

If a non-Japanese chef wishes to prepare some Japanese traditional dishes (such as *sushi, tempura* or *yakitori*) it would be better not to offer it to Japanese guests until you are sure that the chef has mastered the dish.

Guide and tour materials. Guidebooks and maps should be bilingual, and include information about: business hours of attractions and shops, where what goods are sold, some simple history of the location or region, and useful comments and tips for tourists.

Product presentation. Excellent product finish and packaging are desirable. Japanese tend to feel that products lacking attention to detail are not finished, or that service which still needs a finishing touch is crass. Avoid the use of plastic bags. Although the Tokyo-level of gift wrapping should not be attempted, at least place individual items in separate paper bags.

Hotel rooms. Excessively small rooms, uncleaned, with broken appliances and items missing, are the commonest complaints of Japanese tourists abroad. The Australian tourist industry, which in 1989 experienced a massive boom in Japanese tourism, is expected to suffer a 30 per cent decline in 1990, due in no small measure to lack of care with hotel rooms.

Japanese-language signs and assistance. Japanese language signs are still insufficient or entirely absent in most parts of the world. Remember that most of the Japanese arriving in your country are there for the first time, so they need a lot of assistance. This includes the use of Japanese language in restaurant menus, throughout airports, for street directions in leisure or theme park sites, in parks as standing guide maps, in shopping centres to direct them to information booths, washrooms, event sites, etc. Major tourist attractions need interpreters on hand.

Japanese signs at the front desk area of hotels, plus simple directories, would demonstrate a good service orientation by the hotel towards Japanese customers. Hotel rooms do not necessarily need all signs in Japanese, but a booklet in each room in Japanese that covered the basics would be useful: operating hours for restaurants, laundry service hours, telephone use instructions, how to use the television set and how to check valuables, as well as emergency procedures and fire escape locations.

Immigration officials who speak some Japanese have an important role to play at airports. Hawaii Airport has a Japanese person who checks the immigration and customs card of Japanese tourists while people are standing in queues awaiting processing. Printed handouts and information sheets in Japanese at customs and immigration points would also help.

Japanese Managers Abroad

Much of what has been written, especially about service, applies equally to your dealings with Japanese managers abroad. In addition two other factors should be borne in mind:

1   *Your English Communications.* Although the Japanese do learn English, still it is Japanese English, not the English that you speak or have learnt. While it has its own idioms, it does not usually equip the Japanese to speak idiomatically with native speakers of English anywhere. Moreover, Japanese English understandably has little or no slang, and the Japanese would understand little except the most commonplace and dated of Hollywood-purveyed slang.

To communicate effectively with the Japanese using English is no easy task, since it requires you to learn a new and more artificial kind of English, which has no idioms (such as 'what a hot potato', 'he's pulling the wool over our eyes'), or slang, which uses much shorter and less complex sentences (with double negatives, complex conditional clauses, etc., deleted) than those you customarily use, is spoken more deliberately, more slowly and more evenly in tone than your normal English. Those who have lived long in Japan, especially teachers, learn this style as a matter of survival, though it can have its disadvantages. Bernard Barber tells the story of a trip to Paris where, as he walked to lunch with a French colleague, he related in English some news from the Tokyo office of McCann-Erickson. But he had spoken only for a short time when the Frenchman turned wrathfully on him, saying, 'Why are you speaking to me like a child? Do you think I cannot understand idiomatic English?' What Barber had forgotten to do, of course, was to switch off the sanitized and Japanized English that he used on a daily basis with his Japanese staff back in Tokyo (Barber, pers. comm.).

Conversational English problems are one thing. Another set of problems arise when you have to make formal presentations to the Japanese in English. More preparation than you would usually make is called for. Do your homework on the audience, their expectations, their interests and specialities, the location and the equipment available. Have copies of your talk available, in both English and Japanese, for distribution immediately before you begin. Very detailed planning of your slides, and of what you will say as you present each one, is most important. Do not talk too much, or for long.

If an interpreter is to render what you say into Japanese, give her a copy of your talk and the slides in advance, and go over it with her.

Her contribution will certainly help to improve the quality of your talk. Very likely, she will pick up English expressions that will be meaningless or confusing to the Japanese, even though they live abroad. During the presentation, speak only for 20–30 seconds, stop and allow her to interpret. If you are not to use an interpreter, get another Japanese to go over your talk beforehand and expect the same benefits. In many cases you will find the whole logic of the Japanese approach to communication to be different from your own.

Finally, expect far less audience activity, questions or responses, than you are used to. Accept that there may be no questions asked of you. In any case, prepare yourself in advance to face a group of passive poker faces, some of whom will have their eyes closed through your entire presentation—and don't be surprised if some senior Japanese, whom you have particularly wanted to impress, should suddenly leave the room. Set yourself to concentrate on communicating and eliciting understanding by your audience of what you regard as your key points.

2. *Being sensitive to organizational background factors.* When dealing with Japanese abroad, you should be sensitive to the organizational context to decision-making in the Japanese company. You need to make some assessment of how much autonomy the local Japanese managers have, and the manager that you are dealing with in particular. To what extent must he refer back to Tokyo? What questions are Tokyo likely to ask? If the people in Tokyo know little about your country and have little overseas experience, the chances are that your Japanese customer abroad, and so you also, are going to have a rough time persuading Tokyo to approve innovative proposals. But if they do know your country well, then preparing in advance your answers to the questions you anticipate will be asked by Tokyo may eventually save you time and money.

As I mentioned earlier, there is usually no special value in your seeking out the local Japanese top manager. Decisions are most likely made by middle managers, with probably more guidance from Tokyo than from the expatriate president. In any case, the Japanese will insist on matching you with a person of equivalent status, and unless you too are president of a more or less equal-sized company, you will simply not be permitted to meet him more than occasionally at social functions.

MANAGING AND TRAINING FRONTLINE STAFF ABROAD

I wrote earlier about the importance of cultural affinity in the sales people who deal with Japanese customers abroad. How can we assess this quality?

In the box—'Test your negotiating skills with the Japanese'—is a test especially for non-Japanese, consisting of three linked tests: first, a Test of Japan Affinity, especially affinity for dealing regularly with Japanese executives; second, a Relating Test, which assesses what level of un-ease you feel in your interpersonal dealings with the Japanese; and third, the INCOM Test, which is in two parts: one, called Negskill, measures your ability to bargain; the other, Comskill, measures your ability to socialize readily with strangers.

The point of these linked tests is to assess a number of key facets of your ability to get along with the Japanese. The people who will do best with the Japanese both in face-to-face dealings and in corporate business dealings are those who score high in affinity, low in relating problems, and who are equally able to bargain and to socialize with strangers (read 'Japanese' in this case). Therefore the three tests are a valuable tool for assessing your present staff and evaluating the abilities of those you recruit in the future.

Make Japan the Final Finishing School

You may have the highest quality people, strongly interested in and having affinity for dealing with the Japanese, with some being competent Japanese linguists, and all are motivated by your strong leadership and committed philosophy of excellence of product and customer service. But some finishing touches are needed, which will come from exposing them to Japan itself, so they can study the way marketing, selling and customer services are delivered there, and take to heart ideas that are adaptable in your country. If you are in the tourism or hospitality industries, you and your staff should also study some of the key market groups that you deal with at home: the wealthy young ladies of Tokyo (*ojoosama*), for instance. And there will be many other groups that you ought to study. Where do they shop, dine out, spend their leisure hours? How are they treated, as customers? Interview as many of them as you can, as well, to learn how they see the world. Befriend some, so that they can actually take you with them on their days or nights out. Make Japan your university, even laboratory, to polish the skills you and your staff will need to create or capture the opportunities abroad in serving the Japanese customer.

Test your negotiating skills

How well do you negotiate with the Japanese or others from a very different culture? Let me offer a number of ways for you to assess your negotiating skills, especially *vis-à-vis* the Japanese. These should help you diagnose any soft spots in your approach, and strengthen your capacities for the next time you face anyone across the negotiating table.

1 The Japan Affinity Test

The Japanese lay a very strong emphasis on developing sound relationships with everyone they do business with. So it goes without saying that the people who are likely to have an effective relationship with Japanese businessmen are those who have a genuine interest in Japanese culture and society. And if they have a natural affinity with Japanese business customs and ways of thinking, then the chances of success are even better. Conversely, those who feel little interest in the Japanese or little affinity with the Japanese will probably not achieve very good working relationships. The first test, then, is to see how much affinity you have with Japanese businessmen. There are no right or wrong answers. Each item invites four possible responses. Selecting the large T (or F) would mean the statement is generally true (or false) for you. Selecting the small t (or f) would mean that it is merely more true than false (or *vice versa*).

1 I am very interested in the Japanese and in Japanese culture.

T t f F

2 I am as well prepared for meetings as anyone, Japanese or anyone else.

T t f F

3 I usually feel comfortable, even if someone quibbles about a proposal I make.

T t f F

4 It's important in life to be friendly and soft-pedal the 'business is business' approach.

T t f F

5 I guess the Japanese would regard me as too easy-going.

T t f F

6 Probably I tend to be in a rush and be sloppier in preparation than I should be.

T t f F

7 Once you have a contract to work with, that alone should decide how you respond to any problem.

T t f F

8 I'm a stubborn person who doesn't like to surrender, even if surrender proves inevitable.

T t f F

9 I often work forty-five hours or more a week and enjoy it, even when there's no particular pressure on.

T t f F

10 I tend to be suspicious of the Japanese.

T t f F

11 I feel comfortable even when a Japanese takes a long time to answer my questions.

T t f F

12 I don't think there is any particular reason to make a deep study of the Japanese in order to do business with them.

T t f F

13 In business discussions, I tend to avoid saying what I really feel.

T t f F

14 I usually feel uncomfortable when Japanese people I meet talk about what's happening in areas I know nothing about.

T t f F

15 Some of my best friends are Japanese.

T t f F

Your Score

    1 T(2) t(1) f(0) F(0)
    2 T(2) t(1) f(0) F(0)
    3 T(2) t(1) f(0) F(0)
    4 T(0) t(0) f(1) F(2)
    5 T(0) t(0) f(1) F(2)
    6 T(0) t(0) f(1) F(2)
    7 T(0) t(0) f(1) F(2)
    8 T(0) t(0) f(1) F(2)
    9 T(2) t(1) f(0) F(0)
   10 T(0) t(0) f(1) F(2)
   11 T(2) t(1) f(0) F(0)
   12 T(0) t(0) f(1) F(2)
   13 T(0) t(0) f(1) F(2)
   14 T(0) t(0) f(1) F(2)
   15 T(2) t(1) f(0) F(0)

To get your Japan Affinity score, add up the numbers above of all the answers you have circled. A total score of 26 or more may indicate that you are already *simpatico* with most Japanese. On the other hand, a score of 12 or less suggests that you are not greatly interested in the Japanese, do not have any natural affinity, and/or have as yet too little experience with the Japanese to be able to clarify your attitudes. People with scores between 12 and 25 may either have qualified attitudes to the Japanese generally, still be unsure of themselves in their dealings with the Japanese, or unsure of how to read the Japanese. The next test can offer more insight on problems of these kinds.

2 The Relating Test

With the best of will and interest in the Japanese, there will still be many of us who experience considerable difficulties in face-to-face communications with them. This next test is designed to identify the kinds of problems you might be experiencing; it is designed for those who are already dealing with the Japanese on a regular basis, especially face-to-face.

The Relating Test below is composed of a series of statements. For each of these, we want to know whether or not it crops up as a problem for you in your dealings with the Japanese—and if so, is it a significant enough problem for you to work to overcome.

This test is designed to help you clarify various aspects of your negotiating activity with the Japanese. It gives you an opportunity to assess yourself and to set goals for further development in skills. Below each question are three boxes. The left-hand box stands for 'No Problem', the centre box for 'Only a Minor Problem', and the right-hand box for 'A Problem Needing Improvement'. Tick the answer that is most appropriate. There are no right or wrong answers.

How do you assess your attitude towards the following:

1 Appreciating the impact of my behaviour on Japanese clients.

☐ ☐ ☐

2 Yielding gracefully to the inevitable with Japanese clients.

☐ ☐ ☐

3 Feeling the Japanese do not fully accept me.

☐ ☐ ☐

4 Feeling awkward making formal presentations to the Japanese.

☐ ☐ ☐

5 Feeling awkward making small talk with the Japanese.

☐ ☐ ☐

6 Difficult to tell stories and anecdotes to the Japanese.

☐ ☐ ☐

7 Expressing my true feelings to the Japanese.

☐ ☐ ☐

8 Being uneasy with the Japanese.

☐ ☐ ☐

9 Feeling awkward because I don't understand how the Japanese think.

☐ ☐ ☐

10 Understanding the personality, feelings, attitudes of individual Japanese.

☐ ☐ ☐

11 Being talkative with the Japanese.

☐ ☐ ☐

12 Being relaxed with the Japanese.

☐ ☐ ☐

13 Feeling comfortable when communicating while standing or sitting to the Japanese.

☐ ☐ ☐

14 Feeling comfortable with Japanese people who are formal.

☐ ☐ ☐

15 Feeling comfortable with Japanese people who ask many questions.

☐ ☐ ☐

16 Feeling comfortable with serious-looking, unsmiling Japanese.

☐ ☐ ☐

Your score
Score 0 for 'No Problem' 1 for 'Only a Minor Problem' and 3 for 'A Problem Needing Improvement'.

A score of 9 or more suggests that you have something disabling in your communication encounters with the Japanese. Possibly these are problems that you alone know about, and that the Japanese you deal with are entirely unaware of. You may be the best judge of that. In any case, the question is: What can you do about minimizing these problems? What can help is to select the two problems that you are having most difficulty with and think about the kinds of strategies that might be useful to ease them.

For instance, most communication problems can be eased with some standard strategies—relaxation, especially if combined with positive thinking practices (for instance, repeating to yourself, 'I am a relaxed and effective communicator with the Japanese,' or, 'I am always in command of myself, whatever happens'). But there are other practical techniques you may need to employ as well. You can make comprehension of your English easier (and so reduce the opportunities for misunderstandings) for the Japanese if you use simpler, shorter words, shorter sentences, pause frequently for questions, listen more or wait silently for your Japanese partner to speak.

3 The Income Inventory

Competent negotiators are people with a broad array of skills. They are not only or even necessarily sharp bargainers, they have to be persuasive and insightful, analytical and sociable, and so on. It is particularly important that you have a balance of skills, for the negotiator who is, say, strong in bargaining ability but weak in communication skills is unlikely to be successful. Skill balance is important, and is what we want to ascertain in this next test. An abbreviation of a much longer questionnaire, it will give you two scores—one reflecting your general negotiation skills and one your skills as a friendly communicator with strangers. We will call these Negskill and Comskill. Complete both parts now, so that you end up with a score for each of these.

These questions concern your personal reactions to a number of situations. No two statements are exactly alike, so consider each statement carefully before answering. If a statement is true for you, or more true than false, then circle T. If a statement is false for you, or more false than true, then circle F. Be sure to answer every question.

Part 1: Negskill

1 I rarely challenge the opinions or data of other people in a formal meeting or negotiation, even if I know they are wrong.

T   F

2 I work in bursts of energy, then have periods of slackness.

T   F

3 More than most people, I like being praised.

T   F

4 I am reluctant to admit errors, regardless of how small the mistake may be.

T   F

5 I love to bargain.

T   F

6 I am always the one who tries to see that both sides get a fair deal.

T   F

7 I face difficulties with realism.

T   F

8 I am generous in giving praise for good ideas and contributions.

T   F

9 I tend to resist surrender to the other side on small points.

T   F

10 I am low-key in my reaction to other people.

T   F

Part 11: Comskill

11 I find it hard to imitate the behaviour of other people.

T   F

12 I guess I put on a show to impress or entertain other people.

T   F

13 I would probably make a good actor.

T   F

14 I sometimes appear to others to be experiencing deeper emotions than I actually am.

T   F

15 In a group of people I am rarely the centre of attention.

T   F

16 In different situations and with different people I often act like very different persons.

T   F

17 I can only argue for ideas I already believe.

T   F

18 In order to get along and be liked, I tend to be what people expect me to be rather than anything else.

T   F

19 I may deceive people by being friendly when I really dislike them.

T   F

20 I'm not always the person I appear to be.

T   F

Your score

1	T(0) F(1)	11	T(0) F(1)
2	T(0) F(1)	12	T(1) F(0)
3	T(0) F(1)	13	T(1) F(0)
4	T(0) F(1)	14	T(1) F(0)
5	T(0) F(1)	15	T(0) F(1)
6	T(1) F(0)	16	T(1) F(0)
7	T(1) F(0)	17	T(0) F(1)
8	T(1) F(0)	18	T(1) F(0)
9	T(0) F(1)	19	T(1) F(0)
10	T(0) F(1)	20	T(1) F(0)

Now that you have your scores, our interest is in how balanced the two scores are. If there is less than three points difference between the two scores and both scores are five or more, you have rated yourself as a balanced negotiator. But if this isn't the case, then we can diagnose the lack of balance in the following ways:

When your Negskill score is higher

Let's take this to mean that you are a competent negotiator/bargainer with not-so-effective communication skills. In that case, you probably come across to the people on the other side of the table as cold, or adversarial, or unduly hair-splitting in discussion, perhaps suspicious, overcontrolled, defensive and, in general, psychologically 'off balance'. Whatever the elements, you need to become aware of the impact you are having on the Japanese, and do something about it, such as letting someone else be negotiation spokesman or taking a complete backseat and allowing others to take initiatives with the Japanese. As well, if there is suspicion and antagonism directed specifically at the Japanese because of some imagined slights, you need to recognize that the likelihood is that they are entirely unfounded, and have only arisen because of some cross-cultural misunderstanding aided possibly by your own characteristic suspicion or caution.

When your Comskill score is higher

On the other hand, there are many negotiators whose strengths are primarily in being clear and friendly communicators and who fall down when it comes time to take a hands-on 'business is business' attitude. Lack of experience is a big cause here, so actively searching out experience through role-play practice or planned small negotiations in the office or in local stores can help. People who have experience in negotiation with the Japanese or other foreigners can be questioned for their knowledge and advice. Most of all, you should put every effort into being thoroughly prepared for every negotiation you enter. And if none of this works, remember: it is no shame to discover that you do not have what it takes to be an effective negotiator. In fact, relatively few people are—however hard they try. Even so, you will probably be able to play a very effective role as a member of your negotiating team, especially if, as is likely, you are a friendly communicator with natural affinities with the Japanese.

CONCLUSION

Any book about marketing and selling to the Japanese ought to draw on both the written and the oral history of foreign dealings with the Japanese. What is written is often special pleading, even if the facts are correct and the conclusions valid. We know, for instance, that foreign multinationals now regard Japan as the most profitable market abroad, and that it has always been an excellent market for those who have succeeded. Why, then, has the oral history so often contained horror stories, such terrible complaints about the Japanese and their defensiveness? I have hardly touched on such complaints in this book, for they contribute little or nothing in practical guidance, though they have greatly influenced the thinking of foreign business people who might also have tried harder and persisted longer at trying to be successful with the Japanese.

Horrible oral history might also explain, in a very crude sense, why it is that American multinationals, in spite of receiving returns on their investments in Japan that far exceed those from investments in France and Great Britain, have far less investment in Japan than in those two countries? I know some of the answers that will be given: Japan set up more barriers against foreign investment (but joint ventures in most industries have been possible since the 1950s). Japan is a more difficult to understand market (how then did the successful foreign ventures manage to do so well for so long in Japan?). We feel more comfortable in France and Great Britain than we do in Japan (but this again has never been everyone! The pioneer managers of foreign enterprises in Japan felt comfortable in Japan, or worked at being comfortable). Generally speaking, companies that have failed in Japan have done so because of their own shortcomings or mistakes.

As far as foreign imports are concerned, the situation today is that the market is as wide open as one could get it to be in any country. If you are not right now investigating the possibilities and potential, are not talking to JETRO, using their TOPS service to identify distributor candidates, not negotiating with Japanese parties about maximizing the exposure of your product, you are almost certainly missing out on important long-term growth opportunities. It is true that in the past the playing field for foreign importers was not always so level—there were barriers of many kinds. But that era has passed. Japan is an import-dependent society. One might even say it is addicted to imports, provided they offer what they cannot get from products or services made in Japan.

This huge affluent market is continually diversifying in its lifestyles, in its product and leisure tastes, in its international orientation, in its craving for quality, branded merchandise and products and services. The rich are getting richer in Japan, consuming more and more conspicuously. As Japanese society stratifies more and more, professionals and specialists keep emerging as new segments. As the five-day week in business and education becomes more general, as holidays become more accepted by social mores, as regional development—through industrial parks, theme parks, leisure resorts, marinas and so on—continues to accelerate; as business, leisure and education continue to internationalize, with more Japanese abroad and more non-Japanese professionals, white-collar and blue-collar workers in Japan emerging as distinct market segments—you should ask yourself: Why aren't we there? Why aren't we doing better?

The answers to these questions are also part of the reason why foreign companies have failed in Japan in the past. This is a difficult society to understand and adjust to for many non-Japanese. American managers have, relatively speaking, experienced more interpersonal difficulties with the Japanese—with staff, with distributors, with bankers—than have managers from other Western countries. In other Asian and Pacific countries, American managers perform outstandingly, settle in well, quickly learn about their environment and how to do business with the locals. But they have not been nearly as confident or competent in Japan. British and Australian managers have performed better, and European managers, even labouring under the burden of using English in business as a second language, have fitted at least as well into Japan.

Japan demands of those executives and entrepreneurs who would do well a seriousness of study that they might not pursue in any other country. It needs people with some kind of intuitive feel or affinity for Japan and the Japanese, whether you are doing business with the Japanese in Japan or somewhere abroad. Fluency in the Japanese language is not ever as important as being a capable manager who has an affinity for the Japanese, is interested in them and their culture, and shows it. It is often the case that people with the greatest affinity with the Japanese are other Asians or Westerners of Asian origin. Certainly, the Japanese, generally speaking, feel more comfortable (at least on first encounter) with other dark-haired, olive-skinned, brown eyed people, than they do with green-eyed, long-nosed people like myself. Western women, if they are capable businesspeople, also fit well with the Japanese. They tend to be better, more sensitive communicators than men and to have no problems of acceptance if they have these qualities.

As for learning the language, I have seen so many Western managers slog earnestly at their early-morning Japanese lessons year after year without ever achieving even a modest competence: and certainly never being able to make sense of a meeting held in Japanese, let alone contribute themselves. Of course, there are pleasures in having enough Japanese to make shopping or travel enjoyable. But if they are not priorities, your best path as a busy manager is to learn the minimum Japanese, perhaps a hundred words and phrases, together with the appropriate communication style (which is not the same as language), the body language and non-verbal politeness that many occasions call for in Japan.

Part of the communication style that will help you to fit in with Japanese anywhere calls for humility, self-depreciation done with humour, a readiness to apologize, a friendly but deferential manner to people who are senior to you (such as buyers). In meetings, fitting in with the Japanese means learning a possibly different style and rhythm—being less the salesperson, more a provider of information, feeling comfortable with silences when they occur, trying to read between the lines and figure out what is really happening on the Japanese side, not being deceived by the Japanese manner of fulsome praise and hyperbole into believing that things are necessarily going your way. With the Japanese, we need to be exceptionally, meticulously, precise. Give exact, not rounded, figures. If you don't have the data, don't give guesstimates unles they request them. If you are a would-be supplier of precision-made products or components, put yourself in their shoes. Understand that the Japanese will be suspicous and cautious until they are certain that they can obtain from you exactly the quality they are after.

Anyone writing about Japan, who knows Japan, emphasizes the importance of good human relations in business. To have no enemies, to have amicable relations with all your customers and suppliers and even competitors, never to be adversarial but always seeking for some compromise, some face-saving solution to problems for all the parties involved—this is the philosophy of business Japan, and reality is normally very close to the philosophy. Foreigners who enter into business Japan, whether in Japan or abroad, become involved in this as well. You are not then any more an outsider looking in on the cute or alien Japanese any more—you are caught up in and become part of the story of Japanese business itself.

Learning about Japan, and adapting somewhat to its style, is part of what you have to do. They are commited to being loyal, co-operative and hardworking—so should you be. They will be more formal than you, perhaps less open about their real feelings and thoughts, more emotionally reserved: but perhaps not. There are ample exceptions on their side, just as we know that many Westerners can be more closed as personalities than some Japanese.

We need to fight against the negative and distorted stereotypes about the Japanese that are widespread, if not universal, outside Japan. Some of us do arrive at meetings with Japanese customers with our attitudes firmly back in our home country, loaded down with the rhythms, humour and outlook of our own country, not to mention the stereotypes and business assumptions we almost intuitively, almost secretively, share with some of our compatriots.

We may assume not that people who ask too many questions are unnecessarily picky, but that questions indicate interest and the likehood of an early, favourable, decision. We assume that the Japanese will put themselves in our shoes, realize how much time and money we are spending on these meetings and how other projects are also demanding attention, and that they will not waste our time further, but make a prompt decision.

Another common problem is that we will very likely have a time horizon for success in Japan that is in reality far shorter than that of the Japanese side, although, unless pressed, they may never articulate their view on this because it seems so academic (because uncertain) to them.

It is easy enough to miss a very critical difference between the Japanese market and that in most other advanced countries. When it comes to the marketing of quality imported products, the Japanese distributor's approach is to put the development of market share before short-term profit, to price at a premium level and hold that through all channels, generally to invest in demand development for the long term. Contrast this to so many United States distributors of imported products, where it is sink or swim, with no tender nurturing of the new brand for the long term. Short-term profit drives so many in the USA, and price becomes the factor used to get channels to move the import, whatever its excellence.

If, moreover, our Japanese partners let us convince ourselves that a short-term pay-back period is achievable in the Japanese market, it may be that in the long haul the relationship turns into a sort of marathon race, but with us thinking it is a sprint. Over the initial early distance, we power ahead easily as we shower them with ideas for better marketing and promotion, impatient for early results. But over the long haul, we limp in a long way back behind their heels, and their long-term efforts at creating market goodwill and a viable franchise—supposing that we hadn't long since dropped out of an increasingly disappointing effort. Physically we may be in Japan, or some 'little Tokyo' abroad, but psychologically we are still back home—where it might be entirely all right to shake hands with a man as though you wanted to arm-wrestle him, where being late for meetings might be laughingly accepted as a precious cultural tradition, where going unprepared into meetings and 'winging' it could be a sign of 'high macho', and where, if you did remember to bring your business cards, it might not be amiss to flick one niftily across the table, rather than stand up and pass it over.

Japan is a big bundle of problems and challenges, many being out there in their market and in their ways of doing things, while others are strictly inside ourselves. Perhaps the biggest problem in the real world is that once you enter into a relationship with a Japanese distributor, you may never be able to change to another. When recognition of this comes, so too does the importance of clarifying your long-term goals and objectives and the merit of a well-prepared approach to negotiation.

Profits may not be too spectacular in the first five or ten years of your Japan venture. Can you live with that? When do you want to start getting profit returns? Devise a ten-year business plan and profit picture. Decide on your negotiable and non-negotiable items. When and on what points will you say 'no'? Will you be entering a relationship which could make open-ended demands on your level of investment? Your prospective partner may well try to oversell the short-term potential for your product in the Japanese market. Will you be alert to that? Will you be able to query projections or data they present or accept them uncritically or fatalistically? Discipline yourself to take as much time as necessary to get all aspects of the relationship clear, and do it all in writing. Use specialized bicultural consultants to support you and help interpret the real meaning of what you are being told.

Once you are locked into a long-term relationship, will you become an 'easy mark' to be 'rolled' on price? Many foreign exporters bemoan their loss of negotiating power with Japanese distributors. They find themselves unprepared for so many of the queries and new demands that their distributor or partner makes. There is much to learn in the area of product service, in delivering product quality control at a standard always to please the Japanese distributor, and in managing your own organization back home—especially in persuading the production or quality control or packaging departments why it is so important that the Japanese be given exactly what it is they are insisting on.

Meetings in Japan in the early days can be stressful and a struggle with the ambiguities of Japanese etiquette and service. Where does service end and firm commitment to the demands of your own organization begin? If you never achieve satisfactory answers to these questions, yours will not be an unusual case. If you are going to be successful, you must keep involved, motivate them, teach them and learn from them. You will find your product offering under constant review if the market is an intensely competitive one in Japan or abroad. You need to involve them in the new product development process and elicit their new ideas about niche opportunities. Keep giving them the most detailed product information that you can. And, above all, manage the human relationships, both with the section you normally deal with and with whatever senior decision-makers you have been able to develop a good relationship with. You never know when you will need a friend at court.

THE PROBLEMS WITHIN

To get into tune with Japanese customers, we non-Japanese must, as I suggested earlier, learn to uncouple our 'down-home' attitudes. Study is important, but it is wrong to suppose that you are prepared to step out of your plane and go immediately into meetings in Tokyo without allowing yourself to become attuned to that different world. You can become attuned by taking a little time to read newspapers and magazines—what are the issues of the day in Tokyo or Osaka or wherever?—to talk to Japanese executives and government officials, and to expatriates, on the broad issues concerning the matters you have come to discuss. Also, by all means get out of your chromium-plated hotel and walk the streets, visit the shops, ride the subway: soak up the unfamiliar ambience and remind yourself how different a milieu you have found yourself in.

But if this seems a waste of time, I think you should ask yourself if you are in fact really interested in the Japanese—or is it just their money you are after? There is a big problem here, but I have read nowhere, heard no one who has spoken about the necessity for improving our understanding of Japan and the Japanese, who has given other than economic reasons for this. That we should have a friendly interest in them as individuals is a point on which there has been almost absolute silence. Yet we do not need to read Dale Carnegie on winning friends and influencing people to know that effective communicators everywhere are people who are genuinely interested in others and seek to know more about them.

BIBLIOGRAPHY

American Chamber of Commerce in Japan, 'United States-Japan Trade White Paper 1989', ACCJ, Tokyo, 1989.

Baillie, A.S., 'Subcontracting based on integrated standards: the Japanese approach', *Journal of Purchasing and Materials Management*, Spring 1986, pp 17–21.

Barber, Bernard, 'Japanese advertisements: a world of entertainment', *Journal of the American Chamber of Commerce in Japan*, June 1987, p. 15.

Barrett, N.J. & I.F. Wilkinson, 'Export stimulation: a segmentation study of the exporting problems of Australian manufacturing firms', *European Journal of Marketing* 19, 2, 1985, pp. 53–72.

Bertrand, Kate, 'Marketing to the land of the rising yen', *Business Marketing*, October 1986, p. 71.

Brookin, R.M., K. Wenk, M. Atarashi & D. Schmidt, 'Either educate the market or adapt to it', *Journal of the American Chamber of Commerce in Japan*, June 1986, pp. 55–84.

Burstein, Daniel, 'A Yen for New York', *New York*, 16 January 1989, pp. 26–36.

Bush, Richard, *Export Marketing to Japan*, American Chamber of Commerce in Japan, Tokyo, 1981.

Campbell, N.C.G., 'Buyer/seller relationships in Japan and Germany', *European Journal of Marketing*, 3, 1985, p. 47.

Cavugeil, S.T. & R.W. Nason, 'Assessment of entrepreneur readiness to export' (mimeographed), Michigan State University, undated.

Cendron, B. 'Deluxe brand marketing: harsh realities lie behind dreams and fantasy', *Asian Advertising and Marketing*, June 1986, pp. 42–51.

Chandler, Clay, 'Watches, cars or ice cream, it pays to be exclusive', *Japan Times*, 7 May 1986, p. 22.

Chiesl, N.E. & L.L. Knight, 'Attitudes towards Japanese supply sources', *Journal of Purchasing and Materials Management*, Summer 1985, pp. 32–66.

Christopher, Robert C., *Second to None: American Companies in Japan*, Chas E. Tuttle, Tokyo, 1986.

Courtis, K.S., 'Japan: the course ahead', *Hotel Okura News*, July 1989, 13, 7, pp. 1–3.

Distribution Systems in Japan, Business Intercommunications Inc., Tokyo, 1985.

Economist, The, 19 August 1989, p. 13.

Fields, George, 'Advertising Strategy in Japan', in *Japan Marketing/Advertising Annual*, 1982, pp. 71–8.

Fields, George, *From Bonsai to Levi's*, Macmillan, 1983.

Fujii, John, 'Location, visibility as keys to McDonald's marketing success', *Journal of American Chamber of Commerce in Japan*, June 1986, pp. 75–81.

Golden, J., 'Mood advertising pioneer agitates images, stimulates minds', *Asian Advertising and Marketing*, August 1986, pp. 60–63.

'Guidelines to successful entry into the Japanese market', *Journal of the American Chamber of Commerce in Japan*, Tokyo, 1981, p. 62.

Hiatt, Fred, 'Economic disturbances destroy myths', *Washington Post*, 21 March 1990, p. 18.

Industrial Groupings in Japan (8th ed., 1988–9), Dodwell Marketing Consultants, Tokyo, 1988.

Itoh, Kenichi, 'Sloppiness costing USA lot in consumer trust', *Japan Times*, 7 May 1985, p. 24.

'Japan most profitable market in world according to international poll', *Japan Times*, 24 September 1989, p. 3.

'Japanese manufacturers rush to England', *Asahi Shimbun*, cited in *Japan Free Press*, 18, 1988.

Johnson, Chalmers, 'The problem of Japan in an era of structural change', *IHJ Bulletin*, Autumn, 1989, pp. 1–7.

Kakita, Toshizumi, 'Consumers' behaviour changing—but don't look for a standard', *Journal of the American Chamber of Commerce in Japan*, June 1985, pp. 29–35.

Kilburn, David, 'How Japanese products succeed', *Journal of the American Chamber of Commerce in Japan*, June 1986, pp. 24–95.

Kobayashi, Kaoru, '*Japan: the most misunderstood country*' Japan Times Publishing, 1985, p.54

Koren, Leonard, *283 Useful Ideas from Japan*, Chronicle Books, San Francisco, 1988.

Koyama, Hachiro, 'Who said cracking Japan's market was going to be easy?' *Japan Times*, 7 April 1985, p. 24.

Lee, O. Young, *Smaller is Better: Japan's Mastery of the Miniature*, Kodansha International, Tokyo, 1984.

Lorence, M., 'They're cheap, they're late . . . they're American products', *Business Marketing*, September 1987, pp. 94–6.

Lu, David, *Inside Corporate Japan*, Chas E. Tuttle, Tokyo, 1987.

Macpherson, M.F., 'Can we compete?' *Business Marketing*, 72, September 1987, pp. 90–93.

Manoochehri, G.H., 'Suppliers and the just-in-time concept', *Journal of Purchasing and Materials Management*, Winter 1984, pp. 16–21.

'Manufactured imports surging', *Focus Japan*, July 1989, p. 1.

March, R.M., 'Some constraints on adaptive marketing by foreign consumer goods firms in Japan', *European Journal of Marketing*, 11, 7, 1977, pp. 14–19.

March, R.M., 'The performance of foreign capital foreign enterprises in Japan', University of Queensland, Business paper No. 13, July 1978.

March, R.M., 'Foreign firms in Japan', *California Management Review*, Spring 1980, pp. 42–50.

March, R.M., 'Customer orientation in Japan', *The Imperial*, September 1983, pp. 20–23.

March, R.M., *The Japanese Negotiator: Subtlety and Strategy Beyond Western Logic*, Kodansha International, Tokyo, 1988.

March, R.M., 'The Japanese consumer: insights from studies of market segmentation in Japan, Australia and the USA', in Oliver Yan (ed.), *Consumer Behaviour in the Asia Pacific Region*, Addison Wesley, Singapore, 1990.

Maruyama, Magoroh, 'The new logic of Japan's young generation', *Technological Forecasting and Social Change*, 28, 1985, pp. 351–64.

Masler, Daniel, 'Marketing is one key to prospering in Japan', *Journal of the American Chamber of Commerce in Japan*, June 1986, pp. 12–14.

Matsusaka, Makio (1986a), 'Working with channels of distribution', *Japan Economic Journal*, 29 March 1986, p. 7.

Matsusaka, Makio (1986b), 'When yes, yes, yes . . . is no', *Japan Economic Journal*, 3 May 1986, p. 7.

McKinsey & Company, *Japanese Business: Obstacles and Opportunities*, US–Japan Trade Study Group, Tokyo, 1983.

McMaster, Norman A., 'A question of reference: must Japanese advertising be different to be successful?' *Speaking of Japan*, May 1985, pp. 6–12.

McSweeney, P., untitled paper in *Business Opportunities or Obstacles?* (conference proceedings), Australia–Japan Economic Institute, Sydney, 21 March 1989.

MITI, 'Import expansion measures' (mimeographed), January 1990.

Nakajima, Hideo, 'A recipe for foreign success in Japan', *Journal of the American Chamber of Commerce in Japan*, September 1987, pp. 11–16.

'New simple and light equipment for underwater strolls', *Focus Japan*, November 1988, p. 2.

Nippon Information Service Inc., *Shoku Seikatsu Soogoo Choosa—'81 Shoku Seikatsu no jittai to shoku Sutairu* [General research on food behaviour—realities and style of food behaviour in 1981], Marketing Data Base Project, Tokyo.

Nippon Marketing Systems, *Shoohi Shijoo Benchmark Choosa, No. 16* [Consumer Market Benchmark Study No. 16], Tokyo, 1988.

Nishikata, Masumi, *'Kare o shiraba hyakusen ayau karazu'* [Know your enemy, and be fearless in one hundred battles], *Business Review*, 1980, 14, 2, pp. 14–22.

'Perrier Japon: a sparkling success', *Focus Japan*, February 1990, p. 5.

Prime Minister's Office, 'White Paper on Livelihood', Tokyo, 1989.

'Reebok gets a foothold in Japan', *Focus Japan*, June 1989, p. 5.

Reich, Caroline, 'Japanese philosophy puts power in purchasing partnership', *Purchasing World*, October 1987, pp. 78–80.

Robertson, D.F., 'Planning a joint venture for the Japanese market', *Journal of the American Chamber of Commerce in Japan*, December 1987, pp. 24–37.

Robledo-Hara, 'Eiko Ishioka: changing a nation's style', *PHP/Intersect*, May 1986, pp. 18–23.

Rodger, Ian, 'Crash in Tokyo clouds Japan's economic future', *Financial Times*, 20 March 1990, p. 14.

Sakach, Joseph M., 'Can we compete? Selling to Japan here at home', *Business Marketing*, September 1987, pp. 86–9.

Sugahara, K., untitled paper in *The Japanese: Tourist or Guest?* (conference proceedings), Australia–Japan Economic Institute, Sydney, 1988.

'A sweet opportunity', *Look Japan*, July 1987, p. 20.

Tanzer, Andrew, 'They didn't listen to anybody', *Forbes*, 15 December 1986, pp. 168–9.

Terpstra, Vern, *International Marketing* (4th ed.), Dryden, 1987.

Uchimura, Kei, 'Reebok: in step with the market', *Journal of Japanese Trade and Industry*, 2, 1989, p. 12.

Wilk, Robert, 'Japan's teenagers', *Tradepia International*, Winter, 1987, pp. 12–15.

Wolf, Marvin J., *The Japanese Conspiracy*, New English Library, London, 1983.

Zimmerman, Mark, *How to do Business with the Japanese*. Random House, New York, 1985.

INDEX